THE
ECONOMICS
OF
ILLUSION

A Critical
Analysis of
Contemporary Economic
Theory and Practice

L. ALBERT HAHN

FRASER
PUBLISHING
COMPANY

D1453088

First Published 1949
by Squier Publishing Co., Inc.
New York

Fraser Publishing Company Edition
© L. Albert Hahn 1949
2nd printing, 1985

ISBN: 0-87034-040-9
Library of Congress Catalog Card Number: 77-92488
Printed in the U.S.A.

Publisher's Foreword

The author of this volume is Dr. L. Albert Hahn, an internationally known economist, who came to this country in 1941 after having lived in Germany and Switzerland. He is the author of the *Volkswirtschaftliche Theorie des Bankkredits* (*Economic Theory of Bank Credit*) which appeared in three editions, and of many pamphlets and contributions to scientific journals, as well as innumerable articles in well-known dailies. These writings covered the economic events in Germany from the days of the Great Inflation to the times of the Great Depression. He was one of the first to criticize the ill-fated monetary policy which led to the German inflation and he was one of the few who tried to fight the deflation policy of the Luther and Brüning era, which gave to the deflation crisis in Germany its special feature and paved the way for the subsequent Hitler movement.

Dr. Hahn's publications attracted wide attention in Europe, the chief reason being that he was one of the few economists to unify practice and theory; for he was the leading manager of one of the largest and oldest provincial banks in Germany and, at the same time, taught Monetary Theory and Policy as Honorary Professor at the University of Frankfurt.

This book is published in the interest of making available to the American statesman, teacher, student, business employer and employee Dr. Hahn's thoughts and observations on contemporary economic theory and policy.

SQUIER PUBLISHING COMPANY

February, 1949

Acknowledgments

For permission to use quotations from *The General Theory of Employment, Interest, and Money* by J. M. Keynes I am indebted to Harcourt, Brace and Company, publishers, 383 Madison Avenue, New York, N. Y.

For permission to reprint pages 327 to 334 of *German Monetary Theory*, 1905-1933, by Howard S. Ellis I am indebted to Harvard University Press, Cambridge, Mass.

For permission to reprint articles written by me and previously published I am indebted to:

> *The Banking Law Journal,* Cambridge, Mass.
> Chamber of Commerce of the United States, Washington, D. C.
> *The Commercial and Financial Chronicle,* New York, N. Y.
> Social Research, New York, N. Y.
> *American Economic Review,* Evanston, Illinois
> *The Journal of Marketing,* New York, N. Y.
> *The American Journal of Economics and Sociology,* New York, N. Y.
> *Kyklos, International Review for Social Sciences,* Berne, Switzerland
> *Schweizerische Zeitschrift für Volkswirtschaft und Statistik,* Basle, Switzerland

I wish to acknowledge my indebtedness to Dr. Hans Neisser for his helpful suggestions for Chapters 10, 12 and 14.

I also acknowledge the assistance given by Miss Martha Anderson, Mr. Walter S. Morris and Miss G. Sanders in editing and preparing this book.

L. Albert Hahn

New York, N. Y.
February, 1949

Contents

Appendices

Introduction

By Henry Hazlitt

Dr. L. Albert Hahn has long enjoyed a high reputation in Europe, as well as among German-speaking and German-reading economists throughout the world. But linguistic barriers, unfortunately, are still real. Economic thought is not yet an international unit. It is still broken to a large extent into nationalistic or linguistic compartments, which tend to influence each other only sluggishly and often with a deplorable time lag. That is the only reason why Albert Hahn needs any introduction to American readers.

In the following pages some of his recent thinking is made available for the first time in book form in English. We owe this not to a translator, but (as with other talented writers in the forced exile of recent years) to Dr. Hahn's own acquisition of the skill to compose in a second language since he has made his home in New York.

It is unnecessary for me to give here any exposition of Dr. Hahn's contributions to economic thought, or even a biographical sketch. Both tasks have been done adequately by others. It is enough to point out that Dr. Hahn enjoys an enormous advantage as an analyst of Keynesian fallacies. As he has reminded us himself: "all that is wrong and exaggerated in Keynes I said much earlier and more clearly." This intellectual head start enables him to approach and dissect the errors of the Keynesians on their own ground and on some of their own premises.

Dr. Hahn got his education in a hard school. He lived through the dreadful inflation in Germany. He witnessed other European inflations at first hand. He saw the breakdown in practice of the

1

specious theories that had supported those inflations. It was not merely increased scholarship and thought, but his daily experiences as a business man and as a banker, that led him to desert his pre-Keynesian Keynesianism.

There is no more important task for the economic theorist today than to disentangle the network of confusion and error that now goes under the name of the Keynesian Revolution. Until this work has been thoroughly done, clarity and real progress in economics will not be possible. There is no more sophisticated, penetrating and thorough guide in this task than Albert Hahn.

New York, October, 1948

1. Introductory: Cycles in Monetary Theory and Policy

If the luck of a monetary theorist is to be measured by the variety of things he has experienced during his lifetime, then, indeed, I must be considered fortunate, for I lived through times of the widest changes in the monetary field: from the relative stability of the era before 1914, through the inflationism of World War I and the more violent excesses of inflation that followed; through the deep and stubborn deflationism from 1929 onwards, then through the ups and downs of the thirties; and finally the mounting inflation of the recent decade, that has gripped the whole world and has again in parts of Europe and in the Orient passed beyond the limits of control. Throughout most of these periods monetary theorists, by and large, were engaged in rationalizing, justifying and defending the excesses of those responsible for monetary policy. My situation, on the other hand, was often that of a Cassandra who saw the ominous implications of what the majority of theorists considered harmless or even beneficial.

I have attempted to counter to the best of my ability the noxious extremes to which monetary policy and theory seem to swing, pendulum-like, as if subject to a historical law. My first publication, the *Volkswirtschaftliche Theorie des Bankkredits,*[1] it is true, was an inflationary book in an inflationary time; it was under-

[1] Tübingen, 1st ed., 1920; 2d ed., 1924; 3d ed., 1930.

standable, however, as a reaction against the hyper-classicism of prevailing theory in which the effects on the economy of manipulation of money and credit were entirely ignored. It is, to my present way of thinking, a typical soft money book and I attribute its success mainly to the fact that any soft money book—any book that promises prosperity by the relatively easy means of monetary manipulations—is eagerly taken up by readers who have recently witnessed the beneficial effects of inflation in its first phases.

Monetary policy, abandoning conservatism with the beginning of World War I, became extremely inflationary in Europe from about 1920 on; and monetary theorists—laying the blame for the depreciation of the currency to deficits in the balance of payments rather than to inflation—lent support to the prevailing policy. The aim of the articles I wrote during this period was chiefly to *combat the inflationary policy* of the German Reichsbank and its underlying philosophy. These articles were published in 1924 under the title *Geld und Kredit*.

In articles covering the stabilization and post-stabilization periods I pointed out what I considered the shortcomings of the policy of the Reichsbank under Schacht's first presidency. They were assembled in 1929 under the title *Geld und Kredit, Neue Folge*. The reader who is interested in these two books will find their contents listed in Appendices IV and V.

When in 1929 practice and theory again became deflationary in most countries, and especially in Germany, my fight was directed *against deflationism*, particularly of the Bruening-Luther brand which, I was convinced, would undermine the economy to the breaking point. The Nazi revolution was, in my opinion, largely the inevitable result of the deflationary policy of the last pre-Hitler government. By lectures and articles in daily papers, notably the *Frankfurter Zeitung*, and in journals, I tried in vain to combat this policy. Of longer articles that were published separately, *Ist Arbeitslosigkeit unvermeidlich?* (Is Unemployment Unavoidable?) and *Kredit und Krise* (Credit and Crisis) may be mentioned.[2] Like that of all similar endeavors, their effect was frus-

---

[2] Berlin, 1930; Tübingen, 1931. These articles, as well as those mentioned above, are available in the New York Public Library.

trated by the strongly anti-inflationary editorial attitude of the influential *Frankfurter Zeitung* and the *Deutsche Volkswirt* which, even after the pound sterling had been devaluated, saw in every monetary adjustment an attack on the value of the mark and persistently warned against what they called *unzulässige Währungs-experimente* (inadmissible currency experiments). As occurs all too frequently, the people, politicians, and economists had forgotten the past and were solely under the impression of the immediately preceding experience—the hyper-inflation of 1921-23.

In the entire world the great depression led to theoretical views that are again clearly on the soft money side.

I felt compelled to change sides once more. My fight during the last decade has been *against* what I consider a dangerous swing to the other extreme, towards *inflationism.*

As theory and policy during the last decade have been strongly influenced by the late Lord Keynes and his followers, my recent work is squarely addressed to the refutation of Keynesian theory. The articles I have published in the last few years represent, therefore, my criticism of Keynesianism and a further elaboration of what I wrote in the *Neue Zürcher Zeitung* (November 1920, 1936) immediately after the appearance of *The General Theory of Employment, Interest, and Money.*

These articles are reprinted in this volume with only slight alterations—some omissions to prevent repetitions, and a few supplementary footnotes.[3] I am conscious that today I would express many things differently and, above all, that somebody else, more familiar with the English language and the technique of expressing theoretical statements usual in this country could do better. However, in view of the almost entire lack of anti-Keynesian literature, I have felt obliged to surmount my inhibitions in order to relieve this situation to the best of my ability.

As will be evident from this volume, one of my chief objections to Keynes' theory is that it, like all previous inflationary theories of employment, presupposes that the members of the community are

[3] A summary of this volume will appear in German in "Ordo," *Zeitschrift für Ordnung von Gesellschaft und Wirtschaft,* 1949, and in French in *Economie appliquée,* Archives de l'Institut de Science Economique Appliquée.

blissfully ignorant of the changes. In other words, that it pre-supposes one can take away from some and give to others without arousing "compensating reactions" on the part of the former. That is why I have not called this book "Money and Credit, third collection"—which it actually is—but *The Economics of Illusion*, after Chapter 14, in which I emphasize this angle of approach.

It will be further evident from the following that to my mind Keynesianism is, with relation to its position within the history of economic thought, nothing but another one-sided swing of the pendulum monetary theory has often experienced—this time toward the distinct overestimation of the possibilities and effects of monetary manipulations and changes.

Generally speaking, I cannot help thinking that what is today praised as the "Keynesian Revolution" should, more accurately, be called the "Keynesian General Confusion." Not every paradox is correct just because it is a paradox. And what may be an interesting and intriguing mental exercise for specialists who are certain never to lose the firm ground of common sense and fundamental economic insight, becomes irritating and misleading heresy when swallowed whole by minor minds and fanatics. In fact, I sometimes think Keynes wrote his book with his tongue in his cheek. He was doubtless often surprised at the seriousness with which his colleagues took his theses. And if to all this one should remark that I am incapable of grasping the Keynesian intricacies, I would have to console myself with what an old Berlin banker said to an apprentice who was desperate because he was unable to comprehend what a client had written: "Young man, if you are not able to understand his letter, it is probably because it is not understandable."

In rejecting Keynesianism, I am in a peculiar position. Keynesianism is a sin of my youth, for as early as 1920 in my *Volkswirtschaftliche Theorie des Bankkredits* I presented what to me are the basic Keynesian statements.[4] As I confessed later,[5] "all

---

[4] Remarks on my priority are to be found in Gottfried Haberler, *Prosperity and Depression* (1939), Wilhelm Lautenbach, "Zur Zinstheorie von John Maynard Keynes," in *Weltwirtschaftliches Archiv* (Vol. 45, 1937), Heimann, *History of Economic Doctrines* (1945), and others.

[5] In my first criticism of *The General Theory* in 1936, mentioned above.

that is wrong and exaggerated in Keynes I said much earlier and more clearly." Unfortunately I cannot refer to an English translation of my book to prove my claim to priority to English readers. However, Howard S. Ellis gives a very good résumé of my theories in his *German Monetary Theory* (Harvard University Press, 1934). In order that the reader may judge for himself, and because I refer several times to my work in the following articles, the chapter of Ellis's book summarizing my theory is reprinted in Appendix I. For the same reason, part of Gottfried Haberler's extensive résumé and criticism of my book, which appeared in the *Archiv für Sozialwissenschaft und Sozialpolitik*,[6] has been translated (Appendix II). Another reason for adding these two excerpts is that what the authors say, with full justification, against my theses can be said with the same justification against Keynes, but has not been.

Chapter 16 is a study of the relation between Keynes' *General Theory* and my *Volkswirtschaftliche Theorie des Bankkredits*, and includes some remarks on the fate of what may be called German pre-Keynesianism. If one compares the passages quoted from the two books, I think that one cannot but be amazed at the similarity not only of the essence of the ideas but also in some instances of the wording.

In publishing this volume I am prompted by a sense of duty rather than by hope that they may prove a timely warning signal. Life has taught me that men, including economists, are influenced chiefly by their latest experience. Until very recently they were still under the spell of deflation and had forgotten the preceding inflation. Monetary opinion spreads like an infectious disease. Economists make the same mistake as businessmen and stock exchange traders who during a boom see only the bullish argument and during a depression only the bearish argument. Perhaps it is asking too much of a generation engaged in the undoubtedly attractive occupation of working out ever more refinements of the Keynesian theory—see, for example, the multiplier literature—to examine the fundamental question whether the basis of Keynes'

[6] Vol. 57, pp. 803 ff. (Tübingen, 1927).

work is valid and whether all their zeal is not expended on an undeserving cause. They seem to have lost the ability to think along classical lines and may no longer be able to go in for such an examination. Blinded by the allegedly overwhelming importance of demand, they fail to see the implications of costs.

The situation will, I fear, prove dangerous when this country again faces real economic difficulties. It would be an economic policy of illusion to rely, on the one hand, on forecasts of economic developments by economists and government agencies and, on the other hand, on governmental interference to prevent depression and unemployment. As long as the world is not entirely totalitarian, neither the objective data of the future nor the subjective reactions of millions of individuals can be predicted. That is why all models, estimates, and forecasts are either right purely by chance or, if they hedge against future developments, worthless. Unforgotten are the forecasts of a postwar depression (see Chapter 5). The mistake common to all forecasts is that they try to predict the unpredictable. Specific amounts of goods are supposed to come to the market manufactured at a rate of productivity calculated in advance to meet a demand fixed by inveterate investment or consumption habits. The forecasters do not take into account the fact that the slightest change in certain objective factors, such as wage rates, or the slightest modification of the psychological atmosphere can cause fluctuations in the markets that set at nought the calculations based upon estimates of productivity, of pent-up demand, saving habits, and so on. As far as governmental interference itself is concerned, one should never forget that serious economic disturbances are the consequences of basic maladjustments. The effect of correcting or not correcting such maladjustments is infinitely greater than any artificial creation of demand by government in an economy that, in most sectors, is still free. Therefore an economic policy that concentrates on artificially filling up an investment or spending gap rather than on fostering adjustments—and thus creating demand in a natural way —is doomed to fail in any severe crisis.

2. Should a Government Debt, Internally Held, Be Called a Debt at All? *

Professor Alvin Hansen and Mr. Guy Greer, in an article in *Harper's Magazine*,[1] have taken the position that a large and rapidly increasing public debt is, as such, no reason for concern. This opinion, although frequently attacked, has been adopted by many other writers and has had a strong influence on the thinking of this country on the problems in question.

The present writer has been deeply concerned with the practical problem of inflation during the last twenty years and has taken an active part in literary discussions of this problem in Europe;[2] his objections to the mentioned opinions may therefore be of interest.

Generally speaking, he thinks that the whole approach to the problem, as expressed in the article mentioned, must be contradicted as highly dangerous. For in underestimating the dangers of inflation one increases these dangers, which can be avoided by full recognition of the difficulties.

The approach which minimizes a large and rapidly increasing public debt contrasts distinctly with the orthodox principles of

° Appeared first in *The Banking and Law Journal*, July 1943.

[1] April 1942.

[2] A very explicit description of the monetary discussions in Europe during the inflation will be found in Howard S. Ellis's *German Monetary Theory*, Cambridge, 1934. Reference is made in Mr. Ellis's book to my position in the discussions and to my publications. The pages dealing with my position in matters of credit theory are reprinted in Appendix I.

finance as developed during the last centuries. The proponents of orthodoxy have always emphasized the desirability of a comparatively small public debt and have favored balanced budgets, rigid control of government expenditure, and independence of note-issuing banks from the government. Even the governments of today, both Allied and Axis, follow these principles in attempting to recover as large a part of the war expenditure as possible through taxation. Moreover, every businessman, as well as the average layman, is apprehensive of rising debt, whether because of war or because of peacetime deficits.

Now it is to be admitted that the orthodox view is, to a certain extent, one-sided. But is it so entirely antiquated and so rooted in prejudice and economic ignorance as it is made to appear? I do not think so. I believe rather that the orthodox opinion contains certain truths, to disregard which would be highly dangerous.

"The Money Goes Back into the System"

Mr. Hansen's optimism is chiefly based on the thesis that "The money goes right back into the system to the holders of the bonds." By this he means that from a collective point of view the creation of an internal government debt is merely a bookkeeping matter, since in the economy of a nation as a whole, governmental debt is compensated by the claims of the bondholders. To everyone who lived through the German inflation, this argument arouses strong though very unpleasant memories, for it is obviously identical with the dictum formulated in Germany during World War I: "The money remains in the country" (*Das Geld bleibt im Lande*). This dictum solaced the consciences of the German authorities as they followed the lax fiscal policies which resulted in inflation and the misery that came in its wake. But what of the statement itself? Is it true? It is not only true—it is too true. It is a truism like the arithmetical equation that ten minus ten equals zero. This argument, of course, can be applied at whatever level of government debt one might choose to mention—anywhere from $1.00 to trillions and trillions.

Quite correctly the authors point out that governmental debts create a problem of distribution only, and that the present pays for the war, so that the payment is not deferred to the future. "Collectively the cost is paid, but final determination of just how it should be divided up is postponed." Dr. Hansen concedes: "Here is a problem that has to be solved." But this is not a problem; it is *the* problem. It is the problem with which we are concerned and in comparison with which the possibility of compensation between debt and claim, which seems so important to Hansen, is of only formal significance.

It Is More Blessed—and Easier—to Give Than to Receive

From a purely theoretical point of view, nothing is easier than to take from one and give to another if both are under the jurisdiction of the same government and the same police power. The whole country does not become richer or poorer, viewed as a whole. Theoretically, one need only to sentence every creditor of the government to pay himself principal or interest on the bonds he holds. In practice, however, a country is not an economic unit as long as it is not communistic. In practice, again, for governments it is—if not according to the scriptural phrase, more blessed—then surely easier to give than to receive. To spend, one need only resort to credits out of the savings of the nation and eventually, if necessary, to the money-creating power of the note-issuing banks. To obtain receipts, on the other hand, one has to consider hundreds of objections. One has to overcome the resistance of various political parties and pressure groups which try to shift the tax burden from their shoulders to those of others. That is how the gaps between government income and expenditure are created in the first place.

Now it must be admitted that a strong, energetic, and inflation-conscious government can overcome these difficulties in the absence of unfavorable circumstances, but it is clear that the larger the debt, the smaller the adverse circumstances need to be to bring on disaster. Thus, public opinion considers rapidly mounting debt an evil, although in some cases an unavoidable one. In this, public opinion seems to be right, and the formal, logically correct arguments of Hansen to be wrong.

Incidentally, it may be recalled that Keynes, whose authority stands so high among certain theorists in this country, prophesied that after World War I the French internal debt would undoubtedly lead to a depreciation of the French franc to about 20 per cent of its prewar value, on the theory that this debt would not be bearable —a theory which seems to be incompatible with Hansen's thesis.

"A Government Debt Internally Held Should Hardly Be Called a Debt at All"

Based on the fact that "the community as a whole has paid for whatever it has accomplished while the job was being done," Mr. Hansen states that government debt internally held is so completely different from an ordinary personal or business debt that it should hardly be called a debt at all. Now, to begin with, the premise that the community is paying for the war as it goes needs one very important qualification. It is true that the needs of war are overwhelmingly furnished by current production, and recognition of this is undoubtedly progress over previous theoretical analysis which emphasized the importance of "stores"—an analysis which, by the way, was not so incorrect for bygone periods. But anyone who saw the state of Europe after World War I, not only in the vanquished but also in the victorious countries, understands that even nowadays wars are furnished by production of the past. The longer the war lasts and the nearer it comes to the homeland, the more it is financed by the real capital of the nation; stocks, plants, and equipment being either destroyed or no longer replaced during the war. Insofar as this is the case, the government debt is not the equivalent of current production but the production of the past: the capital of the nation. In this sense, government debt is indeed different from private debt, but not something better: it is something worse. Private debts are ordinarily incurred against transfers of goods from one member of the community to another, whereas this sort of government debt is counterbalanced not by real wealth but by its destruction. In the case of the United States, it seems unlikely that the real capital of the nation will be destroyed in any degree corresponding to that of the European countries. On the other hand, it does no harm to keep in mind that wars are serious matters which mean destruction of wealth, and it is wiser to prepare the populace for this contingency than to inform them that no long-term sacrifices will be necessary.

Moreover, there is another sense in which a government debt must be called worse than a private debt, even apart from the conditions outlined above. When a private businessman gets into difficulties, the economy of the community as a whole is little affected since this is a matter of interpersonal relations. When a government, however, gets into difficulties this means state bankruptcy or inflation, eventual social upheaval, and thus suffering for the whole community. The possibility of governmental financial difficulties, however remote they are, should always be kept in mind. After all, there exist budgetary problems, despite all statements as to the equality of debits and credits in the national balance sheets.

The Overpowering External Debt as the Real Cause of Inflation

"What did happen in Germany and certain other countries was uncontrolled inflation which was disastrous, but was in no wise occasioned by failure to pay off the government's internal debts. The cause lay rather in a combination of circumstances, among which was the uncontrolled increase of internal debt, coupled with overpowering external debt." This argument of the fundamental differences between internal and external debt is partly identical with the above-described "compensation argument"; partly it goes beyond it.

Now there are certainly big differences between external and internal debts. But here again the authors have exaggerated the differences and underestimated the similarities. It is, of course, obvious that it is easier to pay interest and amortization on a government loan if it is possible to tax all those who possess the new assets which correspond with the new indebtedness of the government. But insofar as the necessary taxes are not levied on the "new capitalists" (as they can be only partly), the amounts have to be obtained through increased taxes on other members of the population. To these, it is entirely the same whether the amounts are finally channeled to an internal or to an external creditor. If a part of the population has to pay tribute, it suffers the same whether those to whom it is paying tribute reside within or without the country. This is shown by the history of France before the Revolution and, incidentally, by the entire history of medieval Europe. As far as Germany is concerned, gigantic internal reparation payments (in favor of war victims, for example) would, financed in the same way, have had, if not the same, then at least very similar inflationary effects as did the reparation payments to the Allies.

In postwar Germany, the superiority of internal debts over external debts was attributed to the fact that the latter disturbed the balance of payments. It was argued that a disturbed balance of payments caused rising prices of foreign exchange and hence rising prices internally, i.e., inflation. This "balance of payment theory" was very convenient for the Reichsbank since it seemed to exculpate its leaders for the monetary breakdown which ensued, by placing the blame for the currency disaster on the efforts to pay reparations. It also was a convenient argument in the fight for the cancellation of the reparations, since it seemed to show the incompatibility of reparation payments and currency stability. In reality, this entire "balance of payment theory" was rather weak in its theoretical foundation. Currency depreciations have, as the German Quantity Theorists proved at that time, their ultimate cause in an increase in the quantity of money. Thus, what caused the monetary disaster was not the reparations as such but the inflationary way they were financed. The correct argument for their cancellation was not that they ruined the currency but that they ruined the population—and would have also ruined it if the collection had been tried through taxes instead of through inflation, which latter is merely an unjust and rough method of collection. The inclination to balance the budget in favor of an external creditor will, it is to be admitted, often be smaller than it would be in favor of an internal creditor. Only in this indirect way would the external debt prove to be worse than the internal debt.

The collection of money from the members of a community is a difficult task as soon as very large amounts are involved, so that one should not speak of "only an internal debt." As shown above, a country does not form an economic unit.

The people of a country do not have a common pocket, and the difficulty of getting money from the pocket of one into the pocket of the other is distinctly greater than that of getting it from the right into the left pocket of a single individual.

"THERE WILL ALWAYS BE ENOUGH BOND BUYERS—THERE WERE EVEN IN GERMANY"

Everyone who has studied the German inflation will agree that the thesis that there are always buyers of government obligations was correct only up to a certain point. Reference is made in this connection to the fine studies concerning the German inflation, published in English by Graham, Williams, Bresciani-Turoni, and others. All these authors agree that from about the spring of 1922 on, the following situation developed: the obligations of the government for new expenditures, as well as for the renewal of obligations coming due, were no longer purchased by the public and not even by the banks. They had to be taken over by the Reichsbank against newly created money. Unlimited issuance of government obligations had undermined confidence in the currency so that no one was willing to retain his mark securities but purchased goods and foreign exchange. It was primarily this plethora of paper money, newly created to pay off maturing debt, which was one of the chief reasons for the development of the runaway inflation. What had been potential inflation in the past, held in check by confidence in the currency, became actual and dynamic as public confidence dwindled.

As a negative proof of the relationship between government debt and inflation, one can refer to the stability of the rentenmark through which the German inflation was liquidated. One of the chief reasons for the stability of the rentenmark was the fact that the inflation had practically wiped out the internal debt of the Reich. No internal debt having to be repaid, the government was able to make the new money scarce and thus preserve its value under otherwise very difficult circumstances.

This brings us to an important point which Mr. Hansen does not mention. From the days of Ricardo, if not long before, the possibility of making money scarce has always been considered the necessary and sufficient condition for the maintenance of the value and purchasing power of currency. Without this possibility, it maintains its value only on the assumption of full confidence in the currency.

As long as this condition is present there will be no need to produce a scarcity of the money in circulation in order to maintain its value, but a cautious monetary policy must be prepared for less favorable circumstances, especially for spells of mistrust in the currency followed by an increase in the velocity of turnover. Short-term government debts are therefore especially undesirable if inflation is to be prevented; and the consolidation of the government debt for terms as long as possible is therefore correctly the aim of the United States Government as it is for every other government.

Incidentally, there exists *one* situation which no one seems to think of, in which a huge governmental debt must lead to difficulties —the situation of a genuine boom. In such a boom interest rates must go up as soon as an easy monetary policy is abandoned in view of its inflationary effect. Also in this situation government securities are bought by the public but only if they bear higher interest. It remains to be seen if and to what extent the higher interest burden of the government can and will be compensated by higher tax returns during the boom.

"It Is True That a Rapidly Growing Debt Is Sometimes Accompanied by Inflation, but Inflation Is Caused by Something Quite Different"

To some extent, this statement is true, but again the theoretical separation of the rapidly growing government debt from inflation is highly exaggerated. A large and rapidly mounting debt is not alone the cause of inflation, but in the classical inflations of history it has played a decisive role and this, not by chance, but by necessity. One need only recall, for instance, the history of the *assignats* during the French Revolution to see how close these relations can be. The French Government of that time faced large expenditures without having the power or the will to collect the means for them through taxes. Ever new loans were constantly being offered to the public. There came a day when these were no longer absorbed and the government had to fall back on inflationary issuance of paper money which gradually depreciated and eventually broke down entirely. What caused this inflation was indeed not the large debt as such, but rather that the government and the parliament became accustomed to the possibility of increasing it endlessly. This made them mentally and technically unprepared to increase taxes and reduce expenditures. It is this unpreparedness, and not the ever-mounting debt, that is the real reason for the inflation. But then it would also be true that the breakdown of the morphine addict is due to the fact that he is deprived of the drug and not to his being addicted to it.

All this does not mean that inflation in the United States will occur or that it is unavoidable. Nothing is so certainly avoidable as inflation, since it is only one method of distributing the cost of governmental expenditure, and a rough and unjust one at that. What can be distributed in a rough and unjust way can also be distributed fairly. But to do this one must learn the lesson of history and not act like the speculators before the 1929 crash who, when warned of the overvaluation inherent in security prices of that time, replied: "*This* time circumstances are quite different."

REDISTRIBUTION OF WEALTH AND THE THREAT TO THE ENTREPRENEUR'S PROFIT

"Repayment of the amounts specified in such [government] bonds as are issued could not possibly mean anything more than redistribution of the burden of payments already made." The formal truth of this statement is obvious, but its implication is overlooked. The redistribution of the burden of payments is nothing else than a redistribution of wealth to take place in the future but dictated by the present. This would not be the case if the people whose assets had increased during the war were also the ones on whom the new taxation would fall. Mr. Hansen points out quite correctly that the wealth represented by the new government bonds will not accumulate in the hands of a rich few. Therefore, the distribution of the burden will be a distribution of earnings and through that of wealth in the direction of an equalization of the present "too great inequalities of wealth and income." Hence, the real significance of a huge government debt is that it is an invisible mortgage, not on the nation as a whole, but on the wealth of those who have above average income and capital.

Mr. Hansen recognizes the significance of this invisible mortgage quite clearly. He points out that the highly progressive taxes on these incomes lead to economically undesirable effects insofar as they discourage the entrepreneur from risk-taking ventures without which private capitalistic economy cannot function and expand. But for Mr. Hansen this is merely *a* problem, whereas it is (as mentioned above) *the* problem. He suggests as a solution the lowering of taxes for new and expanding investments. This suggestion is interesting, not so much because it would solve the problem as because it displays the dilemma that confronts those who would attempt to reconcile a highly social tax system with the progressive income structure necessary to activate an economy which relies upon risk-taking private ventures. Regarding the suggestion itself: can one honestly assume that entrepreneurs will believe in the continuance of lower taxes for new enterprises as long as existing enterprises are heavily and progressively taxed? If entrepreneurs, especially those who operate through the corporate form, have been disappointed with promises of moderating taxes in the past, will they have much confidence in similar promises with respect to the future? Does anyone think that, when shares of existing corporations decline in value under the influence of new taxes, the shares of new companies will be able to command prices which will make their issuance possible?

The solution suggested by Mr. Hansen is clearly not practicable, but it does point in the right direction. Entrepreneurial profit cannot be threatened to the point where it discourages risk-taking ventures. No private entrepreneur takes risks when faced with losses of 100 per cent and profits in a much smaller percentage. As future profit alone cannot be exempt from this threat, the present profit will have to be treated with equal care.

But the question of taxation of entrepreneurial profit is not one of mere skill and goodwill in fiscal policy. It involves the general attitude toward the future of the American economic system. Like all the other large capitalistic nations, the United States is faced with the decision between private capitalism and state socialism. It is an illusion to believe that they are reconcilable in the long run. The aim of socialism—namely, equalization of income—must, when sought by highly progressive taxation, prevent the working of capitalism which can exist and be dynamic only with risk-taking and proportionate rewards. A system of mixed socialism and capitalism cannot work, although we all seem to think and wish it would. It inevitably leads to state socialism. Old enterprises die and new ones will not be ventured, so that the problem of unemployment has to be solved by the state. It is possible that the decision between capitalism and state socialism may have to be made some day anyway, but the least that can be said of a high government debt is that it will accelerate the decision.

3. The Illusion
of the War Boom *

Undoubtedly an increasing number of people begin to consider the war boom as a highly beneficial phenomenon. They see in its mechanism a simple remedy, if not *the* remedy, for most economic difficulties and especially unemployment. "The war has proved that full employment can be created through government spending. It will be hard to convince the American people that what can be done for war cannot be done for peace." Such ideas have been expressed not only by laymen but also by men who claim to have been trained in economic science.

Nevertheless, the argument is of a typical vulgar-economic character which means that it is based on popular economic misconceptions rather than on a scientific approach.

It has always been considered the chief duty of economic science to unmask and fight popular economic illusions which appeal to the masses because they are simple and, allegedly, panaceas. To fight the "employment through spending" idea has undoubtedly become increasingly difficult in recent times, although its fallacies have been demonstrated by the practical and theoretical experience of centuries. It is indeed easier, more comfortable and popular, to indulge in new spending schemes and to promise the "compensation" of economic difficulties through government spending than to show the basic reasons for these difficulties and to advocate their elimination. I think that it is high time to replace the "compensa-

* Appeared first in *The Commercial and Financial Chronicle*, February 17, 1944.

tion idea" by a sound "correction theory." For not only will the compensation idea, if applied in practice, lead to implications entirely unforeseen by most of its adherents; it will also prove the more ineffective in any severe crisis the more one has relied on the government power to "compensate" existing maladjustments.

Coming back to what may be called the "war boom in peacetime" idea, it seems to us to contain several basic fallacies or illusions.

Wartime Activity Contra Peacetime Productivity

If man works he does so not just to be busy but in order to be able to consume, to live. The worker produces goods which he either consumes himself or—as is the rule in modern times—exchanges for goods produced by others. Activity in wartime is only partially for civilian consumption. The other part—and in some countries at war the overwhelming part—is for war purposes. This purpose can be much more important for the sake of the survival of the community than private consumption is. Nevertheless, in a private economy in which goods are produced because the producer ultimately wants to enjoy the results of his effort, war activity is not and cannot be called a productive activity. From a strictly economic point of view, it means being busy, struggling, making efforts, even if and just when these efforts are very hard. In a rich country such as the United States, where the standard of living is high in spite of war production, these facts are not so easily recognized. But an investigation, for instance, into the German war economy shows what war activity really means in an economic sense: there the population is, on the one hand, forced to work so hard and so long, and is, on the other hand, so curtailed in its consumption that a state of forced labor has developed. For it *is* forced labor if one squeezes out of the worker as much as he can stand without breaking down completely, without leaving him time for leisure, recreation, and pleasure, and gives him only the minimum of food indispensable for mere existence. War production means that people work not for their own well-being but for collective purposes, even if for very important ones. Thus admiring the war boom and war production actually means admiring production for collective purposes.

Taking such a system over into peacetime and making it the backbone of peacetime economy would mean that the individual would no longer have the right to decide if, what, and how much he wants to consume and how much work he is inclined to put into the satisfaction of his needs. This would mean that a communist instead of a free economy has developed.

WAR WORK IS NOT PAID FOR

A further illusion that leads to admiration of the war boom is created by the fact that everybody earns plenty of money and seems to be well paid. But in fact this is just an illusion. As far as the community works for the war effort and not for civilian consumption, the community as a whole does not receive payment. It is true that payment for war work that is not spent on civilian consumption does not evaporate but piles up in the form of savings in the accounts or in the pockets of the individuals. Nevertheless, for the community as a whole, these savings are nonexistent, so that the work through which they have been made was done for nothing. The reason is very simple. As is well known, Professor Alvin Hansen and his followers state that a governmental debt internally held is no debt at all because every new governmental debt is compensated by a new claim against the government in the hands of the population so that, on the balance, the community has not become poorer. The argument which tries to prove the non-existence of a governmental debt can, however, also be used—and more correctly—to prove the non-existence of claims against the government if these claims are internally held. In fact every new war bond held by a member of the community increases the national debt for which the community is responsible. The work put into the war effort is not paid for. It is done free of charge. Never will the community as a whole receive payment for it.

Thus to recommend that the war boom pattern should be continued in peacetime means advocating a national economy in which a good deal of the work is permanently done without payment. Work without payment is again a characteristic of a communist and not of a free economy.

Wars Do Not Create Wealth

One of the reasons why people feel so comfortable during a war boom is that everybody seems to become wealthier. However, this increasing wealth, too, is an illusion. Wars do not enhance the wealth of nations; on the contrary they diminish it, at least in those less fortunate countries in which the natural supplies are limited and become exhausted through the war, and in which equipment is seriously run down. Why is it that in contrast to former times, the impoverishing (or at least the not-enriching) effect of the war is overlooked so often nowadays? Formerly, the population contributed to the conduct of the war by providing horses, weapons, etc., and this without compensation, especially when the citizens went to war with their own equipment. Nowadays, every contribution is paid for, and the total amount of all payments—as far as they are not taxed away—remains with the community in the form of government war bonds. The illusion of the enriching power of modern wars is created by the fact that every individual counts his bonded claims against the government as among his assets, while forgetting that as a member of the community he is liable for the government's debts. Therefore, financing wars by taxation always meets more resistance than financing by loans. The two methods lead to the same result: purchasing power is drawn away from the individual, whose consumption is curtailed in favor of the war effort. This is also why, in the case of financing through loans, it is really the present and not the future which carries the burden of the war. Not the burden, but the question who ultimately has to be taxed for it, is deferred into the future, and everybody thinks it will not be he but the other fellow who will have to pay for what he himself has received. Hence the popular misconception that in the case of the loan it is not the present but the future generation which has to bear the burden of war. Actually, the burden is carried by the present generation, even though it is unaware of the fact.

Again we see that the war boom is nothing desirable in the long run. It means feverish activity that results not in increasing but in stagnating, or even decreasing, wealth.

Government Debts, Too, Have to Be Paid Some Day

The illusion of the wealth growing during wartime has one of its roots in another fallacy: that neither interest nor amortization on government bonds ever has to be met through taxation. Some of Keynes' more radical followers in this country share this illusion. They assume that government obligations can ever again be met by issuing new government bonds. If this were correct, then indeed a large and increasing government debt would mean large and increasing wealth; on the one hand, the community would have billions of new assets for which, on the other hand, nobody would ever be liable.

Experience proves that the perpetually increasing debt is an illusion. No government conscious of its responsibility has ever relied on the alleged ability of the public to absorb any amount of new government bonds. Diminishing the government debt in peacetime in order to be prepared for the increased needs of wartime has always been the aim of government. It has been felt that there is a limit to government borrowing, because at a certain point the public repudiates new loans; then the deficit has to be met by printing paper money, i.e., open inflation. Throughout history this has happened every time a government debt grew beyond the economic capacity of a country—e.g., in the French Revolution with its famous methods of borrowing. A more recent example was Fascist Italy with her methods of financing the war. Although her national economy was under the strictest control, it was (according to a report by Badoglio's first Minister of Finance) in such a state, even before the Allied invasion, that the public refused to take over further government debts and the government had to resort to open inflation.

Therefore he who advocates perpetuation of the war boom—or rather the methods through which the war boom is financed—through peacetime, stands for a policy which may lead to the destruction of government credit and ultimately to runaway inflation.

What a War Boom Really Proves

Feverish activities during a war boom do not prove that full employment can be created in peacetime for any length of time through governmental spending—at least not if the economy is supposed to remain a private-capitalist one. It simply proves that any amount of activity, limited only by physical possibilities, can be incited under two conditions: (a) that production is carried on for collective purposes and not for the markets, and that the individual is no longer free to decide what and how many goods he wants to consume; (b) that this production is carried on through individuals who (for the reasons explained above) work partially free of charge and who are no longer free to decide whether they want to work under such conditions. It is self-evident that work done by people who cannot refuse production, for people who cannot refuse consumption, can go on without interruption. Here lies the explanation why unemployment does not exist in a communist economy. But an economy which perpetuates this method into peacetime, and makes it the deciding factor for its working, is no longer a private capitalist economy.

There is only one legitimate means of increasing employment in such an economy, namely, by inciting the enlargement of existing and the establishment of new enterprises. This can be achieved by creating conditions under which new investments seem to be profitable.

It may be difficult to create such conditions because of certain maladjustments in important cost factors which have developed in this country. Nevertheless, there is no other way out than to try to remove these maladjustments. Therefore, the endeavor to counterbalance existing maladjustments through government spending—not during short transitory periods, but in the long run—will lead to disappointment. This is elementary. But it seems that elementary things sometimes have to be said.

4. Capital Is Made at Home[*]

Plans for the export of American capital to the European continent after the war are being widely discussed. The opposition generally argues that the loans will again lead to losses, this time for the taxpayer, since they would be granted through the government rather than by private investors. But Europe's need for American credit is taken for granted.

The question must be raised, however, of how far Europe will really need American credit, and how far it will be able to rely on homemade capital. To clarify these issues it is useful and necessary to recall the financial development in Germany between the two wars. The outstanding features of that development are the subject of this chapter.

Briefly, the story is that in 1924 Germany began to absorb high amounts of foreign capital, but by mid-July 1931 the import of capital was suddenly stopped and she was forced to rely on her own resources. In one week she gave up her search for foreign credits and turned to capital autarchy. Nevertheless, as the world has meanwhile come to know to its sorrow, her industrial output was stupendous.

From Capital Autarchy via Capital Imports to Capital Autarchy

Foreign capital did not flow into Germany in substantial amounts immediately after the war, when capital was urgently needed to replace depleted stocks and restore the worn-out industrial and

---

[*] I am grateful to Miss Hedwig Wachenheim for her collaboration in compiling the statistical data used in this chapter. It appeared first in *Social Research*, May 1944.

transportation systems.[1] Nevertheless, in 1924, after the great inflation, Germany's industrial and transportation systems were in
good shape, for meanwhile, except during the dizzy last months of
the inflation, the German entrepreneur had had more capital at his
disposal than he actually needed. Capital was made at home,
through the restrictions that inflation had imposed on consumption.

Nor was it through foreign loans that the budget and currency
were stabilized in the fall of 1923. The stabilization was achieved
through the rentenmark credit granted to the Reich and to industry
and agriculture in the amount of 2,070 million marks,[2] and raised by
the issuance of new mark bills. The latter were really nothing but
the old mark bills. . That they were covered by a mortgage on
industry and agriculture was pure fiction. Nevertheless, the mere
idea that they were covered was enough to reduce the velocity of
the money in circulation, and therefore had the effect of an internal
loan granted by the holders of the bills. Suddenly billions of marks
in savings were available, and thereby billions of marks of capital.
Capital had again been produced by a mere shift in consumption
habits.

With this rentenmark loan the ground for German recovery was
laid. Looking back, it seems highly likely that Germany, with her
industry reconstructed by the inflation and her economy restored
by the rentenmark loan, could have managed without new foreign
capital. To be sure, she needed foreign raw materials, but short-
term credits for this purpose had come in before 1924, and would
also have been available later. At any rate, what was done during
the era of capital imports was much less essential than what had
already been achieved.

[1] A certain amount of capital entered Germany through speculation in mark
notes and exchange, in the form of small loans and through the sale of
securities abroad. It is doubtful, however, whether Germany's industrial
equipment profited from it, since reparation payments had already started at
that time (May 1921). For details see Report of the Second Committee of
Experts to Reparation Commission, April 9, 1924, in Rufus Cutler Dawes,
The Dawes Plan in the Making, Indianapolis, 1925, pp. 490 ff., also pp. 503 ff.;
Economist, August 16, 1921, p. 222.

[2] Of this total, 1,200 million went to the Reich and 870 million to industry
and agriculture; see Hjalmar Schacht, *The Stabilization of the Mark*, tr. by
Ralph Butler, London, 1927, p. 182.

Foreign credits began to flow in after the acceptance of the Dawes Plan. According to generally accepted estimates of the maximum amount granted Germany,[3] she received, from the summer of 1924 to the summer of 1930, about 15 to 16 billion marks in short-term credits (one-fourth from the United States) and 11 billion in long-term credits (one-half from the United States); there was an additional 7 billion in direct investments in securities, mortgages, real property, and the like, making a total of 33 to 34 billion marks. In July 1931, when approximately 3 billion marks had been withdrawn, short-term credits still amounted to 13.1 billion marks, long-term credits to 10.7 billion, and direct investments to 6 billion.[4]

But the spring of 1931 represented the turning point. The Reichsbank lost nearly 2 billion marks in gold and foreign currency in the two months after the crash of the Austrian Kreditanstalt in May of that year. In a panic the German Government sent the president of the Reichsbank to the European money centers in quest of new credits of at least 400 million dollars.[5] On July 9 Dr. Luther arrived in London, on the 10th he was in Paris, and on the 11th he flew home. On the 13th he went to Basle to attend a meeting of the governors of the central banks. The credit of 100 million dollars which had been granted the Reich in June for three weeks was extended for three months [6]—for all practical purposes it was frozen anyhow—but a new credit grant was refused. The creditors were no longer willing to pour money into the bottomless German barrel. Germany was forced to act alone. On July 14 the government announced a bank holiday, and on the 15th centralized all foreign exchange dealings in the Reichsbank,[7] which meant the first step toward full currency control. Germany was embarking upon a new policy: to live without importing capital.

[3] *The Problem of International Investment*, A Report by a Study Group of Members of the Royal Institute of International Affairs, London, 1937, p. 236.

[4] *Statistisches Jahrbuch für das Deutsche Reich*, 1937, p. 538; C. R. S. Harris, *Germany's Foreign Indebtedness since July 1931*, London, 1935, pp. 8-9.

[5] *Financial Chronicle*, July 11, 1931, p. 75.

[6] *Ibid.*, July 18, 1931, p. 336.

[7] Claude William Guillebaud, *The Economic Recovery of Germany*, London, 1939, p. 21.

The world expected a new collapse. True, a heavy deflationary crisis shook Germany. But the deflation was not caused by capital withdrawals or by the lack of new capital influxes; it was government-made, to enable German exporters to compete with the British, who were being favored by the devaluation of the pound.[8]

At the beginning of September 1931 the first moratorium agreement for short-term credits was concluded. In June 1933 a partial transfer moratorium for the service of long-term loans was announced, followed by an almost total one in 1934.[9] Nevertheless, until her war with the United States, Germany continuously repurchased her loans in foreign markets, where they were devalued by default. Thus she recovered from the 1931 crisis not only without capital imports but even while reducing her foreign debt.

Since the turning point Germany has produced capital in tremendous amounts, for domestic investment as well as for exportation. The Hitler era before the war was one of intensive industrial reconstruction, in which Germany's capacity for production in general, and for the production of war material in particular, was enormously expanded. During those six years from 1933 through 1938 the capital produced for domestic investment was as follows (in billions of marks): [10]

1933	5.1	1936	13.8
1934	8.2	1937	16.0
1935	11.6	1938	19.0

Hitler's statement [11] that Germany spent 90 billion marks on her armament from March 1933 to the outbreak of the war in 1939 is corroborated by estimates made in Great Britain and in this coun-

[8] On September 21, 1931, Great Britain suspended the gold standard, and on December 8, 1931, the Brüning government cut all income from interest, wages, social insurance, and relief, as well as prices; see *Reichsgesetzblatt*, 1931, i, p. 699.

[9] Guillebaud, *op. cit.*, pp. 63-65.

[10] Reichskreditgesellschaft, *Deutschlands Wirtschaftliche Lage in der Jahresmitte 1939*, Berlin, 1939, p. 5.

[11] In a Reichstag address of September 1, 1939: *Monatshefte für auswärtige Politik*, 1939, p. 907.

try.[12] And the output of armament represented capital production, inasmuch as it withdrew goods and services from consumption.

As for capital exports, Germany transferred, from the turning point in July 1931 to the outbreak of war in 1939, approximately 4.5 billion marks on her debt service; of this, it must be emphasized, approximately 3 billion was transferred during the pre-Hitler era.[13] In addition, her foreign debt was reduced during these years

GERMANY'S FOREIGN DEBT, 1931-39 [a]

(in billions of marks)

Date	Moratorium Credits	Other Short-term Credits [b]	Long-term Credits	Total
July 1931	6.3	6.8	10.7	23.8
Nov. 1931	5.4	5.2	10.7	21.3
Feb. 1932	5.0	5.1	10.5	20.6
Sep. 1932	4.3	5.0	10.2	19.5
Feb. 1933	4.1	4.6	10.3	19.0
Sep. 1933	3.0	4.4	7.4	14.8
Feb. 1934	2.6	4.1	7.2	13.9
Feb. 1935	2.1	4.6	6.4	13.1
Feb. 1936	1.7	4.6	6.1	12.4
Feb. 1937	1.2	4.2	5.4	10.8
Feb. 1938	0.9	4.1	5.0	10.0
Feb. 1939	0.8	4.1	4.6	9.5

[a] Based on *Statistisches Jahrbuch für das Deutsche Reich*, 1937, p. 538; *Economist*, July 9, 1938, p. 65.

[b] Including the clearing debts which accrued to the short-term debt from 1935; see *Economist*, February 11, 1939, p. 301.

by 14.3 billion marks, as shown in the table above. Of that amount 6 billion marks was accounted for by the depreciation of the creditor countries' currencies,[14] and only part of the remaining

[12] *Banker* (London), February 1937, p. 114; Fritz Lehmann and Hans Staudinger, "Germany's Economic Mobilization for War," National Industrial Conference Board, *Conference Board Economic Record*, New York, 1940, pp. 290-309.

[13] *Banker*, July 1938, p. 14; Guillebaud, *op. cit.*, p. 63.

[14] Allen Thomas Bonnel, *German Control over International Economic Relations*, Urbana, Ill., 1940, p. 118.

8.3 billion represented actual repayments, for Germany was able, as shown in preceding table, to repurchase loans and marks in foreign hands well under par. Nevertheless, very substantial exports took place, and the capital exported was replaced by domestically created capital.

It is very difficult to estimate the creditors' losses. As far as the moratorium credits are concerned, it is generally estimated that the creditors lost 15 per cent when they sold their accounts; this would mean a loss of approximately 825 million marks, since 5.5 billion marks in these accounts was disposed of by 1939. Estimates on the repatriation of the foreign bonds range from 400 to 700 million dollars. Up to 1934, when approximately 300 million dollars in these accounts had been repatriated, the foreign creditors had lost about one-half through sales below par; [15] later their loss was much higher.

These losses, however, are in all likelihood the minor part of the damage that foreign creditors suffered from their German investments, since the whole debt, so far as it was not paid back by the outbreak of the war, must be considered lost, at least for the time being. This would mean that besides their losses on the moratorium credits and repatriated bonds, the foreign creditors lost 3.9 billion dollars (9.5 billion marks) out of the 5.7 billion dollars (23.8 billion marks) that was due them in July 1931.

The burden of this loss was not evenly distributed. The banks that granted the moratorium credits suffered relatively little, as in these accounts all except 780 million marks was paid off. It was the private investor who subscribed to the German loans who had to bear the heaviest burden.

Can It Happen Again?

There seems to be a certain feeling that such a disaster cannot occur again. Has this belief any valid basis? Obviously the answer depends on the cause of the disaster.

Popular opinion sees the cause in the alleged carelessness with which such huge sums were lent to borrowers abroad. This opin-

[15] Harris, *op. cit.*, p. 38.

ion, however, is undoubtedly mistaken. In the first place, it is not appropriate to speak of a lack of care in regard to an action that was taken by nearly all banks and investment houses, in accordance with public opinion of the time, and with the approval of the government. Second, an investment house can really be made responsible only for its examination of the individual debtor's solvency and for the formulation of the indenture. In this instance the creditors proceeded with remarkable thoroughness; with negligible exceptions, none of the loans or credits given to Germany was defaulted through the insolvency or bankruptcy of the debtor.

Another explanation that has been put forward is that the loans were used not for production but for consumption purposes, such as the construction of "stadia, swimming pools, and ornamental buildings." [16] This is true only to a small extent, however, for most of the loans were granted to private industrial firms and public utilities. Furthermore, Germany's productive capacity, whatever may be meant by that rather vague term, was increased sufficiently after 1923 to create a surplus production equivalent to the amount necessary for amortization and interest.

Still another explanation, frequently encountered, is that the default was caused by the German debtors' lack of liquidity; especially the German banks are accused of having borrowed short and lent long.[17] After the bank holidays, however, and the subsequent moratorium agreements of 1931, all short-term loans became long, and interest and amortization payments were nevertheless suspended in 1933.

The best of the usual explanations, and one that seems to be generally accepted nowadays, is that in regard to the loans of that period—in contrast to the big international loans of the nineteenth century—it was no longer possible to transfer the interest and amortization burden to the creditor countries. The argument is accurately summarized in the report of the Study Group of Members of the Royal Institute of International Affairs: [18] "In the nineteenth

[16] Schacht in *Frankfürter Zeitung*, November 19, 1927.
[17] Young Plan Advisory Committee Report, *Economist*, Supplement, January 2, 1932, p. 5.
[18] *The Problem of International Investment* (cited above), p. 13.

century . . . the chief lending country, namely Great Britain, herself constituted a market with unlimited possibilities of expansion for the produce of the countries to which she lent; and her lending served to increase the output of precisely the commodities which she was ready to consume. But when the United States lent . . . there was only a somewhat weak presumption that Germany's capacity to sell goods in world markets would thereby be increased, and virtually no presumption at all that the United States herself would be willing to increase her imports in proportion to the growth of her interest claims."

Undoubtedly this is a very important aspect of the situation. Over and over again, especially during the settlement of reparations, failure to understand that large international payments can be accepted only in goods, not in money or gold, proved fatal. Whoever hopes to get his money back from abroad must be prepared to take goods or services.

Nevertheless, events since 1933 and particularly during the last years before World War II, show that the reasoning of the Royal Institute report is only partly correct. Although the creditor countries, reluctant to accept more imports, rationed them and imposed high duties on them, they could not prevent their arrival from Germany; these measures merely made importation harder for the debtor, who was forced to subsidize his exports. In the matter of a country's ability to make payments abroad, it should never be forgotten that, despite the widely held opinion, no country is predestined to have an active or passive trade balance. A small deflationary pressure on the price level, or a small inflationary rise in the price level, will, under certain conditions, suffice to reverse the trend of the trade balance. This is especially clear from the change in the German trade balance between 1927, the year of the largest capital import, and 1931, the year of the largest capital export. In 1927 it showed an import surplus of 3,427 million marks, and in 1931 an export surplus of 2,872 million, a difference of 6,299 million.[19]

What actually prevented Germany from continuing the service on her debt was something else, as has meanwhile become obvious.

[19] *Statistisches Jahrbuch*, 1938, p. 254.

In examining the reason for the German default, two periods must be distinguished: the first, from the end of 1932 to September 1934; the second, from that date to the war.

In the first period the balance of trade became unfavorable and the acquisition of foreign exchange ceased, simply because Germany started on a policy of credit expansion to combat unemployment. During this credit expansion the exchange rate of the mark was not lowered, although it had previously risen substantially through the devaluation of other countries' currencies. In these circumstances it was only natural—according to all rules of the purchasing-power parity theory, the classical theory of exchange—that the balance of trade became passive; it turned from an export surplus of 1,072 million marks in 1932 to an import surplus of 284 million in 1934.[20] Thus from June 1934 the default on interest and amortization on long-term loans was inevitable.

The second period began with the so-called "New Plan" of Schacht in September 1934. Again the balance of trade was reversed, this time toward an export surplus, brought about by an intricate system of import rationing, not by deflationary measures.

In addition, exports were fostered.[21] The technique of the so-called *Exportförderung* (promotion of exports) changed as time went on, but the fundamental idea was always that through defaulting on her foreign loans Germany could depreciate her foreign bonds. Furthermore, by restricting the use of certain mark balances and securities held by people abroad (*Auslandssperrmark, Effekten-*

[20] *Ibid.*, 1938, p. 254.

[21] In the early days of the Nazi regime exports were promoted by giving the exporter as a subsidy the difference between the low market price paid in foreign exchange for the German bonds repurchased abroad and their nominal Reichsmark value. Blocked mark accounts were bought up by the "Golddiskont" bank at a heavy discount; the discount was also used to subsidize the exporter, as was the gain from the repurchase of the scrip certificates issued after June 1933 in part payment of interest on Germany's long-term debt. In the middle of 1934, however, the issue of scrip was stopped and the buying of German bonds abroad through the Exportförderung was limited to cases in which payment did not become due until twelve months after the sale. From then on exports were subsidized from a fund (800 million marks in 1935 and 1,000 million in 1936) produced by a levy on the annual turnover. Throughout this period exports were subsidized also by the use of blocked marks (*Banker*, February 1937, p. 161).

sperrmark, Auswanderersperrmark), she depreciated these assets too, and was thus able to repurchase them at a fraction of their face value. With the profits from this procedure her exports were subsidized and, in consequence, substantially increased.

But the foreign exchange gained by these methods did not go to Germany's creditors; on the contrary, the creditors were forced through false pretexts to make great and ever new concessions. The foreign exchange was used to finance propaganda abroad, to build up gigantic stores of raw material for the war, and to amass a secret fund of gold and foreign exchange. The Germany that was then professing not to have sufficient foreign exchange for her creditors had all the foreign exchange she needed for her war preparations. Incredible as it seems today, it is clear that a substantial part of Germany's war preparations was financed by her foreign creditors, very much against their will.

Thus Germany's bankruptcy was not caused by her economic situation. A country that is able to turn its balance of trade in its own favor whenever it wishes cannot be considered incapable of acquiring foreign exchange. In the last analysis, the German default was deliberate and political. Germany succeeded through fraud and superior capacity to negotiate, especially on the part of Schacht, who played adroitly on the creditors' weakness and disunity and their governments' unwillingness to protect what they considered the interest of one group.

Finally, it should be remembered that in all countries the position of creditors, in comparison with that of industrialists, suffers from an inherent weakness. Industrialists will continue their export business even if the debts accumulated from former exports have not been paid. They would rather give away goods, if the gifts come out of the pockets of the bondholders, than turn down new business.[22] That is why most countries are reluctant to use all

[22] The German-Swiss dealings are a case in point. Although Germany owed money to Swiss citizens for the credits granted her from 1924 to 1930, Switzerland paid for the German coal deliveries of later years by putting the money at the disposal of German tourists traveling in Switzerland. Instead of seeing to it that her own nationals, who were Germany's creditors, were paid out of the coal deliveries, Switzerland reciprocated by new services. Schacht cleverly used Switzerland's biggest export industry, tourism.

possible means of collecting their external debts, so long as there is a chance of continuing exports to debtor nations.

Can all this happen again? There seems to be no reason why it cannot. On the contrary, the chances are even greater than before, for the debtor countries in Europe have meanwhile learned how independent they can really be of the goodwill of their creditors.

Will Europe Need Capital Imports After This War?

In order to judge whether Europe is going to need foreign credits after the present war, let us look back and see whether Europe really needed the capital imports of the twenties.

Foreign loans and credits to Europe, and especially to Germany, are customarily divided into two classes: stabilization loans, intended either to balance internal budgetary deficits or to balance deficits of foreign exchange; and loans for the reconstruction and expansion of productive capacity.

As for stabilization loans, it has already been mentioned that in Germany both the budget and the currency were stabilized with the rentenmark credits—a strictly internal loan granted by the holders of the rentenmark notes. The stability of the rentenmark itself was assured simply by the fact that it was kept scarce. The transformation of the rentenmark into the so-called Reichsmark, which was based on gold, was quite unimportant. Therefore the gold and foreign exchange acquired by the Reichsbank from the proceeds of the Dawes loan—and in that respect the Dawes loan itself—were superfluous.

But even if in the past gold and foreign exchange were really necessary to stabilize the currency, will they be required for this purpose after the present war? In this connection a distinction must be made between stabilizing transactions that counteract capital movements and those that counteract other items of the balance of payments.

To believe that stabilization loans are necessary to counteract capital movements would be to overlook the profound changes that have occurred in the past fifteen years. The gold standard, so far as it required that paper notes be convertible into gold in all circumstances and for an indefinite time, has been abandoned wherever it has been put to the test. It will never again be considered the ideal solution. Governments and nations alike will never again be willing to suffer deflations just because a foreign creditor has lost his confidence. Nowadays stable domestic credit and price systems are deemed more important than a stable exchange rate. The change in attitude, which began before 1931, became general when Britain went off the gold standard in that year. Gold is no longer sacrificed to restore the confidence of people who wish to withdraw or export their capital. Either the exchange rate is allowed to drop until bull speculation replaces bear speculation in the currency, and the drop is stopped, or the exodus of capital is prohibited, as in Germany in 1931 and in Britain in 1939.

If today governments are thus determined not to sacrifice gold and foreign exchange in order to maintain parity when capital is withdrawn, then stability loans that provide a fund of gold and foreign exchange for this purpose are superfluous. Such funds will not save a currency in a troubled world, anyhow. Control of exchange will be the method, at least in the near future; especially will the defeated countries have to resort to it. Stabilization loans of this type are outdated.

In regard to stabilization loans intended to counteract other items of the balance of payments, it must not be forgotten that the first requirement for currency stabilization is a sound financial and credit policy. In comparison with such a policy stabilization credits are of minor importance. Either the deficit which they are supposed to bridge is of a transitory character, in which case the banks of the country will easily find the needed amounts in the free market; or the deficit is caused by a basic disturbance of the purchasing-power parity, in which case stabilization credits are useless, mere drops of water on a hot stone. Their disregard of these facts is the basic fallacy of the Keynes and White plans. Currency stability, too, is basically made at home.

Germany until 1931 enjoyed not too little but too much credit to bridge the deficits in her balance of payments. The loans she received concealed her basic economic maladjustments and delayed their correction. This made the situation acute when the withdrawal of the credits began, after the world had finally recognized her ills.

In addition to the stabilization loans were those for the reconstruction and expansion of productive capacity. How essential were loans of this type in the postwar development of the German economy?

I have already mentioned the paradox that an essential part of the reconstruction of Germany's industrial equipment, as far as it was worn out during the war, was accomplished during the inflation that ended in 1923. What followed was merely the finishing touch.

It is true that all who did not profit from the inflation were impoverished. It is also true that forced savings or forced capital production in the amounts of those days is certainly highly objectionable. Yet the German inflation does indicate how much capital can be produced by inflationary credit expansion. If administered in less gigantic doses it need not have such severe consequences for the social structure.

To be sure, at the end of the inflation, when the currency was stabilized, a severe capital (or rather monetary) stringency arose in Germany, but this stringency had nothing to do with the need for capital in the true sense of "real" capital. Of the latter there was enough, even more than enough. What happened at that time was a typical scramble for liquidity, such as occurs at the end of every boom—in this case an inflation boom—and such propulsions can be moderated through an easy-money policy by the central bank.

From 1924 to 1931 foreign loans poured into Germany in the huge amounts mentioned above. But whether they actually augmented Germany's productive capacity is open to question. Her balance of payments raises some doubts. Of the net capital import of 17.3 billion marks from 1924 to 1930, only 2.4 billion was used to buy merchandise; the remainder was spent on the transfer of interest payments (2.7 billion marks), on reparations (10.1 billion) and for the import of gold and foreign currency (2.1 billion).[23] Thus only a relatively small part of the gigantic capital influx was

[23] *The Problem of International Investment* (cited above), p. 238.

used for really productive purposes, and we may therefore conclude that only a small part was needed for such purposes.

Modern highly industrialized countries seem to be capital autarchies—that is, they make their capital at home. And they are able to do so because their economic systems are elastic with respect to their productive and their credit-creating capacity. They are no longer either Robinson Crusoe's island or colonies of the nineteenth century, from which many people even today derive their conception of capital production.

As for productive elasticity, it is a commonplace that modern industrialized countries possess more industrial equipment than can be fully employed when demand for goods is declining. And even when demand is not declining, new plants and equipment can be built, roads, houses, railroads, can be constructed, with a relatively small amount of additional labor. Productive capacity is so large and so elastic that the needs for investment and renovation, in addition to current consumption needs, can be satisfied without difficulty—in contrast to Robinson Crusoe's island, which had not even an ax, and in contrast to colonial countries, which have no plants, roads, railroads, ports, or other such facilities. In Europe all these facilities will be available after the present war—if they are not totally destroyed by bombing. A certain restriction in consumption will have to be borne, it is true; Europeans will not be able to travel in air-conditioned trains immediately after the war.

Elasticity of production was the strength of the European countries after the 1914-18 war. They have since acquired in addition elasticity of money and credit. With the abandonment of the gold standard, governments and central banks are no longer forced to restrict their credits in order to maintain the parity of their currency. There is no longer such a thing as need for the so-called external discount policy. Now there exists only the so-called internal discount policy, which is used to manipulate the business cycle and the capital and credit supply. The supply of credit can be raised and the interest rate lowered at will; the effect is merely a change in the distribution of income between debtors and creditors. The "slight inflation" that arises from such inflationary expansions of credit restricts current consumption, through raising the prices of goods, and directs economic activity toward the production of capital goods, as described above.[24]

This method of capital reconstruction undoubtedly has certain disadvantages. If loans from abroad—the alternative procedure—must be repaid and are not just gifts, the nations of Europe have to consider whether the disadvantages of creating capital at home can be borne more easily than what they call "tribute"—that is, payments to a foreign country for interest and capital, with the deflationary crises and the thousands of other inconveniences that can follow in their wake. The decision will depend on the marginal productivity of the imported capital, which may be extremely high if the industrial apparatus is completely destroyed. If this is not the case, they will prefer to make their capital at home by restricting current consumption. If it is given them as a present they would, of course, prefer foreign capital.

The capital exported in the 'twenties turned out to have been largely a gift. Most of the capital exported to Europe is lost, probably forever, as everybody realizes. Why is there nevertheless such an eagerness to export capital again? The basic reason, of which some of the experts themselves may not be conscious, is

[24] Dr. H. Neisser in *Social Research*, August 1944, pages 369-381, has pointed out that my "position is surprisingly close to the position of certain Keynesians, who have argued . . . that the amount of saving necessary for expanding the current rate of output is always automatically created by increasing the current rate of investment." He thinks that capital can be made by inflation only if a totalitarian government can tell the people "how much to save or how much to spend" and if "a certain historically obtained standard of living must be maintained for the major part of the population." To this I would agree to a certain extent, but would raise the question whether a country urgently seeking capital abroad has not to lower rather than to raise "the historically obtained standard of living" by opposing instead of encouraging wage increases.

It is, incidentally, not the aim of this chapter to prove that capital *must* or *should* be made at home rather than be imported, but that it *can* be made at home under certain conditions.

What the article teaches for the problems of today (Fall 1948) is that the effect of a sound internal monetary and fiscal policy on the balance of payments is much stronger than is generally assumed and that no foreign loans, however lavishly granted, can correct deficits in the balance of payments for the long run if the debtor countries indulge in an inflationary monetary and fiscal policy.

perhaps the fact that capital export, especially in its modern form wherein it is combined with the export of goods, means creating a ready market for certain products that could not otherwise be sold because they are too expensive. These goods can compete abroad, not because they are cheap but because the credit that finances their exportation is cheap: the foreign country is offered the expensive goods in conjunction with relatively cheap credit. Thus it could be said that the exports are reduced in price at the expense of those who lend capital or extend credit. This is especially true if the foreign country plays with the idea of not paying back the loan, or of repaying it only in part. Indeed, the importer will tolerate even the highest price if he knows that in the last resort not he but the exporting country pays' for the import. As soon as capital is exported which will not be repaid at all, or will not be repaid fully, capital export becomes merely a subsidy paid to the export interests by the bondholder or, in the case of government-financed loans, by the taxpayer.

Of course, under specific conditions political loans will have to be granted. With them this chapter is not concerned. Nor does this discussion deal with loans for relief and rehabilitation, which are granted for noneconomic purposes. It deals only with loans for currency stabilization and for the reconstruction of productive capacity. If these are contemplated, the history of international loans during the period between the wars should always be kept in mind.

5. Don't Predict Postwar
Deflation—Prevent It! *

The country is swamped with predictions about Postwar Business. They run all the way from lasting prosperity to hopeless depression. How much weight should be attached to these predictions?

In this author's opinion their value is very limited. All estimates about how many millions of workers will be released and how many can be reabsorbed by industry after the end of the war must be considered highly questionable. The respect they command in this country—more than elsewhere—is not justified. Unlike communist and Fascist economies, a free economy is directed not by government orders but by the calculations, hopes, and fears of millions of people; *the objective conditions with which these people will have to reckon, and—even more—the subjective reactions are as unpredictable as the future in general.* Therefore, estimates of future billions of working hours, of the national income, and of the goods to be produced are nothing but a toying with figures. There is little that is scientific about such estimates. All calculations of the so-called deflationary gap—the gap between the purchasing power needed for the maintenance of full employment and the purchasing power to be counted on—will prove to be fallacious; as fallacious as all the calculations of the inflationary gap during World War II have proved to be; and postwar planning based on such specific calculations will turn out to be impractical.

During the last few months the proponents of the pessimistic school of thought—which predicts depression and deflation—seem to

* Appeared first in *The Commercial and Financial Chronicle*, Jan. 25, 1945.

have gained in popularity. This line has been adopted by an important group of economists here as well as abroad. Lately it has been propagated by the distinguished Swedish economist, Gunnar Myrdal, in the Swedish, Swiss, and American press.

This school of thought is not only pessimistic—it is fatalistic. It describes postwar mass unemployment as something that follows more or less perforce from the working of the capitalist system. Such an approach has obvious dangers. Let us, therefore, examine the validity of its arguments a little more closely:

The arguments seem to be threefold. They are: (1) The Argument of Increased Population; (2) The Argument of Increased Productivity, and (3) The Argument of the Delayed Rising of the Standard of Living, generally known as the Oversavings Argument. They are based, at least in part, on certain factual assumptions made in S. Morris Livingston's well-known study, *Markets After the War.*

THE ARGUMENT OF INCREASED POPULATION

According to Livingston, around 10,000,000 more people will be seeking jobs in 1946 than in 1940. How can these 10,000,000 people be employed? The question sounds rather distressing. It seems quite impossible to provide jobs for all these newcomers, even if the labor market absorbs the supply which existed before. However, the question in itself only shows how far the thinking of some economists, even if thoroughly acquainted with the classicists of economics, deviates from the orthodox lines of economic thinking and disregards certain basic truths.

Orthodox thinking precludes unemployment as a consequence of an increase in population. For every newcomer is not only a potential producer, but also a potential consumer. According to classical economic thinking, production and consumption equal each other. Growth of population can be the reason for unemployment only under very exceptional conditions, the most important one being lack of capital necessary for the productivity of the new labor forces. This condition certainly does not exist in our times of very low interest rates.

Unless compelling reasons to the contrary are put forward, an increase in population can never lead to unemployment.

THE ARGUMENT OF INCREASED PRODUCTIVITY

Productivity, according to Livingston, is increasing at a rate of 2½ per cent or even 3 per cent yearly. Where will the purchasing power and the demand come from to absorb the output increased by the higher productivity of labor, once the government no longer requires more than half of the national production? Will the management of industry suggest a huge rise in wages in order to create sufficient purchasing power to absorb the output under full employment?

Let us put aside the highly controversial question whether productivity really is increasing at the presumed rate—there are authors who reach entirely different conclusions—and let us assume that the productivity of labor will have increased at the rate of 2½ to 3 per cent during the war; does this mean that unemployment is inevitable? Again, this question in itself implies the disregard of basic economic truths; it is based on a fallacy.

High productivity of labor means that labor produces more units of goods per unit of labor. Generally speaking, wages increase with the units of goods produced per hours of labor, for the simple reason that competition in industry is likely to raise wages until the extra profit of the increased productivity has disappeared. At least this is the case if the adjustment does not take place through declining prices with unchanged wages, i.e., with rising real wages, an eventuality not probable in the inflationary atmosphere of the postwar world. In no case can higher productivity result in a deficit of purchasing power. What has been paid out, chiefly in the form of wages, will be sufficient to buy the output of labor, whether large or small, because increased productivity will either force wages to rise or prices to fall. To assume that productivity of labor rises while wages remain low—or prices high—at the same time is to make two assumptions incompatible with each other; at least, this is so in a static world in which maladjustments are leveled out.

Of course, in a dynamic reality, wages can remain too low relative to labor productivity. But this would cause a boom and not unemployment, as every cost alleviation does. For new enterprises would appear profitable and would absorb elements so far unemployed. Also, wages could be too high relative to labor productivity. But this would not cause full employment—rather a depression and declining employment, as certain enterprises would be forced to close down because of too high costs of production. In a static world with which the Increased Productivity argument primarily deals, wages must be considered as adjusted to productivity. There is no reason to worry where the purchasing power for the increased product is to come from; purchasing power creates itself.

Higher productivity means higher potential wealth of the country; and a country does not suffer because of increased wealth. Therefore, the pessimistic attitude concerning the postwar economy must be considered as unjustified on this basis.

THE OVERSAVINGS ARGUMENT

Even if the Increased Population argument and the Increased Productivity argument are fallacious—that is, if the purchasing power in the hands of labor would always be sufficient to buy the whole output of the economy—even then, according to the pessimists, full employment could not be maintained: the purchasing power, although sufficient, would remain partly unspent, because the standard of living (i.e., consumption) would rise neither so rapidly nor to the same degree as is necessary to maintain full employment. This, clearly, is the well-known Oversavings argument. In our time it has been used by J. M. Keynes and his school to explain unemployment of a secular character. According to this school, modern economy has reached a state of maturity in which new possibilities for profitable investments are scarce. The economy therefore is in a chronic state of underinvestment which prevents savings from being readily absorbed; thus the resulting oversaving must lead to a deficit in purchasing power—or, as it is commonly expressed, in effective demand.

It is not possible to deal here with the highly controversial question of the validity of the oversaving-underinvestment theory; the following remarks are merely designed to show that this theory can hardly be used as a basis for such vital matters as our diagnosis of and planning for the postwar world. The factual as well as the theoretical foundation of the theory is too weak for this purpose.

The conception that the higher output of labor does not lead to a correspondingly higher consumption by labor cannot be proved to be valid over a longer period of time. Indeed, labor's fight for higher wages can be considered as the fight for a higher standard of living. As far as the period immediately after the war is concerned, it can happen that the average person will spend more than he earns, not less, because the high cash reserves accumulated during the war allow for many an extra outlay.

However, even if we assume that underconsumption and consequently excessive savings will be a feature of the postwar period, does this necessarily mean that these savings will lead to underinvestment followed by underemployment? Here, too, it must be realized how far such an assumption deviates from the classical one —and, by the way, from common sense also. Larger savings mean a greater supply of credit to industry, therefore expansion of industry and consequently higher employment.

Quite apart from this, the assumption that our economy is mature and unable to provide new opportunities for investment has never really been proved. The phenomenon of underemployment and underinvestment before the war proves only that enterprise was averse to expanding, but it does not explain the psychological and factual reasons for this behavior. As Professor Schumpeter in his criticism of Harold L. Laski's *Reflections on the Revolution of Our Time* [1] has stated quite correctly, the theory of the mature economy is nothing but the reflection of the group interest of the modern intellectual. One writer after another repeats this theory, without any one of them giving valid proofs of it.

But even if it could be proved that there are no opportunities for profitable new investments, unemployment would not necessarily follow. Professor Pigou proved this convincingly.[2] Even if the investment of *new capital* should prove to be unprofitable, the employment of *additional labor* could still be profitable, provided the cost of labor is not too high relative to the price of the finished

[1] *American Economic Review*, March 1944, p. 163.
[2] *Economic Journal*, 1943, p. 351.

product. Thus, low profitability of capital could lead to under-investment, but not necessarily to underemployment. The number of workmen an entrepreneur can employ—capital being ample and cheap—depends on what he has to pay for labor rather than for the use of capital.

Profits Create Purchasing Power and Employment

Does all this mean that everything will be for the best in the postwar economy? Not at all. It simply means that there is nothing inherent in the capitalist system that inevitably creates unemployment. Neither growth of population, nor increase of productivity, nor larger savings necessarily lead to depressions. A free economy does not work like a machine at a given speed. It is a living organism in which cells are born and die continually. The fact that more cells are born than die, or vice versa, influences the effective demand so greatly that all other factors are only of secondary importance. This is why—and herein we agree with the pessimists—the importance of the great demand for goods and the large amount of cash that will exist at the end of the war should not be overrated. In a free economy demand must come from money paid for the cost of production, money which eventually flows back to buy the output; an economy relying for any length of time on pent-up demand is doomed to failure anyway.

On what will it depend whether more economic cells are born than die; in other words, whether the economy will expand or contract? It will depend on whether the entrepreneur feels that the returns in new or expanded enterprises will be greater than the costs; in short, on whether new business will seem profitable. If this is the case, a boom and high employment will ensue; if not, the result will be a depression and low employment.

Profitability or nonprofitability of business will depend on the many different factors which are now so widely discussed. It will be of great importance to what extent the future corporation tax will mitigate the double taxation of the investor, existing under the present corporation tax law and deterring him from putting new money into enterprises. It will also be of fundamental importance whether wages rise at a quicker rate than productivity of labor.

Problems in this field will certainly be difficult to solve; but it should not be forgotten that the economic difficulties in the United States do not have their origin in natural conditions (as is the case in Europe with the problems she had to face after World War I and will have to face, to an even greater extent, after the second war), but rather are created by man and can therefore also be overcome by man. It is true, they must be handled with understanding, care, and (most important of all) common sense rather than with conceptions based on unproved theories. If this is accomplished, American business will prosper. If not, it will face depression.

6. Compensating Reactions to Compensatory Spending[*]

In the plans for maintaining full employment after the war that flood the country, governmental "compensatory" spending plays a major role. Only a few proposals mention the question of adjustment that was so prominent in the earlier literature on the liquidation of booms. Most planners do not recognize the paramount importance of the wage level for employment. If they see it at all, the importance given wages in sustaining a high effective demand far overshadows the importance given them as a cost factor. To be sure, there is an opposition. To it adjustments remain a major problem, and compensatory spending in an unadjusted economy seems of highly doubtful value. But in view of the overwhelming number and influence of those who favor "spending without adjustment"[1] and the appeal of their plans to laymen, the opposition must be considered "voices in the wilderness."

To anyone watching the trend of economic thought in this country the situation is not astonishing. It is just an outgrowth of the general acceptance of Keynesianism. For, though some planners[2] are distinctly out-Keynesing Keynes in a way that Lord Keynes

[*] Appeared first in the *American Economic Review*, March 1945.

[1] For a good survey of postwar full employment plans, see Albert Halasi, "Survey of Recent American Literature on Postwar Security," *International Postwar Problems*, Vol. I, 1943, pp. 120-38.

[2] *Cf.* Abba P. Lerner, "Functional Finance and the Federal Debt," *Social Research*, Vol. 10 (1943), pp. 38-51.

himself would surely reject, the planners' basic attitude is distinctly an application of Keynes' *General Theory*.[3] According to this theory, employment can, "as a rule" and "in the general case," be raised or restored by raising effective demand to a sufficiently high level. Why, then, should there be any need for a painful adjustment process?

In this chapter the author tries to explain what seem to him to be the fallacies not merely of some of Keynes' implications but also of the general assumption underlying the entire system.[4]

THE ILLUSION EFFECT OF MONETARY MANIPULATIONS IN CREATING EMPLOYMENT

Lord Keynes contends that "as a rule" and in the "general case" an expansion in "effective demand" increases employment as well as prices. "Effective demand spends itself partly in affecting output and partly in affecting price."[5] The reason is—to put Keynes' argument in the simplest form—that additional labor can be used profitably despite its diminished marginal productivity. This, in turn, is because "the decreasing return from applying more labor to a given capital equipment has been offset by the acquiescence of labor in a diminishing real wage."[6] And labor acquiesces in a diminishing real wage, because usually ". . . the supply of labor is not a function of real wages. . . ."[7] For "it is not their [the workers'] practice to withdraw their labor whenever there is a rise in the price of wage goods."[8]

However, "a point comes at which there is no surplus of labor

---

[3] John Maynard Keynes, *The General Theory of Employment, Interest, and Money*, New York, 1936.

[4] As I take the position that in my *Volkswirtschaftliche Theorie des Bankkredits* (1st ed., Tübingen, 1920) I advanced a "credit expansion theory of employment" very similar to that of Keynes, I have added in the following notes after the citations from Keynes' *General Theory* the numbers of the pages of my *Volkswirtschaftliche Theorie* on which the corresponding ideas are expressed.

[5] Keynes, *op. cit.*, pp. 13, 3, 285, and (in a slightly different wording) p. 296 (Hahn, *op. cit.*, pp. 135, 146, 140, 141, 149, footnote).

[6] Keynes, *op. cit.*, p. 289, and in a different wording, p. 284.

[7] *Ibid.*, p. 8.

[8] *Ibid.*, p. 9.

available at the then existing real wage." [9]   As soon as this point is reached, the supply price of labor is fixed in accordance with the declining purchasing power of wages.   In other words, the supply curve of labor in terms of money wages moves upward with prices which rise because of the expanding effective demand.   From this point on no additional unit of labor can be applied profitably.   The "crude quantity theory of money" once again functions.   "Output does not alter and prices rise in exact proportion to [the quantity of money]." [10]

This is doubtless a correct picture of the process of monetary expansion.   It is generally agreed that monetary expansion in its first phases increases employment.   But from a certain point on, which we may call the "reaction point," reactions on the side of the productive factors compensating the effect of credit or money expansion will set in, and prevent a further rise in employment or even bring about a decline. [11]   And this will be true even in the case not mentioned by Keynes—when price increases should have been avoided, diminishing unit costs offsetting the effects of diminishing marginal efficiency of labor.   In this case entrepreneurs derive extra profits which labor, from a certain point on, will claim for itself, [12] just as it claims for itself, and with success, the increments technical progress brings to its productivity.

Where does the difference between Keynes and the classical attitude lie?   Keynes assumes that the period before the "reaction point," the period free from "compensating reactions," is so long

[9] *Ibid.*, p. 289.

[10] *Loc. cit.*

[11] The experience of the last phase of the German inflation illustrates this point.   From about the middle of 1922 on, wages were made sliding according to the sinking purchasing power of money (*Gleitloehne*).   As a result, employment no longer rose, but even declined.   Inflation spent itself in price rises. For it is one question whether goods already fabricated are purchased at higher prices, and another whether new goods are fabricated.   The latter depends on production being more profitable, i.e., wages and other costs not rising so fast as prices; a fact quite obvious though often forgotten in the wake of the spending enthusiasm of our time.

[12] Sumner H. Slichter, "Labor after the War," in Harris, *Postwar Economic Problems,* New York, 1943, pp. 241-62: "Union wage policy will tend to keep the prospect for profits unfavorable, because unions will press for wage increases despite the continuation of price controls" (p. 245).

and general that it is characteristic of "the economic society in which we actually live," [13] and is thus a sufficient basis for a "general theory of employment." The classicists, on the other hand, consider the "reaction-free" period as usually short and occurring only exceptionally. This apparently unimportant difference in factual assumptions is, as far as I can see, responsible for all the wonders of the Keynesian world so paradoxical to classical thinking.

What prevents labor during the "reaction-free period," whether short or long, from raising its demands for money wages to correspond with its declining purchasing power and/or the profits resulting from increased sales? After all, men work for food, clothing, etc., not for pieces of paper, even if dollar amounts or other denominations are printed on them. Keynes does not answer the question; he merely states the facts so important to his system. It is a complicated sociological economic problem that is at stake. But one thing seems certain. If, during the "reaction-free period" labor does not insist on money-wage increases, it is not because it wishes to receive lower real wages. It can only be because it does not, or does not immediately or fully, realize what is happening when prices begin an inflationary rise. What works is the phenomenon Professor Irving Fisher described in his famous book *The Money Illusion* [14] and what we may therefore call the "illusion effect" of monetary manipulations.

THE ILLUSION EFFECT INDUCING INVESTMENT

According to Keynes' theory, a larger effective demand, leading to a higher level of employment, will depend, given a certain propensity of the community to consume, on the amount of current investments. "The amount of current investment will depend, in turn, on what we shall call the inducement to invest; and the inducement to invest will be found to depend on the relation between the schedule of marginal efficiency of capital and the complex of interest rates on loans of various maturities and risks." [15] So by

---

[13] Keynes, *op. cit.*, p. 3.
[14] Irving Fisher, *The Money Illusion*, New York, 1928.
[15] Keynes, *op. cit.*, pp. 27-28. (Hahn, *op. cit.*, 1st ed., pp. 132, 137.)

lowering the interest rate, investment and effective demand can be increased.

Increasing effective demand through lowered interest rates is what European writers used to call "inflationary credit expansion." It depends not on any spontaneous decision of the community to save more, but on the will and capacity of the banking system to expand the amount of credit and the quantity of money. According to the classic approach it is a case of monetary manipulation.

A downward monetary manipulation of interest rates can undoubtedly induce an increase in investments and effective demand, especially as "rising prices . . . will redistribute incomes to the advantage of the entrepreneur and to the disadvantage of the *rentier*," [16] and as this is equivalent to a further decline in the interest rate or even to a negative interest rate. But just as in the case of lowering wages through monetary manipulation, investments are induced only before the "reaction point" is reached. Then the productive factors whose rewards, although nominally unchanged, have really been lowered will react. As soon as the supply curve of credits is raised in accordance with the decreasing value of money, the investment-inducing effect of interest manipulation disappears. Similar developments which can, incidentally, be observed during every business cycle are the basis of all monetary cycle theories of the Wicksellian type.

That the illusion effect of money at first prevents compensating reactions was demonstrated drastically during the great German inflation. Until about the middle of 1922 the majority of the population, especially the creditors, were not aware of what was happening. They were deceived by the "illusion effect." Loans were still offered in ample quantities and at low rates. When the creditors were no longer taken in by the money illusion, they raised their demands for interest to fantastic levels, wishing to be compensated for the decreasing purchasing power of their money during the lending period. The Reichsbank, thinking it should not tolerate this healthy compensating reaction, tried to keep the rates down by maintaining a ridiculously low discount rate. This low

[16] Keynes, *op. cit.*, p. 290. (Hahn, *op. cit.*, 1st ed., p. 137.)

discount rate was one of the chief reasons for the runaway character that inflation in Germany assumed in 1922.[17]

THE ILLUSION EFFECT OF GOVERNMENT SPENDING

If the manipulation of interest rates downward does not induce sufficient investment, and it probably will not, compensatory deficit spending by the government is recommended. "The State which is in a position to calculate the marginal efficiency of capital-goods on long views and on the basis of the general social advantage," has, as Keynes says, to take "the responsibility for directly organizing investment." [18]

In the case of government spending, too, investment and employment increase because the supply price schedules of the productive factors have, through manipulation, become "really" lower than they seem. Here, too, sooner or later the point is reached where compensating reactions prevent further improvements, or even reverse already achieved improvements. Until then it is the illusion effect of monetary manipulations that prevents compensating reactions.

When the efficiency of a further unit of capital is too small to cover the interest charges, private enterprise refrains from new investments. If governments can invest where private enterprise cannot, it is not because capital is supposed to be more efficient in its hands. (Professor Hansen, for instance, warns against "timidity" and urges consideration of a 50 per cent recovery of principal—not of interest!—as a sufficient return on invested capital.[19]) It is because the interest rates charged the government are much lower than the market rate, or, if capital is allowed to be 50 per cent unrecoverable, even negative. A negative interest rate means that the entrepreneur does not have to make payments but receives payments from those who lend the capital. This is just what happens

[17] Cf. L. Albert Hahn, Geld und Kredit (Tübingen, 1924 and 1929) and Unsere Währungslage im Lichte der Geldtheorie (Frankfurt a. M., 1924).

[18] Keynes, op. cit., p. 164. (Hahn, Volkswirtschaftliche Theorie, 1st ed., p. 151.)

[19] Alvin H. Hansen, "The Postwar Economy" in Seymour E. Harris, Postwar Economic Problems, New York, 1943, p. 23.

in government deficit spending through shifting of the deficit in one way or another to the community, which becomes liable for the amounts.

What bearing the liability will have on the economy depends on whether and to what extent the members of the community have to redeem it by tax payments. Distinction is made in this respect, in literature, between the liability for interest and for the principal.

Sooner or later the day must come when interest no longer can be paid through issuing new government securities, but has to be paid out of taxes. This happens either when private investment is picking up so that government deficit spending has to be discontinued entirely in order to check an excess of effective demand; [20] or it happens, at the latest, when the public refuses to take over the ever-increasing public debt, i.e., when what can be called the saturation point for government securities is reached.

If interest on the public debt has some day to be met by taxation, it will mean a heavy burden on postwar America. For it would come on top of taxation for interest on the war debt, which alone will swallow a substantial part of national income. Nor, incidentally, can the tax burden be minimized by pointing to the growth of the economy which will reduce the ratio of the debt to the national income. The inherent weakness of the "growth argument" is that it assumes the "growth" to be, so to say, natural,[21] whereas it depends to a large degree on economic conditions and will probably never materialize if employment is made dependent upon government spending for any length of time. It is furthermore forgotten that the enlarged future economy will have its own larger problems, be they war, unemployment, or other. It does not therefore seem permissible to mortgage the growth.

The "only-the-interest" argument in contemporary literature on government spending is used to such an extent that the impression is created that only one-fortieth part of every deficit (2½ per cent of the capital) is the real burden, whereas the principal can be for-

[20] *Cf.* Lerner, *op. cit.*, p. 43.

[21] *Cf.* Joseph Stagg Lawrence, *Empire Trust Letter*, No. 6, p. 5, New York, Empire Trust Company, 1944, for a good refutation of the "growth argument."

gotten as a gift.[22] Obviously, when this argument is used, the beneficial effects of spending are made to compare very favorably with the ensuing burden.

However, the "only-the-interest" argument is tenable only if spending can be discontinued because private spending has picked up. The argument is not tenable in the case of spending continued indefinitely in order to counteract a chronic tendency to unemployment.

A curve representing the amounts of bonds or money accumulated by the public does not mount steadily to a saturation point, to run horizontally thereafter. Curves representing data which depend on psychological factors—such as confidence in business prospects, in the value of the currency, and in the future level of prices—never remain on a plateau but rise and fall according to the laws of action and reaction. In other words, once deflationary tendencies are relieved through inflationary tendencies, it becomes highly probable that—through the unloading of previously accumulated money and government securities—deflation turns into inflation, not into stabilization.

What must be done to prevent runaway inflation at such a time? It is not sufficient simply to stop further deficit spending. Certain amounts of existing public debt become due, and these amounts will be larger the smaller the portion of the debt which has been consolidated to longer terms. Suddenly, what seemed a gift for eternity is transformed into a real loan. The bill must at last be paid. In addition to taxation covering all public expenditures, business will then face the burden of high interest rates. For, in order to stem the demand of those who want to profit from the dwindling purchasing power of the currency and therefore borrow from the banks, interest rates will have to be raised. This also hurts legitimate enterprise. In short, a very severe deflation crisis will occur.

The result of all this is that interest on the public debt must be met by taxation. The principal, or at least parts of it, will also

---

[22] *Cf.* Harris, in Harris, *op. cit.*, pp. 172 ff.; also Alvin H. Hansen and Guy Greer, "The Federal Debt and the Future," *Harper's Magazine*, 1942: "The internal debt of a government need never be paid" (p. 492).

some day become a tax burden if government spending is permanent. If this is so, government deficits mean for the economy that net wages, net profits, and net interest received by the factors of production are really lower than their gross earnings. For from gross earnings the amounts should be deducted that will have to be paid as taxes in the future and thus represent a mortgage on present income. Owing to the illusion effect, this is not at once realized.

There is no miracle in government spending. The fundamental fact remains that investment and employment increase only when the supply schedules of the contributors are lowered in real terms. The difference is merely that government spending effects the reduction indirectly and unobtrusively, as does every inflation and monetary manipulation in general.

Incidentally, our analysis shows not only the mechanism at work when one tries to overcome by government investments the alleged "secular stagnation" of the economy, caused by insufficient profitability of new capital investments; it also shows that insufficient opportunities of capital investment can never be the reason for lasting unemployment—even if the "maturity" of the economy were proved.[23] For if investment becomes possible where the prices of the productive factors are lowered, excessive factor prices and not the low "efficiency" of capital are the secular cause of unemployment. Low efficiency of capital can explain why no new unit of capital is applicable to a given amount of labor, but not why no new unit of labor is applicable to a given capital. Even if the capital structure cannot be deepened, labor can be employed and savings utilized at the prevailing depth of the capital structure, if only labor is not more expensive than corresponds to its marginal efficiency. This has been recently restated with great clarity by Professor Pigou.[24]

---

[23] Cf. Joseph A. Schumpeter, review of Harold J. Laski's *Reflections on the Revolution of Our Time*, in *American Economic Review*, March 1944, p. 163.

[24] A. C. Pigou demonstrates in "The Classical Stationary State," *Economic Journal*, 1943, pp. 343-51, how investments which no longer bore interest became profitable again when the value of money increased, after workers had been forced to accept lower wages (pp. 349-50). He comes to the conclusion: "I have been concerned to show that in given conditions of technique and so

When employment is created by means of governmental deficit spending, the day will come when people realize that the real rates of earnings have been reduced and they will demand higher rates. Labor will not be satisfied with the prevailing wage level, less capital will be offered at the prevailing interest rate, and less entrepreneurial activity at the prevailing profit rate. All supply price schedules will move upward. Which of these upward movements will be the strongest depends upon whether labor, capital, or entrepreneurial earnings are expected to be taxed most heavily. The consequences for the structure of the economy are well known; in any case, a further increase in employment will not be possible. And if the government tries to compensate for the compensating reactions by spending still more, again still higher taxes will be anticipated, and so on in a vicious spiral.[25] All this will happen at the latest when the first taxes to meet the larger government obligations are to be levied.

The "General Case"

The fundamental difference between the classical and the Keynesian employment theory is one of factual assumption, not of theoretical analysis. Lord Keynes assumes that the state of monetary illusion is a normal state; that money wage, interest, and profit demands are normally not altered when the rates of earning no longer represent the same real value. The classicists assume as normal that the money illusion is always and immediately seen through and the supply schedules accordingly revised upwards, because people are interested only in their real, not their nominal income. These writers therefore contend that what they call monetary "falsifications" and even swindle do not really change the amount of employment but only the value of the currency. Thus, the whole question of whether Keynes' theory and its practical

on, if wage earners follow a competitive wage policy, the economic system must move ultimately to a full employment stationary state, which is the essential thesis of the classicals. There can be no question at all that in this event the equilibrium that is attained is stable" (p. 351).

[25] Cf. Sumner H. Slichter, in Harris, op. cit.: "The fears which encourage the hoarding of cash may be partly fears of higher taxes, i.e., fears aroused by the deficit itself" (p. 250).

consequences are acceptable boils down to this: does the "illusion effect" of monetary manipulation work so long and so regularly that it can rightly be used as the basis of a *general* theory of employment?

The world Keynes paints is not the real world. To realize this fully one has merely to compare his remarks with any newspaper report about the bargaining policy of labor. Generally and as a rule, whether we like it or not, the "money veil" nowadays is seen through most thoroughly and clearly. Wage demands do not remain unadjusted, for any length of time, to the sinking purchasing power of money, i.e., to higher living costs. They are demands for "real" wages. As a matter of fact, money wages have not lagged behind prices during the last decade. On the contrary, they have run ahead of prices; labor has succeeded in raising its standard of living because its wages have risen with the increase in its productivity.

Our conclusion is that the case Lord Keynes regards as the "general case" is in reality a special case, valid only under special conditions and for a certain time. His theory is a special theory of employment for the case when the money illusion works.[26]

In the "general case," the equilibrium which the economy attains through monetary manipulations is not real, definite, and stable, as Keynes claims, but at best transitory and dynamic. It yields to a real and stable equilibrium as soon as the supply schedules of the participants in the economic process are adjusted to the changes brought about through the manipulation.

CYCLICAL VERSUS STABILIZED UNEMPLOYMENT

In one special case Keynes' scheme works: in the special case of the recovery phase of the business cycle after the liquidation of

[26] There exists, in addition to the incorrectness of his factual assumptions, a methodological reason why Keynes' theory cannot be considered a satisfactory analysis of a stable equilibrium but only of frictional maladjustments: in an equilibrium analysis it is inadmissible to assume that some of the data, the prices of goods, yield to inflation whereas the others, the wages, interests, profits remain rigid. Either everything or nothing must be considered as flexible. In the first case the quantity theory is valid; in the latter case we have a sort of regulated economy in which not economic but price- and wage-fixing laws reign over the market.

the preceding boom. For here, indeed, ideal conditions prevail for
the money illusion. Here the demands for interest are still influenced by the memory of the low profits on capital during the depression. Here reductions of real wages are not watched closely
and, if recognized, not followed immediately by reactions because
real wages have only recently risen through the deflation of prices.
And the burden of government spending is not yet taken into
account; first, because at the beginning the amounts spent are not
substantial; and secondly, because the decision as to which class
will have to foot the bill is deferred and everyone gambles on the
hope that it is the other fellow who will have to pay.

Consequently, monetary manipulations will be effective in short-
ening the transition period from a cyclical depression to recovery.
Lowering interest rates below the prevailing market rates and governmental deficit spending are defensible, even advisable at this
juncture.[27] But all this is nothing more than the discount policy,
open-market policy, and fiscal policy recommended as a means of
mitigating cyclical movements, long before Keynes, by almost every
monetary business-cycle theorist.

Now there is no doubt that Keynes' employment theory was conceived during and under the impression of such a cyclical pre-
recovery and recovery period. This alone can explain his factual
assumptions which are typical for such periods but entirely atypical
for other periods. On the other hand, Lord Keynes certainly does
not intend his theory to be merely a theory of fluctuations in employment during business cycles; these are treated as a special case
toward the end of his work. He deals with the establishment of
stable equilibria with larger employment, as distinct from the increase of employment during the dynamic process of the cycle. He
means his theory to be, chiefly, a theory of noncyclical and thus
stabilized, or—to use the European expression—structural employment and unemployment; [28] in short, a *general* theory. And it is

[27] I consider the refusal of the Brüning government to follow a reflationary
policy in 1931 the most important cause of the victory of the Nazi party.

[28] For the distinction between structural and cyclical unemployment, *cf.*
L. Albert Hahn, *Ist Arbeitslosigkeit unvermeidlich?*, Berlin, 1930. The reader
will find in this booklet a summary of the views on unemployment expressed

just and only as a *general* (not as a business-cycle) theory that it is original, challenging, and different from the classical.   And it is at this point that there arises a phenomenon that is tragic for economic theory and dangerous for practical economic policy: what is really a theory of cyclical unemployment is formulated as a theory of structural unemployment.   And once formulated, it leads its own life, detached from its premises, and becomes the basis and justification for policies concerning situations for which it is not valid, such as unemployment caused by wages which are structurally too high.

To this case Keynes' scheme is not applicable.[29]   In other words, neither lowering interest rates nor government compensatory spending is effective when unemployment prevails at a price level that is neither boom-inflated nor depression-deflated.   The reason is simply that in this case the illusion effect does not work for any length of time and that the reaction period is therefore very short.

If wages have become structurally too high, it is merely because labor had considered them really too low.   Obviously in such a situation rising living costs through monetary manipulation will immediately lead to compensating and (if we may judge by experience) even to overcompensating reactions.

If interest rates are lowered in the case of structural unemployment, creditors revise their interest demands upwards.   For there is not the slightest reason why creditors should tolerate a redistribution of income to their disadvantage through inflationary credit expansion for any length of time.

Government spending to compensate cyclical unemployment can be stopped as soon as the special factors making for cyclical depression, especially those of a psychological nature, are checked. Spending to compensate structural unemployment has to go on indefinitely.   Otherwise the level of effective demand would again be reduced and a deflationary process started, because private en-

in Europe during a discussion which strikingly resembles the one going on at the present time in this country.

[29] Accordingly, in the third edition of my *Volkswirtschaftliche Theorie des Bankkredits,* the Interest Theory of Unemployment was developed as a cyclical theory.

terprise does not invest at the prevailing marginal efficiency of capital.

If government spending goes on indefinitely and therefore represents an ever-increasing burden on the community, the day must eventually come when it outlasts and outgrows the illusion effect, which is, by its very nature, transitory and limited. Compensatory reactions are inevitable.

It seems to be the tragedy of economic science that psychological phenomena like the money illusion become obsolete when they are discovered. If Lord Keynes has discovered the mechanism of lowering real wages through monetary manipulations, he has at the same time destroyed the working of the mechanism by drawing attention to it.

Only in connection with a policy aiming to adjust, rather than compensate, structural maladjustments will government expenditure be useful in the postwar period. Contrary to a widely accepted opinion, there exists no automatic and mechanical parallelism of spending and creation of employment. Nor do "unexhausted resources," as such, guarantee that employment, and not prices, will rise in the wake of spending. If this is not recognized in time, postwar planning, far from bringing about full employment, will delay it by creating the illusion that maladjustments need never be corrected.

7. Interest Rates
and Inflation *

Wherever Government economic policy, the business policy of an individual firm, or the future trends of stock or commodity markets are discussed, the topic of inflation plays a major role. Generally speaking inflation is considered dangerously imminent.

A FORGOTTEN DEVICE

If inflation had been feared ten years ago, the raising of interest rates would have been suggested as the simplest and most natural means of defense. Raising of discount rates—the interest rates applied by central banks—recommended itself as the classical and traditional policy of central banking developed for more than a century. It appeared also as the logical consequence of the monetary business-cycle theories prevailing at that time. The theorists, and especially the followers of the eminent Swedish economist, Knut Wicksell, were of the opinion that in order to stabilize the price level, one had only to regulate the quantity of money; and that this, in turn, could and should be achieved by making the supply of credits from the money-issuing authorities more expensive.

Today, the recommendation or the mere mention of a restrictive discount and interest policy as a means of checking inflation appears almost ludicrous to the overwhelming majority of economists and businessmen in this country. This shows the extent to which ideas

* Written before the abolishment of the O.P.A. in July 1946: the article appeared first in *The Commercial and Financial Chronicle*, December 22, 1946.

on this subject have changed and traditional views been replaced by what, in the opinion of this author, must be called a general confusion of minds.

Uncertainty of Diagnosis

This confusion begins even at an earlier stage when the existence of inflation is questioned. Besides much inflation talk, there is much deflation talk around; and the danger of the divergence of opinion is that it seems to be especially pronounced in the government. The O.P.A. is decidedly inflation-minded, whereas the Secretary of Commerce has frequently expressed his fear of deflation. Incidentally, this uncertainty of the government in the inflation and deflation controversy supplies an early and conclusive confirmation of those skeptics who have doubted governmental ability to stabilize the business cycle. It is clear that governmental business-cycle stabilization is possible only under the assumption that private enterprise can err in regard to the future development and therefore be prone to indulge in overoptimism or overpessimism, whereas the government that must counteract the excessive expectation of private enterprise has a clear and certain vision of the future. Now, on the first occasion when cycle stabilization is put to a practical test, it turns out that government officials are subject to errors and uncertainties like other human beings, so that their ability to stabilize the cycle cannot be relied upon.

Those in government as well as in business who fear inflation base their diagnosis, as is well known, on the presence of a huge pent-up demand and purchasing power. This author considers this diagnosis basically correct. Pent-up purchasing power is nothing else than deferred inflation, as the history of almost all postwar periods proves.

Those who are deflation-minded base their opinion on the fear that lowering of the "bring-home pay" would create a deficit in effective demand. This argument is of course in many cases political rather than scientific. It is presented to show the necessity for raising hourly wages. Where it is seriously meant as an economic argument, it does not take into account that the demand pent up through many years of war, the credit expansion of the rehabilitation and reconstruction period ahead, and the usual waste of postwar years will add so much purchasing power to the wages of the production period itself that a deficit in the latter, even if it really occurred, would be compensated and overcompensated.

The "Cart Before the Horse" Therapy

As far as the actual policy is intended to be an anti-inflationary policy, it concentrates exclusively on the fight against the symptoms rather than the causes of inflation. It does not endeavor to reduce the quantity of money spendable at the markets, but to prevent the natural effects of the enlarged money quantity—the raising of the price level. It is generally not realized what fundamental changes from previous policies this implies. The laws of the market which alone formerly prevented price-raising, are replaced by criminal laws which penalize the raising of prices according to the market laws. The smooth and inexpensive price-fixing by means of the market is replaced by a very expensive and complicated price-fixing and law-enforcing organization. This, incidentally, creates the very unwelcome phenomenon of hundreds of thousands of businessmen becoming transgressors of the law who otherwise would have never come in contact with the courts; this, because of the paradoxical situation in which they are placed by a system of prices fixed contrary to the laws of the market.

The reasons why neither the O.P.A. nor any other governmental agency has even considered fighting inflation by monetary measures are manifold:

First of all, it seems to be entirely forgotten that it is not only possible but natural for a currency to be held scarce in order to uphold its purchasing power over goods. Forgotten seems to be the method whereby under the gold standard the value of the currency was preserved, the so-called discount policy of the central banks. Nobody thinks any longer of reducing the quantity of money when the coverage of bills by gold deteriorates. One either reduces the coverage requirements or devaluates. The concept of a totally elastic currency seems to have replaced the concept of the currency in which the quantity is restricted in one way or the other. It is natural that, in a world in which the supply of money is thus considered as unlimited, the feeling for the necessity of curtailment of the quantity of money is weakened.

Furthermore, fear that the low interest rates of the Federal Reserve Banks could lead to inflation has been abated by the experiences of the 'thirties, when the supply of extremely cheap money led not to an inflationary but rather to a deflationary situation. One forgets, however, that this was the result of the abnormally low investment demand created by various, especially political, factors of that time. Today, expectation of unlimited markets due to pent-up demand must create a very strong need for money through withdrawals of bank deposits and requests for new credits from the side of business—not to mention the demand from the side of the still entirely unbalanced government budget. In such a situation on the demand side, low interest rates create inflation, whereas raising of interest rates could prevent inflation.

Finally, there seems to be a certain inclination to deny the effectiveness of higher interest rates on the grounds of an alleged inelasticity of the demand for credits. One argues that the interest rate is nowadays of such minor importance in the cost calculation of industry that even a very high rate would not deter demand, other conditions being favorable. To this it must be replied that this argument—besides being inapplicable in industries requiring vast amounts of capital, as in the building industry—forgets entirely the indirect effects of low interest rates. Low interest rates, enduring over a period of time, raise the price of common stocks whose earnings seem reasonably assured because the public capitalizes these earnings at a much higher price-earning ratio. This means that venture capital can be raised through the issuance of new stocks at cheap rates and in practically unlimited amounts, at least by the big corporations of the country. Thus, during the boom of the 'twenties in the period before the crash, an extremely high price-earning ratio—at that time created through crazy earning expectations—allowed industry to obtain any amount of money which, spent in one way or another, strengthened the forces of inflation.

HIGH INTEREST RATES NOT NECESSARILY COINCIDENT WITH UNEMPLOYMENT

The aversion to raising interest rates has its roots also, of course, in the widely held theory that easy money means high employment and tight money means low employment. If this theory were correct, high employment could in times of a strong demand for credits be achieved only at the price of inflation. However, the theory is basically wrong. True, if the supply of credit is kept scarce, enterprises requiring large amounts of capital are doomed. But enterprises requiring lesser amounts of capital but more labor can carry on provided only that too high wages do not render these enterprises unprofitable. Full employment can be achieved at any interest rate level, as shown by experience in colonial countries. If low interest rates threaten to lead to inflation, the relief of business enterprises has to be sought through other means, especially through a reasonable tax and wage policy.

FISCAL POLICY VERSUS ECONOMIC POLICY

The appeal that low interest rates offer is derived, too, from the fact that they enable the Treasury to finance and refinance the government debt on cheap terms. That the government is, so to speak, creditor and debtor in one person, because it fixes the rediscount rates of the Federal Reserve System, leads indeed to large savings for the government and thus for the tax-payer. However, the artificially low interest rates on government securities create an artificial abundance on the entire credit market. All other creditors—private as well as institutional—have to revise their interest claims downwards in order not to be excluded from a market where they are in competition with the cheap money coming directly or indirectly from the Federal Reserve Banks.

Without wanting to argue whether fiscal considerations should be taken at all into account when economic policy is discussed, it may incidentally be pointed out that the structure of the war debt would have to be changed before one could return to an orthodox interest policy. Substantial parts of the debt, especially those financed by the Savings Bonds A to G, practically represent what

one used to call a floating debt. Therefore, in case of a marked
rise in interest rates, necessitated for instance by an inflationary
boom, billions in bonds would be presented for redemption in cash
which would increase the forces of inflation. Obviously, this floating debt would have to be consolidated in the traditional way into
a truly long-term debt through offering higher interest rates for
truly long-term bonds. This might not even mean an additional
burden on the Treasury, for there would always remain a strong
spread between long-term and short-term interest rates. So the
Treasury could easily pay no interest at all, or relatively low interest, to those who wanted to retain, for reasons of liquidity, bonds
payable at sight—and who now, paradoxically, receive interest equal
to those on long-term bonds; whereas, on equally liquid bank accounts, no interest is received.

Needless to say, the return to orthodox financing methods would
also result in serious difficulties for banks and other government
bond-holding institutions. The long-term bonds they hold would
of course depreciate with higher interest rates, creating catastrophic
losses which would have to be taken over by the government in
order to prevent socially and politically unbearable bankruptcies.
The return to a sound way of financing is always as costly and
difficult as the departure from this way seems easy and advantageous.

Summing up, we may say: the fight against inflation concentrates
indeed on the suppression of the results rather than the causes of
money abundance. The O.P.A. and the law enforcement agencies
have taken over responsibilities that formerly were the Federal
Reserve Board's. Increase of the quantity of money is tolerated,
but its natural effect on prices in accordance with the "Quantity
Theory of Money" is prevented. One is reminded that during the
high days of the Nazis, the German president of the Reichsbank
boasted that the National Socialists had won a victory even over
the Quantity Theory. But it turned out to be a Pyrrhic victory.

PRICE STABILITY WITH WAGE INSTABILITY

The policy of fighting inflation with price ceilings is, however,
not consistently carried through. The policy of ceiling prices must

logically be combined with the policy of ceiling wages. Such a combination of policies was pursued and to a certain degree achieved during the war. It has now been replaced with a policy of fixing prices but not wages: wages are to be determined by collective bargaining according to the ability of the individual industry to absorb higher wages through increasing productivity. It has already been mentioned that a wage-boosting policy is unnecessary so far as it is meant as an antideflation device. For whatever reasons it is advocated, it is obvious that it intermingles in a peculiar way with the otherwise anti-inflationary policy of the government. It is true that it will not create inflation, at least not directly. However, if wages are no longer—as in a free labor market—fixed according to the productivity of the marginal but of the intermarginal enterprise, this must obviously lead to a stoppage of the former. For, if in the large enterprises, which derive high profits from gigantic turnover, labor is entitled to share these profits, then workers will just leave the smaller enterprises and join the larger and largest ones. This must lead, at first, to unemployment and thus even to deflation and later to a concentration process that is surely highly undesirable for many reasons. If, and as soon as, prices are raised under pressure of small businesses so that they too can pay the high wages of their large competitors, then unemployment and the concentration process is, of course, halted, but an inflationary spiral is started.

THE PILING UP OF PURCHASING POWER

In spite of everything that has been said above and could be said further, one has to reckon with a continuation of the prevailing policy. Government as well as public opinion is too strongly committed to it. Nevertheless, our analysis is not just of theoretical but of highly practical importance, for it leads to the perception of what can be reasonably expected as results of this policy; if one cannot change a policy, one should at least be prepared for its consequences.

The immediate consequence of the policy must be a huge and unprecedented piling up of spendable purchasing power in the economy through money and credit creation. For there will be a practically unlimited and undefended supply of money and credit facing a huge demand. Governmental expenditures financed by deficits will go on, though on a smaller scale than during the war. Furthermore, private enterprise and the government will proceed with huge investments in this country as well as abroad. They will believe they are entitled to make these investments because the huge amounts of idle funds held in the form of cash or short-term government securities will create the illusion of a tremendous abundance of wealth. In reality, all these funds are already invested directly or indirectly in loans to the government and to business firms. The fact that they can actually be invested anew arises exclusively from the possibility that every owner of these funds can dispose of them without incurring losses. This again is caused by the preparedness of the Federal Reserve System to rediscount government securities at negligible rates. The rate of interest that forms when demand and supply for credit are forced to balance without the additional money obtainable through the Federal Reserve System was formerly called in theory the "natural interest rate." There is no doubt that the "natural interest rate" is very high at this juncture. If one allowed it to become effective, the illusion of the abundance of the capital markets would disappear. Nobody considers funds "idle" when he receives high interest on them.

Low interest rates are—at least partly—responsible for the boom on the stock market and could be responsible for additional strong price advances—especially if the interest-lowering is carried still further in accordance with the British precedent. These advances would not represent an inflationary boom in the ordinary sense where people anticipate higher earnings through inflated asset values. It would be a recapitalization boom, caused by the fact that earnings are capitalized by ever lower interest rates. It creates a situation in which venture capital, too, can be obtained abundantly and at low interest rates. This again means, of course, that dormant purchasing power is transferred into actual inflationary purchasing power.

FRUSTRATED INFLATION

In the ordinary course of events this would mean strong and general advances of all prices of goods and services. However, as mentioned above, such general price advances have been and will be forbidden. This is why many people believe that all the accumulation of purchasing power can do no harm, as long as the O.P.A. remains in power. To this one has to reply: first, there is no doubt that for a certain time what can be called a "frustrated inflation" will work. And it must be admitted that, as long as it works, the ensuing prosperity is of an ideal character, inasmuch as it represents prosperity without price increases—a "turnover prosperity," as one could call it. Not only does this prosperity lack the essential prerequisite for the development of the depression, the price inflation, but it would be of a comparatively long duration. The pent-up purchasing power, not being able to spend itself in price increases, guarantees effective demand for goods over a much longer period of time than does a purchasing power that is allowed to push prices upward.

However, this sort of "frustrated inflation" cannot go on forever—especially in peacetime when the psychological and patriotic inhibitions against breaking the price ceiling no longer work so strongly as during the war. Price ceilings can never be applied universally. There are always realms—for example, the market for used furniture or for certain services—which will not and practically cannot be controlled. On these markets the prices will show a slow but decisive increase. The resulting distortion of price and wages—the margin developing between those that are controlled and those that are uncontrolled—will eventually result in just that general raising of the price and wage level which one wished to avoid, and which will render the economy vulnerable and exposed to reverses.

But even where price rises are avoided, the economy will prove increasingly vulnerable. Wages are under the permanent upward pressure. The ensuing wage increases—where they do not lead to unemployment—are bearable only because the huge turnover due to the enormous pent-up demand cheapens and alleviates production and distribution. It is a very high-strung system, in which the price-cost relationship remains tolerable only so long as everything works full blast and at high speed. As soon as the slightest slackening in demand sets in, many enterprises will have to shut down because of the losses they suffer. Exactly as at the onset of every depression, the boom will collapse through the losses that the marginal enterprises begin to undergo; except that this time not the decline of prices, but the decline of turnover will be the initiating cause.

CYCLE AS USUAL

Our conclusion is: the prevailing monetary policy—and incidentally the prevailing fiscal policy, too—will prove to have been not contracyclical, but procyclical and contrastabilizing. There will develop a situation that will embrace, if not all, at any rate many of the features that are usually called unhealthy; whereas the healthy aspects of the boom—increasing employment—may not necessarily be present. For it could be that labor, during this boom, would tend to be progressively replaced by labor-saving capital investment if the policy is continued of making the use of labor more expensive and of making the use of capital cheaper.

Furthermore, there is bound to develop an additional upward movement on the stock markets, for it is the peculiarity of the aforementioned "victory over the quantity theory" (on the markets for goods and services) that more and more unspendable funds accumulate, of which at least parts are never converted into government securities, but seek to be exchanged into stocks of private corporations.

But after this boom there will follow a collapse of serious proportions as soon as a slackening of demand sets in or is feared. For with this slackening of demand the cost-price relation and therewith the profit situation will deteriorate rapidly. Nor will the continuation of easy money give any protection against depression when the forces of this boom have exhausted themselves.

If one wants to prevent a deflationary depression, one must prevent an inflationary boom. If one wants to prevent an inflationary boom, one must prevent inflation in every form. If one wants to prevent inflation in times of strong need for credits—by the government or by private industry—one must make money scarce. And if one believes that this method is antiquated and can be replaced by other devices—an opinion which is not at all so original as its originators believe, but which has been held over and over again during the course of history—one will face disappointment. Interest rates are not, as seems to be assumed nowadays, a vicious invention of creditors. They have the function of rationing a scarce supply of credit among those who need it. As long as one wants to avoid the step incompatible with a free economy—of having credits rationed through the government—a revision of interest rates upward remains the only method of keeping inflation in check.

At the end of World War I, the above-mentioned economist, Knut Wicksell, wrote an article called "Put the Discount Rates Up," in which he warned that maintaining interest rate far below the natural interest rate would inevitably lead to worldwide inflation. The article was much praised, but nowhere heeded. Inflation ensued, even in those countries where the budgetary situation would have not necessitated it. In view of the prevailing state of mind, it is very probable, and to be feared, that history will repeat itself.

8. Exchange Rates Run Wild[*]

One of the most amazing things to an economist traveling nowadays in Europe is the awkward and truly grotesque conditions that have developed as a consequence of governmental interference, restrictions, and regulations in the foreign money markets. It seems as if the public and even the experts in the United States are only inadequately informed about these conditions.

To begin with, if one were to try to describe these conditions as identical with the system invented by Schacht, this would be an offense to him. For whereas Schacht's system worked almost faultlessly, the new European systems do not work at all in essential respects. They are caricatures rather than reproductions of Schacht's system.

This is not to be blamed on the men who introduced these systems. It is caused because governments are only able to prevent the working of the laws of supply and demand under very special conditions, such as are present when a nation is either at war or under totalitarian control. Here every move of the citizen, every letter and every telegram he writes and receives, every telephone call he makes, is subjected to strictest censorship. In democracies at peace, where the citizen remains free and independent in his essential civil rights and where his private moves are investigated only under special circumstances, the laws of supply and demand continue to work in the field of foreign exchange, if only in an

---

[*] Appeared first in *The Commercial and Financial Chronicle*, August 22, 1946.

imperfect way, on the black markets. In the person who expects further depreciation of the nation's currency by abuse of governmental or pressure group power, the wish for future security is stronger than the fear of the penalties for contravening the exchange regulations, especially if they do not include the death penalty à la Göring.

The prices paid for foreign exchange or gold on the black markets represent, so to speak, the secret ballot of the citizens on the fairness of the governmentally fixed exchange rates. They show the citizens' real opinion of the value of their currency and to what extent they believe it is overvalued by the government.

Frustrated Inflations

The period after World War I was featured by exceedingly strong inflations of the currency with correspondingly strong inflations of prices of goods and foreign exchange. At the beginning, it is true, the exchange rates rose substantially faster than the internal price level—giving effect to the so-called sell-out of the countries. But in the long run the quantity of money in the hands of the public, the prices of goods and services, and the prices of gold and foreign exchange moved up in conformity. There were endeavors to hold prices down through a system of price ceilings and exchange rate controls, but neither the former nor the latter worked for any length of time. The inflation ran its course. Based on the experience gained during and after that war, one was able during World War II to check to a certain degree the creation of superfluous purchasing power, especially by means of severe excess profit taxation. Nevertheless, monetary inflation has still been strong because the enormously increased number of employed have not been and perhaps could not be, taxed in such a way that the purchasing power would remain on its former level. However, if inflation was not prevented in its causes, it was prevented in its effects. A very stringent system of price and wage controls tried to prevent the increasing purchasing power from achieving its natural effect: the raising of prices and wages. What ensued was not prevention of inflation, but frustration of its consequences.

Frustrated inflations marked World War II and its postwar period in all countries—in some to a greater degree than in others. As a result all economies became divided into two distinct areas: one where prices were regulated, and the other where the governments either did not want or were not able to enforce price regulations— the area which includes the black markets. It is into this second area that purchasing power overflows when it is prevented from exhausting itself in the first area by price ceilings and/or rationing. In large countries such as the United States, where the internal markets have such overwhelming importance and ideas of capital flight are for various reasons unknown to the populations, the purchasing power overflowing from the first to the second area is directed towards the legal purchase of real estate, certain luxury articles, and securities, and towards the illegal buying of certain consumer goods on the black market.

In the much smaller countries of Europe, which are more dependent on international trade than is the United States, and in which the population is extremely exchange-rate-conscious, the excess purchasing power is directed not only towards nylon stockings and cigarettes (luxury articles whose importation is allowed only in very small quantities) but also towards the acquiring of foreign currency and bank balances. This is partly because these can again be used for the illegal purchase of illegally imported luxury articles, and partly because foreign currency and bank balances are considered means of conserving the value of one's assets. For the domestic currency has—most outspokenly in France—lost its function as a means of conserving value, retaining only its function as a means for payment. Not so strongly as during the great inflation in Germany and Eastern Europe, but nevertheless quite distinctly, dollar bills and gold have replaced internal currency for hoarding and saving purposes.

BLACK AND GRAY FOREIGN EXCHANGE MARKETS

The traveling economist needs quite some time before he finds his way through the maze of the various official, semiofficial, and unofficial exchange rates. To the degree to which dealing on the respective markets and the fulfillment of transactions violate the regulations or laws of one or more countries or only certain conventions binding some banks, the markets are characterized by colors ranging all the way from black over gray to white. The various kinds of "money" in question, and the prices at which they are traded in the various European countries, is an extremely interesting subject, but one that could be treated only within the framework of an extensive study.

Nevertheless, a certain understanding of the conditions on the black and the gray markets can be gathered if one reviews the prices at which the various foreign exchange values are quoted in Switzerland. Switzerland itself—though free from most currency restrictions (e.g., concerning the exportation of currency)—must also be considered a country in which the government controls international payments as far as foreign trade is concerned. For where such payments are not affected by international clearings, the foreign exchange for imports has to be purchased at the official rate from the National Bank; however, where specifically Swiss foreign trade interests are not concerned, dealing in every sort of foreign money has been entirely legal from the Swiss standpoint since the end of the war. During the war dealings in foreign bank notes were forbidden in order to prevent the Germans from disposing of stolen bills in neutral Switzerland.

On the markets for *bank notes,* only small denominations—American bank notes of not over $20—are dealt in freely. Large denominations are salable, if at all, only at a strong discount, the reason being either that their importation into the countries of origin is forbidden, or that paying them into bank accounts is controlled for illegal (especially internal) black-market transactions. The so-called *black* or *internal payments* that are traded replace the ordinary checks on or transfer orders to foreign banks. They are sold in Switzerland by small firms that specialize in these matters because the banks of standing do not trade in these markets. The counterpart in the foreign country is not a bank, as is usual, but a private individual or a small firm that pays out the purchased amount at the residence of the recipient. In this way, a traveler who needs money for living expenses in France can acquire the francs from somebody in France who needs Swiss francs in Switzerland without a single check or letter between banks passing the frontiers.

In most countries of Europe, outside Switzerland, these transactions are clearly illegal. Swiss francs, for instance, can be acquired in France legally only for importation of specific goods by special license. The purchase in Switzerland of dollar payments from Swiss credits would be illegal from the standpoint of the United States as long as the frozen Swiss accounts are not deblocked. Some transactions in United States dollar checks and transfer orders are, however, entirely legal also from the American standpoint. These are concerned with payments from Swiss accounts that have been licensed for some reason by the United States Treasury, but in which the dollars received are not taken over by the Swiss National Bank at the official rate of frs. 4.30 to the dollar. (At this rate the National Bank buys only dollars received in payment for exports and—in limited amounts—for certain other purposes, e.g., the support of charities.) All other dollars are called "finance" dollars as distinct from "commercial" dollars. They are traded and quoted freely and the quotations are, like most prices for currencies and transfer orders, listed in newspapers and bulletins.

A QUOTATION LIST

The following are the prices at which foreign *paper money* was quoted in Zürich on Aug. 3, 1946. The official exchange rate is added in the last column so that the discount of the free market rate in comparison with the official rate can be seen without difficulty.

	Demand	Offer	Official Rate
Dollar	3.32	3.47	4.30
Pound Sterling	10.32½	10.42½	17.34
French francs	1.35	1.45	3.60
Belg. francs	4.80	5.00	9.90
Dutch fl.	41.50	43.00	162.00
Swedish kr.	105.00	110.00	17.40
Portuguese esc.	13.00	13.75	. . . .
Czech. kr.	3.25	3.75	. . . .

The following gives the quotations for the so-called "*internal payments.*" The official rates are again added in the last column.[1]

	Internal Payment	Official Rate
Paris (100 ffr.)	1.45	3.60
Brussels (100 bfr.)	5.25	9.90
Italy (100 lire)	.80	1.91
England (1 pound)	10.50	17.34
U.S.A. (financial dollar)	3.40	4.30
Portugal (100 esc.)	13.60	17.40
Sweden (100 kr.)	102.00	102.60
Holland (100 hfl.)	42.00	162.00
Argentina (100 pes.)	84.00	106.00
Spain (100 ptas.)	14.00	39.50
Turkey (1 l tq.)	1.35	3.30

It is clear from the above that dollar bills and financial dollars are traded at a discount of about 20 per cent.

For gold coins the following prices are paid: [2]

	Napoleon	Eagle	Sovereign
Switzerland (official)	30.50	7.50	38.45
Belgium	57.00	13.70	75.00
Italy	50.00	. . . .	65.00
Portugal	. . . .	13.70	40.00
Turkey	50.00	. . . .	63.00
Egypt	. . . .	. . . .	62.00

The quotations represent the prices paid for gold coins on the black markets in the various countries, calculated in Swiss francs at the black-market rates for the latter. It can immediately be seen at what a tremendous premium, in comparison with the official rate in Switzerland, gold coins are traded all over the world.[3] For instance, the Napoleon—the gold 20-franc piece—is worth almost 100 per cent more on the black market in Belgium than it is officially worth in Switzerland.

---

[1] These quotations are taken from the weekly bulletin of the well-known private bank of Julius Baer & Co. in Zürich.

[2] Again according to the bulletins of Julius Baer & Co.

[3] The gold premium is not only much higher than the premium for Swiss francs but also fluctuates from country to country in terms of Swiss francs too.

The official price of gold in Switzerland is the price at which the Swiss franc is stabilized for the time being. The National Bank, however, sells gold or gold coins not to every bearer of her bills, but only—and this in very small quantities—to people who are known to her as reliable. The result of this semigold standard— where everybody can sell and not everybody can buy gold at the official rate—is the development of a black market for gold in Switzerland too. This market, known to the authorities, exists even though trading above the official prices and, even more, the exportation of gold are strictly forbidden. The black-market prices for gold and gold coins seem to be roughly 50 per cent higher than the price corresponding to the gold standard of the Swiss franc.

From all this it is obvious that on the scale of values gold ranks at the top; then follows the Swiss franc; then the United States dollar and the currencies of the dollar bloc; then the pound sterling; and finally such truly weak currencies as those of Holland, Belgium, and France.

Awkward Consequences

The imagination is not equal to figuring out the awkward situations that develop from what may be euphemistically called the arbitrage between white and black exchange rates. It is not possible to describe the multitude of abnormalities one hears of the longer one stays. A single story may suffice. The fact that it has been published in a well-known Swiss magazine shows to what degree these things are publicly known. It seems that a correspondent of *Time* heard it in London. He met a man who traveled to Switzerland with the £75 allowed every British subject for a trip to Switzerland. He changed his pounds in Switzerland at the official rate of fr. 17.34, receiving approximately fr. 1,300. Of these he spent fr. 100 for all sorts of nice things. With the remaining 1,200 Swiss francs he bought on the black market 120,000 French francs which were delivered to him when he went to Paris. Here he spent 5,000 French francs for black-market dinners, etc. With the remaining 115,000 French francs he bought on the black market pounds at the rate of fr. 700, thus receiving about £160. This means that he returned to London, after having spent quite a lot of money for all sorts of luxuries and travel, with £85 more than he had had when he left! [4]

This was possible, of course, because the traveler was able to change his pounds into Swiss francs at the official rate, whereas all transactions that followed back to pounds were traded on the black markets, where the Swiss franc has a much higher value.

Incidentally, in United States dollars too, a profitable transaction is possible which, while not so spectacular, is legal, although not quite fair. The National Bank of Switzerland pays to the American traveler fr. 4,250 for $1,000 for living expenses in Switzerland during every calendar month. If he stays one month and one day he receives for $2,000 francs 8,500. Supposing that he spends 3,000 francs—which is ample for one month's stay—he keeps 550 francs, for which he can buy dollar bills at the rate of 3.50, thus obtaining about $1,600. This means that he has lived a whole month in Switzerland for $400 instead of the $750 representing the counter value of the 3,000 francs he really spent. If he buys American money orders, which are traded freely in Switzerland at the price of about 3.20 (though the cashing of the money orders for Swiss accounts seems to be illegal from the American standpoint), his profit is even larger.

THE BLACK MARKET AND THE MORALS OF THE PUBLIC

The profits that black-market traders can make at the expense of the community is not the worst consequence of the existing margin between white and black exchange rates. The real damage is that it undermines more and more the respect of the public for the law. The feeling is created that the black market prices represent the true value of the foreign money and that it is the government which does an injustice to its citizens when it forces the exporters, or—in the case of the confiscation of foreign bank balances and securities— the investors to deliver their property against a compensation in internal currency that is calculated at the low official rate.

[4] As the black-market prices have meanwhile sunk somewhat, the above transactions, while still possible, are no longer quite so profitable as they were.

The absence of any feeling of guilt over trading on the black markets renders contraventions of the law more frequent. In fact the contraventions have become so universal that they can be prosecuted in only a very small percentage of cases. In certain countries every waiter is prepared to change foreign money at the black-market rate. The entire situation shows that the power of the government to regulate prices against the laws of supply and demand has its limits. The only reliable way to regulate prices is through controlling the quantity of spendable money by a strict financial and interest-rate policy. To those who believe that an inflation can be checked for any length of time in spite of easy taxes and easy money, an informational trip to Europe is strongly recommended.

Orgies of Bureaucracy

One can imagine how huge a bureaucratic apparatus is needed for the working of the artificial systems. For not only do the official prices have to be enforced by all sorts of police measures against the forces of supply and demand; there also has to be an organization that protects the economy against exchange rates that are "wrong" in essential respects—the official rate of foreign money being, for instance in France, too low to maintain an equilibrium in the trade balance and to prevent it from becoming too passive; the black-market prices, on the other hand, being due to the risk premium they contain—too high and disturbing the balance of trade in the opposite direction towards too big activity.

The fact is that in every European country huge organizations have been created whose only purpose is to enforce "wrong" official exchange rates and to paralyze their economic consequences—organizations which would of course be superfluous under a free currency system. Below is a survey of the respective "frustrations" introduced in various countries:

1. *In countries with weak currencies,* i.e., currencies with a tendency to weakness at the official rates, especially towards the Swiss franc and the United States dollar.

Regarding frustration of the *official rates:* As the official rates of the foreign exchange are lower than the rate at which the trade balance would be in equilibrium, thus giving it a tendency of becoming highly passive, it is necessary—

(a) To strangle *imports* not limited by high foreign exchange rates through all sorts of artificial practices such as import quotas, rationing of the foreign exchange for import purposes, and so on.

(b) To stimulate *exports,* in which there is not sufficient incentive because foreign exchange rates are too low, by all sorts of direct and indirect subsidies.

Regarding frustration of *black-market prices:* The very high black-market rates of course create a very strong appeal for the illegal export of all sorts of goods which the government wishes to retain in the country, because they are consumed by the masses— such as food smuggled in great quantities from Italy to Switzerland—or because they represent internationally recognized values— such as jewelry and gold that the government wishes to use for its own purposes.

It is clear that a very extensive antismuggling organization is needed for counteracting the high stimulus to illegal exports. As a matter of fact, the fights between the custom officials and smugglers at the various frontiers have become in some districts regular battles, with many dead and wounded.

Strangely enough, the high black-market prices for foreign exchange do not prevent the *importation* of certain valuables into countries where the price of goods is higher than in the foreign country even if the foreign exchange is calculated at the black-market price. This is the case, for instance, with gold bought at the official and even at the unofficial rate in Switzerland; it is smuggled in great quantities to France, although this transaction is strictly forbidden by the Swiss as well as by the French Governments.

2. *In countries that are on the other side of the fence,* i.e., in which the *currencies show a tendency to strengthen* at the official rates. Here all other currencies (including United States dollars) are quoted unofficially below the official rates. Thus an opposite problem develops. Switzerland is practically the only country remaining in this category today, since Canada and Sweden have

noted the consequences of the strength of their currencies and have revaluated them in terms of dollars.

Regarding frustration of these *official rates:* The official rate that is higher than the rate at which the trade balance would be in equilibrium works as an impediment to *imports.* Switzerland would undoubtedly be more competitive on the markets, especially in the United States, if it could purchase the dollar lower than 4.30, say at the rate of "finance" dollars—about 3.40. As Switzerland is extremely import-hungry, especially for raw materials and automobiles, the effect would be beneficial, at least for the time being.

The too high official rate has the effect of a premium on all exports. Because the exporter receives 4.30 for his dollar balances, created through exports, instead of 3.50, he is extremely competitive on foreign markets. The consequence is that exports have to be rationed. This is done, for instance, in the watch industry, by the National Bank taking only a limited amount of export dollars at the official rate of 4.30. The amounts taken by the National Bank are, however, so substantial that a one-sided boom of the watch industry has developed which many consider unsound and exaggerated.

Regarding frustration of *unofficial rates:* if dollars for the purpose of imports were available at the lower rate of "finance" dollars, imports would of course increase.

It is, however, strictly forbidden to use as payment for imports other dollars than those which the National Bank sells at the official rate of 4.30. For the National Bank must get rid of its dollars (purchased from the exporter at the too high price of 4.30) at the same high price of 4.30 to the importer. Nevertheless, this frustration of the "finance" dollar is not quite comprehensible and is fought by many experts in Switzerland. They argue that in an import-hungry country "finance" dollars, too, should be admitted to pay imports; they think that importation would increase to such an extent at the lower dollar rate that not only the floating amounts of finance dollars but also the amounts owned by the National Bank would be absorbed; and they believe that if the latter suffered a loss on these dollars it should be charged to the exporters who allegedly make too high profits anyhow.

THE WAY BACK

Is there a possibility of returning to normalcy? We begin by examining the easier problems that confront the strong-currency countries.

Should we re-establish the gold standard in Switzerland, Sweden, and some other countries?

As has been explained, on the black markets in Switzerland gold is worth roughly 50 per cent more than corresponds to the Swiss gold standard. This is caused by the Swiss National Bank not selling gold freely, but instead strictly rationing it at the official price, so that neither the internal hoarding demand nor the hoarding demand in foreign countries is satisfied.

There is no doubt that the premium on gold would disappear in Switzerland if the National Bank were to sell gold freely at the official price. However, to establish a true gold standard it would be necessary to allow the free exportation of gold; in which case the premium on gold in comparison with the Swiss franc on the black markets of other countries would disappear, the gold being marked down and the Swiss franc improving its price still further.

It is, however, important and interesting to examine the consequences of such re-establishment of a true gold standard even in a strong-currency country like Switzerland. According to the classical scheme, a gold-standard country losing gold experiences—besides improvement of its exchange rate—a deflation because the outgoing gold is paid for by bills which are prevented from being replaced owing to a high discount rate. It seems extremely unlikely that in Switzerland, in spite of the prevailing boom, such a deflationary policy would be tolerated, because there too people have become accustomed to the wrong idea that only under easy-money conditions can full employment be maintained.

However, if one were to try to re-establish the gold standard without establishing a prohibitive discount rate or a system of credit rationing, the bank notes coming back to the National Bank against outflowing gold would be replaced immediately in the economy by bank notes leaving the National Bank on behalf of credits granted by her. In this case, obviously, no deflation could develop, nor would any equilibrium be established in the demand for and supply of gold. Instead, the demand—the quantity of money not being reduced—would remain effective until the last gold coin or gold bar had left the National Bank, thus exhausting her gold reserves in spite of their gigantic proportions—in the way described so masterfully by David Ricardo. For it is not an imaginary gold hunger that pushes the prices for gold upwards, since with hunger alone one cannot buy. It is rather the monetary inflation that produces the high gold prices, which therefore can be suppressed only by monetary deflation. If one wishes to avoid deflation, however, the gold standard can be re-established only at a price for gold that takes into account the existing quantity of purchasing power. In other words, the re-establishment of the gold standard presupposes a devaluation of the currencies against gold.

One of the conclusions reached through a study of monetary conditions in Switzerland is that a truly free gold standard could, at the existing quantity of purchasing power, be re-established in the world currencies only after devaluations. Without devaluations —thorough deflation being extremely unpopular—it will be necessary to continue to frustrate the inflation towards gold by rationing the demand and fixing an artificially low price for the scarce supply; retaining what may be called a pseudo gold standard rather than a true gold standard.

SUPPRESSION OF THE DISCOUNT FOR DOLLARS IN SWITZERLAND

As shown above, United States dollar bills and "finance" dollars sell at about 3.40, whereas export dollars and import dollars are sold at the official or commercial rate of 4.30.

The first question that arises is why one does not treat all dollars alike, establishing one single price for all sorts of dollars at which supply and demand for the entire offered and demanded amounts would balance. In all probability such a price would lie between the official and the free market rates, say at about 3.85. Thus all the difficulties mentioned above would immediately disappear.

It is said in Switzerland that the official rate for the dollar has been maintained at the suggestion of Washington authorities who allegedly fear a loss of prestige if the dollar were to be officially devaluated; but such devaluation has meanwhile been effected in Canada and Sweden without any loss of prestige to the United States. The suggestion would be erroneous in that in Europe the free-market rates rather than the official rates are considered to represent the true strength of a currency, and it is therefore the free-market or finance-dollar rate which would have to be raised to 4.30 for reasons of prestige.

There is no doubt that the free-market rate for dollars could easily be raised in Switzerland if the mechanism of the gold standard were allowed to play between the United States and Switzerland. However, here again the gold standard is frustrated. Just as the National Bank does not sell gold freely, she does not buy it freely. Whereas probably the United States authorities would be prepared to sell as much gold against Swiss francs as they need to buy the floating amounts of finance dollars, the Swiss National Bank does not buy gold for this purpose, although the floating amounts are relatively small now and will become larger only when the Swiss dollar accounts are ultimately unfrozen.

The reason why the Swiss National Bank is reluctant to accept gold freely—or to buy finance dollars—is that she is afraid of the inflationary effects of the Swiss money she has to issue against gold or dollars that she could probably convert into gold at the official United States gold price. However, if one regards the monetary policy of a foreign country as too inflationary, one must decide whether one wants to follow this policy in the interest of the maintenance of stable exchange rates, or whether one wants to become independent of this policy. In the latter case one has to sever the gold standard ties and revaluate the currency—just as one has to devaluate it as England did in the 30's, if one does not want to follow the deflationary policy of other countries. But one cannot eat the cake of stable exchange rates and keep the cake of internal price stability. For the time being, Switzerland has chosen a middle way—keeping the official rate of 4.30 stable and letting the rate of the finance dollar decline. The artificiality of this solution will, however, as time goes on, force a decision. Either the National

Bank will have to buy all sorts of dollars at the present official rate, since those who have invested in United States securities cannot be permanently penalized in comparison with the exporters; and in this case the Swiss monetary policy would become synchronized with that of the United States. Or the National Bank will have to lower the official rate to the rate of the finance dollar, thus revaluating the Swiss franc in terms of dollars. The fight over this question is still going on. The revaluation party argues that inflation on the one side and ever stronger bureaucratic regulations on the other can be avoided only by revaluation. The opposition, consisting mostly of exporters and the hostelries, fears that once the United States reaches full production and begins again to compete at lower prices on the world markets, the revaluated Swiss franc would have to be devaluated again.[5] The Swiss authorities have officially denied their intention to revaluate. Whether they maintain this stand will depend largely on the development of the purchasing power of the dollar, which is closely watched.

Observation of the international exchange rate markets leads to the conclusion that the United States dollar is internationally not so strong as is generally assumed in the United States. There is no doubt that the dollar is basically a currency of great strength. But any currency can be weakened through a policy that does not take into account that even a very rich country can grant foreign loans only within certain limits. If it surpasses these limits they must lead to a higher price level within the country and to the weakness of the currency in the international money markets. It seems therefore that in order to improve the situation of the dollar a certain restraint in the granting of foreign loans would not be out of place.

[5] The fears of the opposition have meanwhile proved to be correct. The Swiss balance of trade has become very passive. On the other hand, the finance dollar has gone up and fluctuates somewhere around 4 francs. There is, therefore, no question any more of revaluating the Swiss franc. Once the dollars from the defrozen accounts are absorbed, the finance dollar will probably reach the official parity. The wait and see policy of the National Bank and their refusal to revaluate has been vindicated in contrast to the revaluating policy of the Swedish Government, which proved disastrous for the country.

SUPPRESSION OF THE PREMIUM FOR FOREIGN EXCHANGE ON THE BLACK MARKETS IN THE WEAK-CURRENCY COUNTRIES

The problem of black-market prices for foreign exchange is identical with the problem of black-market prices on markets in general: the problem of controlling the purchasing power which cannot exert itself on the regular markets and which overflows to the black market.

One method of dealing with the superfluous purchasing power that overflows on the black markets for foreign exchange would be to let the official rates rise to the point where supply and demand are in balance. This was more or less what happened in the weak-currency countries after World War I. With rising official rates, exports from the weak-currency countries would increase. Imports would of course become more expensive, but—owing to the increased exports—probably not scarcer. They could even increase quantitatively, just as on the internal markets the lifting of ceiling prices makes products more expensive but also more plentiful because marginal plants begin to work again.

On the other hand, it is clear that while imports would on the whole increase, distribution among the population would be changed to the disadvantage of the masses, who would have to pay the higher prices without being compensated through higher profits as the entrepreneurial class would be. There is no doubt that a policy increasing imports as a whole but diminishing the share of the masses would be highly unpopular and politically unfeasible.

Another method of suppressing the margin between black and white exchange rates would be to deflate the purchasing power until under the pressure of this deflation the black-market prices receded. This was the method followed by Schacht at the beginning of the stabilization of the mark in 1923. Such a deflation —which would have to include deflation of wages, too, if mass unemployment were to be avoided—would hardly be feasible for political reasons.

Incidentally, whatever method is chosen to narrow the margin between black and official prices, the internal price and wage level would always have to remain relatively low in comparison with the price of foreign exchange rates. For as long as there exists a mistrust of the domestic currency, exporters, investors, and speculators will part with the foreign currency they receive only if the exchange rates take this mistrust into account. A price for foreign exchange at which demand and supply would balance could thus be maintained only at a relatively low wage level. In other words, the population would have to work cheaply in comparison with prices of import goods because it has to bear the confidence premium for the foreign exchange with which imports are paid.

This confidence premium would of course increase in case of anticapitalistic threats by governments or political parties. For it is the tragedy of socialistic experiments in an otherwise non-socialistic economy that they achieve the contrary of what they aim at. They do not better, they actually worsen, the conditions of the masses because it is the latter who ultimately must pay for the fear that socialistic measures arouse in those who possess or produce wealth.

This shows the only practical and politically possible way that would lead to the abolishment of black markets for foreign exchange in the weak-currency countries. It is to restore confidence in the domestic currency. Only in this way can the purchasing power overflowing to the black markets be sterilized without a painful deflationary process. Only in this way can the mistrust-discount of the domestic currency be suppressed. In order to establish confidence in the domestic currency it is above all necessary to balance the budget. Furthermore, everything must be done to give small and large capitalists the feeling that it is not only forbidden but also unreasonable to export their capital. Whether, especially in France, under the prevailing internal and external political conditions a policy of restitution of confidence is possible may be doubted. But what is not doubtful is that without such a policy sound conditions in the field of foreign currency cannot be regained.

How About Bretton Woods?

It is obvious that nothing experienced today in the field of foreign exchange in Europe fits in the slightest degree into the picture that the Bretton Woods agreements presuppose. In fact, Europe is not even yet in the so-called transitory period where currency restrictions work. It is in a pretransitory stage where not even currency restrictions are able to maintain orderly conditions.

Without reopening the discussion about Bretton Woods, one thing can be said: observations of conditions in Europe show—what critics of Bretton Woods have always emphasized—namely, that for the stabilization of currencies the stabilization of underlying political and financial conditions is overwhelmingly essential, and that technical devices and a stabilization fund as provided by the Bretton Woods agreements are of relatively small importance. Therefore one cannot help feeling that in all probability the Bretton Woods fund will not be essential for the stabilization of the postwar currencies. There is a good chance that for all practical purposes it will be replaced by individual credit arrangements coupled with certain guarantees to the creditors on the economic and fiscal policy to be followed by the debtor nations.

9. Is Saving a Virtue

or a Sin? *

During the war, saving was considered a decided virtue. The war-loan drives emphasized the necessity of saving and stressed its beneficial effects. Correctly so, for if the huge purchasing power created by a government's war expenditures is not counterbalanced by restraints on private spending, inflation must ensue.

There is no doubt, however, that after the extraordinary wartime and postwar expenditures have ceased, the inimical attitude of prewar days towards saving will prevail again. Once more we shall hear that saving diminishes the so-called "effective" demand for goods and, therefore, employment—in short, that saving is a sin. Again those will be ridiculed who adhere to the conservative opinion that saving does not reduce "effective demand," and that increased spending by governments or private individuals is no palliative able to restore demand and employment—in short, that saving remains a virtue.

To find a correct answer in this sin-or-virtue dilemma is obviously of the highest importance. For on this answer depend not only the decisions of individuals in many questions of everyday life and the decisions of governments on questions of economic and tax policy, but also the decision whether essential parts of our civic ethics are still valid. Is it still "ethical" to provide for a future rainy

* Appeared under the title "The Effects of Saving on Employment and Consumption" in the *Journal of Marketing*, July 1946; the German version, "Ist Sparen eine Tugend oder ein Last r?", in the *Neue Zürcher Zeitung*, Aug. 1946.

day, for old age, or for the education of one's children, by curtailing present consumption?

Saving is still a virtue, not a sin. Ten or fifteen years ago it would have been neither necessary nor difficult to convince the public that the war-loan slogans on the advantages of saving hold good also in peacetime. The "virtue" argument was solidly entrenched. Savings were considered indispensable to economic expansion and progress, and the layman was trained to follow the explanation and the proof of the argument even where it did not lie on the surface.

Things have changed meanwhile. Lord Keynes, that great exaggerator of partial truths, laid the foundation of what is called the "mature economy theory." And that theory, in turn, gives support to all "spending-is-a-virtue" theories.

A host of writers have considered it their duty to exaggerate Keynesian exaggerations still further and to vulgarize them in order to popularize them. The result is that the fundaments on which our economic, political, and moral decisions seemed to rest solidly have been shaken. Our sentiments, concepts, and convictions have become thoroughly confused. Yesterday's virtue is today's sin.

To fight against this modern trend is neither easy nor popular. For the public at large seems to have forgotten how to weigh economic problems in an unsophisticated common-sense way, which was the way of the English classicists, especially of Adam Smith and David Ricardo. And a theory that recommends prodigality among public and private households as an easy way out of difficulties is, of course, more palatable than one that calls for thrift. However, too much is at stake to forego the fight against what in the long run can only have disastrous consequences.

Let us begin by describing the classical and the prevailing concepts as simply as we can.

The Classical Concept

According to the classical concept of the problem of saving—as of most economic problems—the interests of the individual and of the community are in full harmony. He who saves serves his own as well as the nation's welfare.

He improves his own welfare because saving implies the transfer of means for consumption from the present, where his earnings are ample, into the future where his earnings may become scarce through old age and sickness. Furthermore, saving will increase his means through the interest he receives.

The nation as a whole, on the other hand, benefits from savings since these savings are paid into a bank or some other reservoir of money from which an employer may borrow for productive purposes, for instance to buy machinery. This means a change in the direction of productive activity.

Through saving, production is diverted from goods for immediate consumption to goods which cannot themselves be consumed but with which consumer goods can be produced. Production is diverted, as one puts it, from a direct to a roundabout way of production, a "long-production way" in which the end-product is available for consumption only after substantial delay.

The roundabout way of production has the advantage of greater productivity. Let us assume—the example is illuminating if not very realistic—that 100 men are able to produce 1,000 shoes in the course of a year when working with their hands. If, however, during one year these 100 men produce shoe-manufacturing machines, and during the second year produce shoes with the help of these machines, then the net result of their work will be not 1,000 shoes a year, or 2,000 in two years, but 20,000 shoes or even more.

But the labor put originally into the production of the manufacturing machines is available for consumption in the form of shoes only after the second year—even if we assume that the machines are fully worn out and amortized after one year's use. Furthermore, during the second year production needs twice the amount of capital. Formerly the employer had to pay wages only for one year; now he has to lay out the wages for the first and the second year until he can recoup them by sales of the shoes. Production has become more capitalistic.

The high productivity of the more capitalistic production methods has further favorable effects. Because much less labor is required per unit of production, the employers can—and by competition are forced to—pay interest on the capital borrowed, to raise wages, and to lower prices. The standard of living of the nation rises.

This process is renewed over and over again, because increased savings permit primitive direct methods of production requiring small amounts of capital to be replaced by roundabout indirect methods requiring large amounts of capital. Colonial and pioneer peoples realized this when they tried to import as much capital as possible, from older nations with a high rate of saving, into their young country with its low rate of saving. And the United States realized it and imported huge sums of foreign capital to build railroads.

Those who look thus upon the effect of saving will of course regard everything as favorable that increases savings. They will, for instance, regard an inequality of income as perhaps unjust but never as harmful to the economy, for it is easier to save out of high incomes than out of low ones. Their decisions in many questions of daily life will be influenced by such a sympathetic attitude toward saving. They will become strongly "puritan" and try to influence their surroundings and especially their children in a puritan spirit.

Likewise, they will consider thrift an important, if not the most important, duty of government finance. The thriftier the government, the lower will be the taxes on production and consumption. The lower consumer taxes, the higher the standard of living; the lower the taxes on production, the greater the possibilities of expanding production, thus increasing the wealth of the nation. Adam Smith and David Ricardo, the great English classicists in the economic field, have emphasized the fact over and over again.

THE PREVAILING THEORY

According to the prevailing theory, the interests of the individual and those of the community are not necessarily in harmony. Those who save serve their own advantage, but can easily endanger the community by doing so.

In its simplest form the argument runs as follows: those who save desist from buying and hereby render a certain quantity of goods unsalable. This is not harmful as long as an entrepreneur

takes over the money as a credit or the like and uses it for investment—for example, for buying modern machinery to improve his
output. This demand replaces the demand of the savers.

The flow of money from the saver to the entrepreneur is, however, not coercive. It can be interrupted and obstructed, and it
was interrupted and obstructed during the last decade before
World War II. The means available through saving cannot be
fully invested, because new opportunities for profitable investment
are lacking. Such opportunities are present only when new inventions—or growth of populations—promise an adequate profit for the
invested capital. Today we no longer live in the age when railroads, electricity, or the automobile were invented. There are no
more "innovations." Our economy is mature. It has become stag-
nant.

If the foregoing argument is correct, then saving no longer means
that "effective demand" is switched from a potential consumer to
an entrepreneur, but that its aggregate amount is reduced. Goods
become unsalable. Operation of plants is curtailed. Unemployment ensues with all its disastrous social, economic, and political
consequences.

This is what is usually called the oversavings-underinvestment
theory of unemployment. From it follows automatically an unfavorable attitude towards saving that is diametrically opposed to
the classical concept. Everything that tends to curtail consumption is considered pernicious; everything that serves to increase it
seems advantageous.

Inequality of income appears harmful, because it increases saving. Confiscatory taxes on higher income brackets are recommended. The same holds true for undistributed corporation dividends, because their accumulation in the corporation reduces the
ability of the country to consume.

All this leads, of course, to a break with the old, and to the introduction of an entirely new, economic morale. If saving is contrary to the interest of the nation, then the watchword is: not
curtailment, but increase of consumption; not accumulation of purchasing power for the future, but spending in the present. There

is no longer any room or motive for puritanism in economic convictions.

And if the adherents of the new theory refrain from preaching outright waste, it is not because it would be inconsistent with their theory, but rather because they feel that it would be considered too much in contrast to common sense and, therefore, compromising to the new creed.

In the realm of public finance this creed leads to recommendations that are entirely revolutionary. Formerly, when economic activity slackened, maladjustments were considered the reason and their removal the remedy. Now, as soon as effective demand by individuals begins to slow down, the government is supposed to spend so much that the demand remains at its old level.

Since taxes would curtail private consumption even more, spending must be continued in spite of growing budgetary deficits—"deficit spending," formerly considered permissible only in emergencies such as war. As unemployment seems to have become a permanent evil, permanent deficit financing, formerly viewed as the most dangerous financial policy, nowadays appears as the most progressive.

Whether the government investments are profitable or not is considered of secondary importance. Keynes himself went so far as to praise the building of the Pyramids because of their employment-creating effect. But the building of pyramids is, in any circumstances, one of the most useless of enterprises, since they serve as a residence not for the living but for the dead—and for very few dead at that.

SAVING POSTPONES, IT DOES NOT PREVENT, CONSUMPTION

Let us try to show the basic fallacies of the theory. To do this, we have to examine what really happens in an economy after saving sets in (or increases), when savings become greater than dissavings.

The main point of attack on savings is, of course, the contention that they render products unsalable, because the saver's demand for consumer goods falls off. The demand is destroyed over a period that lasts until savings as a whole decrease, i.e., until the distant period when withdrawals of savings—dissavings—again out-strip savings. However, things are not so simple as this argument assumes.

Consumption is not a single occurrence. It happens over and over again because economic life is an ever-beginning and ever-continuing process. All the time, people begin to work anew, are paid for their work, and spend out of their income.

Now, if in any given year people do not spend all that they have received, this does not mean that the consumption schedule of a country falls into disorder for all time. It simply means that the demand of the given year is taken out from the beginning of the schedule and put, so to speak, at its end, while the next year's demand is not affected. The effect of saving on the spending schedule is therefore that the whole schedule is postponed for one year.

Saving and spending are thus not mutually contradictory. Savings mean delay in—not absence of—spending.

This is a very important point. It shows why saving cannot really hinder production and employment. If the annual demand for products has not vanished but is postponed for one year, production need not be curtailed but should instead be changed in such a way that the end-products appear after two years, instead of after one year, on the market where they can be sold without difficulties. One must—we return to our example of manufacturing shoes by hand—build machines during the first year with which shoes can then be produced in the second year. The incentive to invest in machines is the necessary correlative to delayed consumption.

But savings do not merely stimulate investments in machinery; they also make these possible. For the money saved and turned over to entrepreneurs furnishes them with the additional capital they need for buying machines and thus enables them to follow a more capitalistic pattern of production.

However, adherents of the "mature economy" thesis will reply: even if the sale of shoes is guaranteed in the second year, the entrepreneur will not be willing to invest in new machines unless his investment brings him a profit in comparison with the less capitalistic way of production. Such profits are allegedly lacking because of the dearth of new inventions. However, as Mr. George Terborgh has shown,[1] the more capitalistic method of production practically always leaves an extra profit—though perhaps a diminishing one—in comparison with the less capitalistic method.

But even if this were not the case and no extra profit would accrue from more mechanized production methods, there is not the slightest reason why the entrepreneur should not choose this way when interest rates reduced by increased savings render the more capitalistic way increasingly advantageous as long as demand and production are maintained. And even if this advantage should entirely vanish—which is highly improbable—there would still remain an outlet for the savings as long as there was unemployment. For every newly engaged worker has to be equipped with tools requiring capital. And there is, as will be shown later on, nothing like a labor force that is permanently unemployable under any conditions.

So saving creates its own investment opportunities. This means that it creates real wealth, for if anything can be called wealth of a nation, it is the increased stock of machinery, inventories, and other means of production which accumulate when more capitalistic methods of production are chosen. All this means that the new economic creed is not correct.

DEMAND SHRINKS DURING CYCLICAL DEPRESSIONS; BUT SAVING IS NOT THE CAUSE

We do not mean to assert by all this that the flow of purchasing power to the markets of goods and services is never interrupted, that goods and services never become unsalable. Such an assertion would be contradictory to practical experience. Every one of the cyclical crises of history has begun with a severe congestion of the markets. However, one would be deceived by an illusion if one considered these congestions to be caused by savings.

As we have shown, saving has the effect that the demand for consumer goods arises at the end of the second instead of at the

[1] *The Bogey of Economic Maturity,* Chicago, 1945.

end of the first year; whereas at the end of the first year, demand for production goods—our shoe machines, for example—sets in.

The dislocation of demand during a depression has an entirely different character. During a depression, the demand for consumption goods is reduced not only at the end of the first but also at the end of the second and all subsequent years, as long as the depression lasts, and is not replaced by demand for production goods. But when the depression is over and recovery sets in, the demand schedule postponed into the future by the depression is, so to speak, shifted back into the present again. Demand gains speed and omitted consumption is made up for during the boom.

Dislocations of demand through saving are caused when somebody curtails present consumption to provide for needs in the very distant future. Dislocations through cyclical depressions are caused by buyers' withholding their purchasing power for fear of a further fall of prices—just as they had spent their money freely during the preceding boom in the hope of further price advances. Dislocations through saving remain until savings are surpassed by dissavings. Dislocation through depression ends with the end of the depression when prices have declined and the decline is considered sufficient by the buyers.

If in a state of cyclical depression savings in the real sense of the word are increased, the depression is thereby not rendered more severe. The contrary is the case. Saving as such only replaces demand for consumer goods by demand for production goods. Within the framework of a general dwindling of demand, it is still better that demand for production goods should remain relatively stronger than demand for consumer goods. For the indirect way of production—using production goods—is still the more productive way.

Do the oversaving-underinvestment theorists recognize the special reason for, and the characteristics of, a cyclical dwindling of purchasing power, and the fact that it is entirely independent of saving? Most of them do not. Most of them argue that for whatever reason consumer demand fails to materialize, it is the duty of the entrepreneur to replace the consumer's demand and to invest for production. If shoes are not bought, they say, entrepreneurs should buy shoe-producing machines. If they do not do so, the ensuing discrepancy between saving and investment must be considered responsible for the dwindling purchasing power, deflation, and all other consequences.

This line of argument is caused by an illusion. The illusion is created by the abundance of money and credit that develops during every depression at a certain time and indeed indicates an oversupply of loanable funds. This oversupply materializes because the consumers bring to the banks the money they do not for the time being want to spend, and because the entrepreneurs are not ready to use it.

However, this situation does not alter the fact that it is not underinvestment caused by the lack of investment opportunities, but a general dwindling of consumers' demands which is responsible for the conditions on the market during a depression. The entrepreneur who refuses to buy machines is, so to speak, only the representative of the future consumers of the machines' end-products, as illustrated in our example of the shoes.

The entrepreneur refuses to buy machines as long as he cannot count on selling the shoes at all, or at the old price. The outlet into present as well as future consumption is blocked, and for neither condition can the entrepreneur be blamed or held responsible.

Cyclical disturbances of demand are not created by saving or oversaving, but are by their very nature transitory. It is the basic fallacy and the tragedy of the modern theory that it regards the cyclical depression of the 'thirties as representing a permanent change of the economy. For this confusion has forced its adherents to advance such untenable—and unnecessary—theories as the stagnation and mature economy theories, and to indulge in pessimistic prognoses for capitalism and free enterprise.

This whole approach is clearly an outgrowth of the overwhelming effect of the Great Depression, and it will vanish when the memory of the Great Depression has vanished. For it is obviously unreasonable to state that the soil has become sterile because nothing grows during the winter.

CHRONIC UNDEREMPLOYMENT AND UNDERINVESTMENT

There exist not only cyclical transitory disturbances of demand and employment, but also disturbances of a chronic character which extend over a long period of time. This fact cannot be denied. When the recovery reached its peak in 1937, millions of workers were still out of work. This unemployment must be regarded as noncyclical and chronic.

The oversaving-underinvestment theorists, as mentioned above, explain underemployment by referring to the entrepreneur's reluctance to invest in a mature economy in which profitable investment opportunities are lacking. We have already shown that this explanation is unsatisfactory. Low profitability of new investment can be no obstacle to a more capitalistic production and corresponding new investment, if savings force and make possible the more capitalistic way. Savings create their own investment opportunities.

The correct solution can be grasped if one examines the real reasons for the entrepreneur's reluctance to invest nowadays. He is reluctant, as everybody familiar with practical business knows, not because the interest to be paid for idle capital is higher than the additional profits more capitalistic methods of production would yield in comparison with the less capitalistic ones, but because other costs have risen too much in comparison with the price the entrepreneur can expect for the end-product.

Among these other costs, wages and taxes are the most important. For, after all, interest rates are not the only costs of production, and the prices obtained for the product are not the only reward for the use of capital, as the theory of the lack of investment opportunities seems to suggest.

The answer to what causes chronic underinvestment and underemployment is thus very simple. The cause is not unprofitability of capital as such, but unprofitability of other production factors, especially labor, which has to be paid either directly or in the price of machines that contain labor. Production containing labor cannot be sold when it costs more than it nets.

This, incidentally, was the answer of the classicists when they were concerned with the question of unemployment. It is also the businessman's answer; when he explains why he does not care to invest, he mentions wages and taxes. The prevailing theory does not seem to see the wage and tax problem in the same way the businessman does. It has, in this respect, lost contact with practical life and has become purely mental speculation in a purely fictitious world.

Saving or oversaving does not create unemployment. It is rather the other way round: unemployment caused by excessive production costs creates underinvestment.

This sort of unemployment can be a feature of an economy with low savings, just as full employment can be a feature of a high-saving economy. If the shoemakers who produce shoes by hand demand excessive wages, they will face unemployment, whereas the men working with machines may be fully employed if their wages are not excessive. And the probability that wages are too high in a high-saving economy with high productivity is, of course, smaller, because high productivity leaves a margin for higher wages.

It is clear from all this that chronic unemployment cannot be fought by curtailing savings. Adjustment of cost to price is the only remedy; increase of wages in this situation is entirely out of place.

Increase of wages is often recommended because it allegedly raises and maintains effective demand. However, it raises only the effective demand of the worker who is lucky enough to stay on his job. The aggregate purchasing power of the working class sinks with the increasing unemployment caused by the unprofitability of the marginal enterprise.

CONCLUSIONS

Our conclusions are as follows:

1. Basically, the old saying remains valid: saving is a virtue and not a sin. Those who save serve their own good, and, far from doing harm to the community, they serve its well-being. Private and common interests are still in harmony.

2. During cyclical crises and depressions, demand can dwindle and goods and services can become unsalable. This happens, however, not because consumers save, but because all members of the

economy—consumers as well as producers—withhold purchasing power temporarily. This withholding is caused by a lack of confidence, especially concerning the future price structure. Its duration can be shortened by any means that will restore confidence, but never by propaganda or measures against saving.

3. In order to restore confidence in the price structure, the government is justified in compensating, and even obliged to compensate, the lacking private demand by proper expenditures for which it acquires the means by loans, not by taxes. But such "compensatory" deficit spending must really remain a remedy for transitory periods. The underlying idea must always be to repay the ensuing government debt during the next period of prosperity. Deficit spending must never become permanent spending.

4. In the long run and outside the business cycle, the level of employment or unemployment in an economy depends on the relation of production costs to the prices obtainable for the product. Saving improves this relation, because it improves productivity and thus the possibility of digesting higher costs. Again, propaganda or measures against saving do not improve but rather deteriorate the level of employment.

5. Adjustment of costs to prices remains the only remedy for chronic unemployment. Government spending is not adequate to combat chronic unemployment, for such spending would have to be continued permanently. Permanent deficit spending, however, means cumulative government indebtedness. This leads sooner or later, as shown by historical experience, to inflation or government bankruptcy.

6. Government intervention in order to fight chronic unemployment can only consist in the fight against everything that hinders adjustment of cost to prices, especially against all monopolistic manipulations of prices and wages. For without such manipulations, in a free economy costs would tend to adjust themselves to prices, through competition among the unemployed production factors. It follows, incidentally, that it is shortsighted to demand guarantees for 60 million or any other number of jobs from a government which does not control prices and wages. It is just as if a patient were to demand from a physician a guarantee for his

health though the physician lacks the power to prevent him from indulging in excesses.

7. Thrift is and remains the fundament of every private enterprise. The thriftily, not the wastefully, managed enterprise survives. The wealth of a nation rests not only on the industry but also on the thrift of its citizens.

8. Thrift, and not wasteful spending, is the fundament of public finances. In the long run, high expenditure means high taxes, and high taxes mean low consumption. They mean more expensive and, therefore, curtailed production.

9. The new teachings, in spite of their unquestionable success, are nothing else than a deviation from sound common-sense principles. History shows that such deviations have often occurred, because the easy way out, especially in matters of currency and finance, is always attractive until the inevitable disappointment restores the conviction that in the long run the hard way is the only way out of difficulties.

10. Mercantilism and
Keynesianism *

Nothing is so instructive for the evaluation of scientific and political ideas as the history of those ideas. It teaches us that conceptions claiming novelty and originality have nearly always, during the course of history, been not only conceived but refuted. The knowledge of this history can therefore prevent scientific discussion from moving always in circles; it can prevent undertaking hopeless economic experiments for the testing of which the past has already paid; and finally it can deprive some scientific or political opinions of the appeal of paradoxicalness that make them seemingly irresistible to many people.

In the field of monetary theory and policy, history teaches us, further, that ideas about the role of money in the economy swing like a pendulum from one extreme to the other. Times when the power of monetary changes is overrated alternate with times when it is underrated. Times when a reasonable synthesis of opinion is achieved appear to be rare and brief.

There seems no doubt that in our time the pendulum has again swung strongly in the direction of an overestimation of the possibilities of influencing the economy from the money side. By the followers of the late J. M. Keynes, whose opinions prevail especially in this country, it is considered self-evident that by increasing purchasing power (or "effective demand") employment can be increased and unemployment combated. It might therefore be appropriate

° Appeared first in the *American Journal of Economics and Sociology*, July 1947.

to recall briefly the teachings of the school that has shown more enthusiasm for monetary manipulations than any other during history. We mean the teachings of the *Mercantilists*.

THE THEORIES OF THE MERCANTILISTS

The relationship of Keynesianism to Mercantilism of the sixteenth to the eighteenth centuries is well known. Keynes himself has pointed to it.[1] He has said much in praise and in defense of mercantilistic theory and policy and against arguments presented by its classical critics.

The ideas of the Mercantilists contain—in this we have definitely to agree with Keynes—theoretical insights on money which are astonishing for those times. This is why the general prejudice against them is surely unjust. But can it be concluded from this, as Keynes seems to assume, that Mercantilism can be used in support of Keynes' ideas, especially regarding the stimulation of business activity? We doubt it.

The main conclusion of the Mercantilists is—in Keynes' formulation—that "a favourable balance [of payments in international trade], provided it is not too large, will prove extremely stimulating."[2] This stimulation happens, according to the Mercantilists, by a simple mechanism: the favorable balance of payments draws precious metal into the country. This increases the circulating purchasing power. This again means increased demand for labor and thus higher production.[3] Such a mechanism can indeed work; however, as Keynes correctly remarks, only under the condition that "the increase in the domestic level of costs [does not] begin to react unfavourably on the balance of foreign trade";[4] a condition which the Mercantilists fulfilled by "discouraging rises in the wage-unit."[5]

---

[1] J. M. Keynes, *General Theory of Employment, Interest, and Money*, New York, 1936, p. 333 ff.: Notes on Mercantilism, the Usury Laws, Stamped Money and Theories of Under-consumption.

[2] Keynes, *op. cit.*, p. 338.

[3] I can see no essential difference between this process and what is today called "the foreign trade multiplier."

[4] Keynes, *op. cit.*, p. 336.

[5] *Ibid.*, p. 340.

If the Mercantilistic employment theory is thus based on the idea that increased purchasing power results in higher employment, provided wages remain fixed, they have indeed anticipated Keynesianism. For Keynes, too, holds the theory that increased demand leads to increased production; and his theory, too, is valid only if wages and costs are prevented from rising with and through the increasing demand.[6]

This condition was fulfilled in the times of the Mercantilists. Today it is all but fulfilled.[7] Therefore the paradoxical situation arises that Keynesianism is indeed applicable for an analysis of Mercantilistic but not of modern economy; and that on the other hand Mercantilism cannot be used to support modern Keynesianism.

However, we do not want to examine further the factual conditions under which the Mercantilistic-Keynesian employment theory is valid. What we want to show is that this theory embraced in fact all essential features of modern "Effective Demand Analysis." As far as I can see, the man who developed this analysis most conclusively is John Law who, although generally not counted among the Mercantilists proper, is undoubtedly to be considered the strongest and most interesting exponent of their ideas.

John Law was a man of fabulous ascent and terrible downfall. At the peak of his good fortune (1717-1720) he was master of billions but he died (1729 in Venice) in extreme poverty. Seldom has a man been more loved and admired and also more hated and despised. His relation to Mercantilism can be compared to the relation of Keynes to the New Deal: he was not the originator of the movement but he was the most able and mature formulator of its ideas. Law's chief works [8] are not the works of a crank, as has been maintained by Charles Rist [9] and many other authors, but of

---

[6] *Ibid.*, p. 289.

[7] See Chapter 6, "Compensating Reactions to Compensatory Spending."

[8] John Law, *Money and Trade Considered as a Proposal for Supplying the Nation with Money*, Glasgow, 1760 (first published at Edinburgh, 1705); *Mémoires sur les banques* and *Lettres sur les banques*, 1717. Cf. Faire, ed., *Economistes financiers du dix-huitième siècle*, Paris, 1843.

[9] Charles Rist, *History of Monetary and Credit Theory*, New York. First printed in English in 1940.

an extremely ingenious thinker who reached conclusions amazing for his time.

Law by no means identifies abundance of money with abundance of goods, for which many Mercantilists have been correctly reproached. On the contrary, he states explicitly that money as such has no value through its use: "Money is not the value for which goods are exchanged but the value by which they are exchanged: the use of money is to buy goods, and silver while money is of no other use." [10] Money is not wealth but money creates wealth. For "National power and wealth . . . depend on trade and trade depends on money" [11] ". . . nor can more people be set to work, without more money to circulate, so as to pay the wages of a greater number." [12]

CREATION OF EMPLOYMENT THROUGH CREATION OF "EFFECTIVE DEMAND"

But how is it that according to Law money creates wealth? Law's reply differs in form but not, so far as I can see, in essence from the reply that Keynes gave nearly two and a half centuries later. It is already a complete "analysis in terms of effective demand." We quote the famous passages from Chapter 7 of Law's *Money and Trade:*

Suppose an Island belonging to one man, the number of Tenants 100, each Tenant 10 in Family, in all 1000. By these the Island is labour'd, part to the Product of Corns, the Rest for Pasturage. Besides the Tenants and their Families, there are 300 Poor or Idle who live by Charity. There is no money; but Rents are paid in kind, and if one Tenant has more of one Product, and less of another than his Family has occasion for he barters with his Neighbour. [13]

One sees that there are 300 unemployed and 1000 farmers employed for only half the year. "For this reason," continues Law, "'tis proposed to the Proprietor that if a Money were established to pay the Wages of Labour, the 300 Poor might be employed in manufacturing such Goods as before were exported in Product; and

[10] Law, *Money and Trade* . . . , p. 188.   [13] *Ibid.*, pp. 182-83.
[11] *Ibid.*, p. 110.
[12] *Ibid.*, p. 21.

as the 1000 that labour the Ground were idle one half their Time, they might be employed so as their additional Labour would be equal to that of 500 more." [14]

And he concludes: "But as this addition to the Money will employ the People that are now Idle, and those now employ'd to more Advantage, so the Product will be encreas'd, and manufacture advanced." [15]

This is obviously the same idea that Keynes expresses in the words: ". . . it will be possible to increase employment by increasing expenditures in terms of money" [16] and later ". . . as effective demand increases, employment increases." [17]

But what is the deeper reason for the creation of employment by the creation of new money or demand? Keynes explains the mechanism very clearly by analyzing the reason for existing unemployment. If people are unemployed, it is because their wage demands are higher than the value of their product. If new money is created, the prices of the products increase in terms of money whereas wages remain stable.[18] So new money transforms former unemployed into employed by reducing the reward of labor in comparison with the value of its product. Keynes himself, it is true, believes in the employment-creating power of an increase in the quantity of money only for the "general case" because only in the "general case" can wages be considered stable. His followers, however, have formulated the theory in an absolute form, forgetting the special Keynesian assumptions. For them, increase in purchasing power increases employment *always* until all unemployed are absorbed.

We have already mentioned that nowadays money wages can no longer be considered stable when an inflationary monetary policy tends to lower real wages. In the Mercantilistic period, however, the mechanism as described by Keynes could work, because the omnipotent State had absolute control over labor conditions: workers were forced to work wherever the government wanted, and wages were fixed—and at very low levels—by governmental author-

[14] *Ibid.*, pp. 183-84.   [17] *Ibid.*, p. 289.
[15] *Ibid.*, p. 198.   [18] *Ibid.*, p. 284.
[16] Keynes, *op. cit.*, p. 284.

ity. It is well known that, in case of need, workers were even driven by force into the factories, and a not unimportant part of labor supply was recruited from among the inmates of prisons and orphanages.[19]

CREATION OF PURCHASING POWER THROUGH CREATION OF NEW PAPER MONEY

If the increase of purchasing power means more employment, and more employment means more wealth, then the problem of increasing wealth is obviously the problem of increasing purchasing power. And here, at the question how the quantity of purchasing power (of money) can be increased, Law arrives at those statements and claims through which he gained, more than through everything else, the attention but also the execration of his contemporaries and later generations. He claims not only that bank notes or paper money should be created, but also—and this is the decisive part—that these should be created in any amount demanded and for which real estate could be given as security. If the authorities ". . . do not give out money when it is demanded, where good security is offer'd 'tis a hardship on the person who is refuted, and a loss to the country: for few if any borrow money to keep by them; and if employ'd it brings a profit to the nation, tho' the employer loses."[20]

Thus according to Law's theory the size of the credit supply in a country is no longer dependent on the amounts which have been saved, or, incidentally, on the amounts of capital goods that are available. With paper money to be created *ad libitum* every credit demand can be met at the prevailing interest rate without any disadvantageous consequences. It was this theory that served as a theoretical justification, not only for the bank which he himself was to create later on, but also for the entire sympathetic attitude towards the creation of banks of deposit and banks of issue during the eighteenth and nineteenth centuries. It led to the idea that

---

[19] *Handwörterbuch der Staatswissenschaft*, "Merkantilismus," 1925, Band VI, pp. 548-49.

[20] John Law, *op. cit.*, p. 168.

the founding of a bank, and especially of an issuing bank, is under all circumstances beneficial for every country; an idea that considerably later was formulated by Henry Dunning Macleod in the words: "A bank is a gold mine."

It will be noted that Law's opinions are, to a certain extent, more conservative than those of the modern proponents of the "easy-money policy." His idea is that every demand for credit can be satisfied through creation of new money at the same interest rate—i.e., that the scarce supply need not be defended by rising interest rates. Modern easy-money policy as proposed by Keynes [21] goes further in that it advocates lowering of interest rates below the prevailing level in order to incite new demand. Generally speaking, however, it is clear that John Law can be correctly considered the founder of the modern "easy-money policy."

The Experience of John Law's Bank

As is well known, Law had full opportunity to try to create employment through creation of new purchasing power, and to create new purchasing power by the issuing of paper money. In 1717 he founded his famous Issuing Bank, which, at the end of 1719, created what was probably the greatest boom of all times with more employment than was desired. But the beginning of the year 1720 brought what was probably the biggest crash of all time.

The bank had created paper money without hindrance or inhibitions. Every demand was satisfied—the demand of the private economy, whose need for credits rose during the boom, as well as the demand of the government which financed its deficits through the help of the banks. The financing of the government's deficit, incidentally, took place as the result of pressure from the government and very much against Law's will. The creation of paper money led at first to an increasing discount of the bills in comparison with bullion, then to their repudiation: the public no longer accepted the paper money. And all this, though all the well-known techniques were applied with which governments, deteriorating their money, fight the citizen who wants to conserve his capital.

[21] Keynes, *op. cit.*, pp. 27-28.

The hoarding of bullion was suppressed, the use of coins allowed for small payments only. Export of bullion was punished. Wearing or importing diamonds and pearls was forbidden. Manufacture of silver objects was prohibited, and the paper money became legal tender in the entire country.[22]

It has been said that the débâcle occurred because Law was an inflationist—that is, he consciously aimed at the depreciation of money. Nothing is more false. He believed that he could create employment by creating money and that he would be able to cease the issuance of new money the moment full employment was reached. He was, therefore, not an "inflationist" but a "prosperity spender." Like his modern successors, he believed that prosperity created through inflation could be stabilized at a high level. He overlooked the fact that the inflationary boom is followed either by deflationary reaction or by a runaway inflation—this latter in case an attempt is made to prolong the boom artificially. For the stimulus of inflation works only so long as costs have not adapted themselves to rising prices. Therefore, prices have to be raised ever anew by the creation of new money in order to provide the necessary stimulus for the maintenance of the boom. The ever-renewed issuance of new money, however, leads in the long run to the ruin of the currency. Law's experiment, in any case, ended in severe economic depression, the bankruptcy of his bank, and the devaluation to zero of the paper money it had issued.

If a great financier dies at the peak of his power, it is said at his grave that he was a financial genius. If, like Law, he dies after the collapse of his creations, or if after his death it is discovered (as in the modern case of Ivar Kreuger) that he was bankrupt, people say that he was a ruthless speculator who ruined his contemporaries and his country. If Law's "system" lives in the memory of posterity as the creation of a visionary, a swindler and a crook, it is because he died broke. But his theories would be objectionable even if by chance his bank had survived him for a certain length of time.

---

[22] Cf. Handwörterbuch der Staatswissenschaft, "John Law," 1925, Band VI, p. 261 (3).

THE CRITICISM OF THE CLASSICISTS

Law's theories are interesting not only because of their similarity to modern ideas. A knowledge of them is indispensable if one wants to do justice to the teachings of the great English Classicists in the field of monetary and general theory. It has become customary nowadays to think of the Classicists as a sort of antiquated and obsolete out-of-the-world people whose assumptions "happen not to be those of the economic society in which we actually live," as Keynes [23] charges. In reality their theories were based on the very practical experiences of their times, and if certain (though by no means all) of their views were one-sided, this is explainable by the fact that they represented the reaction to a very extreme swing of the pendulum to the unconservative side.

MORE MONEY LEADS TO HIGHER PRICES, NOT TO HIGHER EMPLOYMENT

What the Classicists set against the ideas of Law (whose name, by the way, they did not mention because they considered him unworthy of notice) was the "Quantity Theory of Money," which they did not invent but which they reproduced and reformulated. In so doing they expressed the basic truth of monetary theory to which science will always return after excursions into the realm of fantasy, quackery, and the illusion that basic economic maladjustments can be corrected through monetary measures. The classical formulation of the quantity theory is found in the famous fourth paragraph of the twenty-seventh chapter of David Ricardo's *Political Economy:* "A circulation can never be so abundant as to overflow; for by diminishing its value, in the same proportion you will increase its quantity, and by increasing its value diminish its quantity." [24]

It is clear that within the framework of a quantity-theoretical attitude there is no room for the idea that employment can be increased by increasing purchasing power. If one creates additional money, prices and wages, but not employment, will increase.

[23] Keynes, *op. cit.,* p. 3.
[24] David Ricardo, *Principles of Political Economy and Taxation,* 2nd edition, London, 1819, p. 448.

Employment will increase not when money increases but when } capital—tools and the means of subsistence for the worker—increases. } Adam Smith expresses this idea in the second chapter of the second book of *The Wealth of Nations* in the following way:

In order to put industry into motion, three things are requisite: materials to work upon, tools to work with, and the wages or recompense for the sake of which the work is done. Money is neither a material to work upon, nor a tool to work with; and though the wages of the workman are commonly paid to him in money, his real revenue, like that of all other men, consists, not in the money, but in the money's worth; not in the metal pieces, but in what can be got for them.

The quantity of industry which any capital can employ, must, evidently, be equal to the number of workmen whom it can supply with materials, tools and a maintenance suitable to the nature of the work. Money may be requisite for purchasing the materials and tools of the work, as well as the maintenance of the workmen. But the quantity of industry which the whole capital can employ, is certainly not equal both to the money which it purchases, and to the materials, tools and maintenance, which are purchased with it; but only to one or other of those two values, and to the latter more properly than to the former.[25]

It follows that according to the Quantity Theorists an increase of purchasing power can never lead to an increase in employment. The increase in purchasing power leads to an increase in prices, and, because the workers need the same amount of means of subsistence, to a corresponding degree of wage increases. The increase of money exhausts itself and is absorbed by these price and wage increases. There is no money left for the employment of additional labor.

It is clear that this line of thought is exactly the contrary of Law's. Whereas he believed that the additional money can be used profitably for the employment of workers hitherto unemployed, the Quantity Theorists contend that the additional money spent itself in increased nominal prices and wages. No wonder that in their system there was no room for what one calls today fluctuations of employment caused by fluctuations of "effective demand."

[25] Adam Smith, *An Inquiry into the Nature and Causes of the Wealth of Nations*, Vol. I, 8th edition, London, 1796, p. 440.

Loanable Funds Cannot Be Increased Through Creation of Additional Money

For the same reasons, the Classicists deny that it is possible to increase the amount of purchasing power loanable to entrepreneurs by the issuance of new paper money. They consequently deny, too, that it is possible to lower interest rates or to prevent their rising by increasing the quantity of money.

> I do not dispute [says Ricardo in his famous essay, "The High Price of Bullion" [26]] that if the Bank were to bring a large additional sum of notes into the Market, and offer them on loan, but that they would for a time affect the rate of interest. The same effects would follow from the discovery of a hidden treasure of gold or silver coin. If the amount were large, the Bank, or the owner of the treasure, might not be able to lend the notes or the money at 4, nor perhaps above 3 per cent; but having done so, neither the notes, nor the money, would be retained unemployed by the borrowers; they would be sent into every Market, and would everywhere raise the prices of commodities, till they were absorbed in the general circulation. It is only during the interval of the issues of the Bank, and their effect on prices, that we should be sensible of an abundance of money; interest would during that interval be under its natural level; but as soon as the additional sum of notes or of money became absorbed in the general circulation, the rate of interest would be high and new loans would be demanded with as much eagerness as before the additional issues.

Only through increased savings can loanable funds be augmented and interest rates lowered.

> To suppose that any increased issues of the Bank can have the effect of permanently lowering the rate of interest, and satisfying the demands of all borrowers, so that there will be none to apply for new loans, or that a productive gold or silver mine can have such an effect, is to attribute a power to the circulating medium which it can never possess. Banks would, if this were possible, become powerful engines indeed.[27] . . . Profits can only be lowered by a competition of capitals not consisting of a circulating medium. As the increase of bank notes does not add to this species of capital, as it neither increases our exportable commodities, our machinery, or our raw materials, it cannot add to our profits nor lower interest.[28]

[26] 4th ed., London, 1811.
[27] *Ibid.*, pp. 35-36.
[28] *Ibid.*, p. 36.

The reason is simply that the increase of currency increases prices. The power over machines, material, and labor that the entrepreneur acquires through the credits is only apparently but not actually enhanced. It is true that displacements and dislocations of the power to command production factors occur. The owner of the old money is expropriated in favor of the entrepreneur who is endowed with the new money. In a masterly way Ricardo depicts these consequences of an inflationary credit expansion:

> But however abundant may be the quantity of money or of bank notes; though it may increase the nominal prices of commodities; though it may distribute the productive capital in different proportions; though the Bank, by increasing the quantity of their notes, may enable A to carry on part of the business formerly engrossed by B and C, nothing will be added to the real revenue and wealth of the country. B and C may be injured, and A and the Bank may be gainers, but they will gain exactly what B and C lose. There will be a violent and unjust transfer of property but no benefit whatever will be gained by the community.[29]

The Pendulum Has Again Swung Backward

As we have mentioned at the beginning, periods that overrated the power of monetary changes have alternated with periods underrating this power.

The aim of science should be, in this as in every other field, to achieve a synthesis of divergent concepts. Such a synthesis was reached by David Hume in his *Essay on Bank and Paper Money,* 1752.[30] He describes the strong effects of inflation on production during transitory periods and the ineffectiveness of purely monetary measures for longer periods. He recognizes the reason for this: inflation no longer works as soon as the various data of the economy have become adjusted to the increased quantity of money. Thus Hume avoids the overestimation of the Mercantilists as well as the underestimation of the Classicists.

People seem to learn only from their latest experience. Under the effects of the disastrous inflation, German monetary policy

[29] *Ibid.,* p. 37.
[30] *A Select Collection of Scarce and Valuable Tracts and Other Publications on Paper Currency and Banking,* ed. by J. R. McCulloch, 1862.

turned extremely deflationary in the early 'thirties. The consequence was such an increase of unemployment and such an up-
rooting of the entire social structure that the Nazi revolution was
made possible.

The experience with deflation during the Great Depression in
the Anglo-American countries, though less serious, was serious
enough to imbue people with a terrible fear of a repetition of
deflation and a great respect for reflationary measures. In the
framework of this situation, Keynes' book and its influence on his
contemporaries can be understood. In this author's opinion, the
atmosphere which created this influence and which was so strongly
enforced by it represents a swing of the pendulum away from
the classic toward the pre-classic state of affairs—a swing that can
only lead to deceptions. It is to be hoped that theory and policy
will again revert to a reasonable synthesis of the divergent
concepts.

11. Wage Flexibility Upwards[*]

All business-cycle theories work on certain basic assumptions. One of the more important, if not the most important, of these assumptions concerns the movements of wages in relation to advancing and receding prices, for the resulting rise and decline in real wages have been, and are still being, cited by many writers as the cause of fluctuations in employment during inflationary and deflationary movements.

It is the intention of this study to prove that the prevailing assumptions must be modified if a realistic, rather than a purely speculative, theory of business-cycle movements is to be developed. In order to show the consequences of what we think are the correct assumptions, we shall proceed with the same analytical method that Lord Keynes used in his *General Theory*.[1] As a matter of fact, we shall regard as entirely correct the functional relationships as outlined by Keynes; what we object to is not his theoretical concept. In the course of time, however, certain basic assumptions about wage inflexibility, which were introduced by Keynes as valid "in the general case" and "as a rule,"[2] have been tacitly assumed to be present in every case, with the result that far-reaching theoretical and practical conclusions have been drawn unconditionally. Keynes's responsibility for this situation, which to the present author

[*] Appeared first in *Social Research,* June 1947.

[1] Keynes, *The General Theory of Employment, Interest, and Money,* New York, 1936, Chapters 2, 20, and 21.

[2] *Ibid.,* pp. 3 and 13.

seems very dangerous, lies in the fact that he failed to emphasize sufficiently that his theoretical conclusions are valid only under very specific conditions. Perhaps he felt this responsibility when he spoke in his posthumously published article of "modernist stuff, gone wrong and turned sour and silly." [3] Perhaps he regretted his wholesale rejection of the "characteristics" assumed by classical theory which, as he says at the beginning of his *General Theory,* "happen not to be those of the economic society in which we actually live, with the result that its teaching is misleading and disastrous if we attempt to apply it to the facts of experience." [4]

Some Historical Remarks

In classical theory, the idea that wages are sticky in comparison with prices plays no important role. Classicists were concerned chiefly with long-term analysis and were therefore not interested in changes of profit margins resulting from lags which they considered transitory. A remarkable exception is David Hume's famous description of the short-run effects of inflation and deflation in his essay on money,[5] in which, incidentally, almost all correct notions of modern theory are anticipated, while unwarranted generalizations are avoided.

In neoclassical literature, especially where business-cycle theories are developed, wages are generally assumed to be "moderately" sticky in both upward and downward directions. The increasing profits that entrepreneurs derive from a lag in wages behind rising prices offer an explanation for credit and employment expansion. And the declining profits or the losses that entrepreneurs suffer from a lag in wages behind falling prices serve to explain credit and employment contraction. A multitude of other minor features of the business cycle are also explained by what Schumpeter calls "the race between prices and wages." [6] On the other hand, it is

[3] Keynes, "The Balance of Payments of the United States," in *Economic Journal* (June 1946), p. 186.

[4] Keynes, *General Theory,* p. 3.

[5] David Hume, *Essays Moral, Political and Literary,* London, 1907, part II, Essay 3, "Of Money," p. 294.

[6] Joseph A. Schumpeter, *Business Cycles,* New York-London, 1929, p. 1019.

assumed that after a certain time the wage-lag disappears and wages become entirely adjusted to rising and falling prices. These final adjustments offer the explanation, at least in part, for the turn from prosperity to depression or from depression to recovery.

This was essentially the position that Keynes, too, took in his *Treatise on Money*.[7] In his *General Theory*, however, not only does the stickiness of wages play a much stronger role within the whole system but also the basic assumptions themselves are strengthened. The inflexibility of wages is seen as a quasi-permanent and general, rather than a transitory and self-liquidating, phenomenon. This leads, on the one hand, to the idea that lowering of money wages can no longer be relied upon for the attainment of full employment, and, on the other, to the conclusion that lowering of real wages by raising prices will, within a certain range, always be an adequate means of increasing employment. Indeed, this conclusion represents the core of Keynes' views on the connection between investment and employment. Because "the supply of labour is not a function of real wages,"[8] and because it is not the workers' "practice to withdraw their labour whenever there is a rise in the price of wage-goods,"[9] "it will be possible to increase employment by increasing expenditures in terms of money."[10] The "decreasing return from applying more labour to a given capital equipment has been offset by the acquiescence of labour in a diminishing real wage."[11] And all this will be the case "until a point comes at which there is no surplus of labour available at the then existing real wages; *i.e.* no more men (or hours of labour) available unless money-wages rise (from this point onwards) *faster* than prices"[12]—which is, by definition, the point of full employment in the Keynesian sense. It need not, as is so often believed, coincide with the point of full employment in the everyday sense, because, unfortunately, the supply price of labor, as fixed by unions, can move upward, even if there are millions of unemployed workers "available at the then existing real wage."

[7] Keynes, *A Treatise on Money*, London, 1930, vol. 1, pp. 283 ff.
[8] Keynes, *General Theory*, p. 8.   [11] *Ibid.*, p. 289.
[9] *Ibid.*, p. 9.   [12] *Ibid.*, p. 289.
[10] *Ibid.*, p. 284.

It is obvious that if the Keynesian assumptions are not correct the essential parts of his entire system are shaken. His "investment theory of employment," with which he replaces the classical "wage theory of employment," is tenable only for a system in which wages are not variable. Outside of such a system his contention that increasing "effective demand spends itself, partly in affecting output and partly in affecting price" [13] becomes of dubious value, just as do most of the conclusions drawn from Keynes, especially the advocacy of an easy-money policy and of government deficit spending.

Post-Keynesian literature seems to take the parallelism of investment and employment for granted. This suggests that the correctness of Keynes' basic assumptions is tacitly accepted.

It might be pointed out that less productive labor can be paid for not only out of the profit margins from lagging wages [14] but also out of the profit margins from rising productivity of labor or capital. This presupposes, however, that wage rates remain unaffected by such increasing profit margins, a matter to which we shall return.

The Classico-Keynesian Assumption

It may remain undecided whether Keynes' assumption of protracted inflexibility of hourly or piece wage rates in an upward direction was correct at the time of its introduction. Today it is

[13] *Ibid.*, p. 285.

[14] In my book, *Volkswirtschaftliche Theorie des Bankkredits*, 1st ed. (Tübingen, 1920), where I presented an "investment theory of employment" very similar to that of Keynes, I even then explicitly renounced the idea that less productive labor can be paid for out of falling real wages, stating that "the wage increase is not only nominal but real; for the price of goods will tend, because of the competition among entrepreneurs, always to equal their costs. As these will have increased only by the outlay for wages and not by the outlay for capital, the prices of goods will have risen only so far, that is, by less than wages. Thus there remains a real increase in the remuneration of labor, since the compensation of the other participants, though nominally the same, has been devaluated by the increase in the prices of goods" (p. 137).

In *General Theory*, Keynes later presented the same idea in the following form: "Since that part of his profit which the entrepreneur has to hand on to the rentier is fixed in terms of money, rising prices, even though unaccompanied by any change in output, will re-distribute incomes to the advantage of the entrepreneur and to the disadvantage of the rentier, which may have a reaction on the propensity to consume" (p. 290).

certainly incorrect. By this statement and all that follows we do not, of course, mean to imply that in reality complete flexibility has already been achieved. There are always special reasons why the adjustment of wages to prices is not yet instantaneous.

For example, there was the hesitation of labor during the winter of 1946-47 to claim full compensation for rising costs of living, a situation probably attributable to the sharp increase of real wages per hour during the war. Or, when an economy comes out of a very deep depression during which real wages have increased substantially, owing to the Keynesian wage rigidity in a downward direction there may indeed be an "acquiescence" of labor to declining wages, at first. An increase in weekly working hours may be considered compensation for reduction of real wages per hour. It was probably this situation that led Keynes to his assumption of wage rigidity in an upward direction.

It is also true that living costs need not always move up with prices; therefore wage demands may not be raised in accordance with the increase in prices, especially in commodity prices. If living costs really lag behind prices in general, this means that other production factors are no longer receiving their previous reward in real terms. The owners of houses may be receiving a lower real rent because of long leases. The retailer may be selling his goods at cost instead of replacement prices. Such "inflexibilities," however, are temporary and their end can be clearly foreseen. Thus we do not believe that the lag between prices and living costs is sufficiently substantial or protracted enough to invalidate our thesis that wages move up with prices.

And finally, wage agreements may frequently prevent labor from asking for an immediate adjustment to changes in the cost of living, however much such adjustment is desired. Since entrepreneurs know that the agreements will end sooner or later, for any long-term investment they will calculate their wage costs on the basis of the future higher, rather than the present lower, wages.

Our conclusion is that if any general statement on wage movements can be made nowadays, and especially for this country, it is to the effect that wages move up with prices. Labor, especially in all those cases in which it has fought for higher nominal wages in the belief that its real wages were too low, will not tolerate a lowering of real wages by inflation, but will immediately claim higher wages. Nevertheless, as stated before, we do not contend that wage flexibility will always prevail. We merely state that it will prevail "as a rule" and "in the general case," just as Keynes assumed that a protracted "Keynesian range" prevails "as a rule" and "in the general case." But even if this contention is rejected, it will surely be granted that it is interesting and necessary to describe an "ideal-typical" state of affairs in which these conditions are fulfilled. Economic theory always gains more by picturing the future on the basis of present trends than by examining the present, which is generally outdated as soon as it is fully understood.

Accordingly, we introduce a new set of assumptions: with regard to the downward direction the Keynesian assumption of quasi-permanent inflexibility remains unchanged, whereas for the upward direction it is replaced by the classical assumption of complete flexibility of wages and their capacity to move up to the same extent and at the same pace as prices. We consider this assumption, which we shall call the "classico-Keynesian assumption," much more realistic than the one currently accepted.

This "classico-Keynesian" assumption is not at all incompatible with Keynes' system. On the contrary, Keynes makes explicit provision for the case of wages moving up simultaneously with prices.[15] But he assumes that the upward movement of wages will never be "fully in proportion to the rise in the prices of wage-goods"[16] as long as there is substantial unemployment. Thus, what we are really doing by introducing the new assumption is to shorten to negligibility what one could call the "Keynesian range," and what I myself have called the "reaction-free period";[17] in other words, the "illusion effect," by which changes in the value of money are veiled, is *immediately* destroyed.

Keynes himself was well aware of what occurs outside the "reaction-free period." As a matter of fact, he noticed clearly the

[15] Keynes, *General Theory*, p. 296.
[16] *Ibid.*, p. 301.
[17] See Chapter 6, "Compensating Reactions to Compensatory Spending."

"apparent asymmetry between Inflation and Deflation" which must develop in a system in which labor is unwilling to tolerate lowered nominal wages when real wages rise, but insists on raising nominal wages when real wages decline: "Whilst a deflation of effective demand below the level required for full employment will diminish employment as well as prices, an inflation of it above this level will merely affect prices." [18] That is, there will be "true inflation." [19] So, though Keynes assumed this case to be only exceptional, he did envision it clearly.

Unfortunately, however, this contingency has been almost entirely neglected in contemporary literature. The possible occurrence of such a situation has not been mentioned, nor have its features been described.[20] This is the more astonishing since the assumption of wage flexibility is much more plausible than the assumption of rigidity. The latter presupposes a very peculiar difference in price anticipations on the part of entrepreneurs and of labor. The entrepreneurs are supposed to recognize that the increased investment leads to higher prices, on which they must rely in order to be able to pay the same money wages for less productive labor. Labor, on the other hand, is supposed either not to recognize the consequences of higher investment or, at least, not to take them into account in its economic decisions and strategy.[21]

WAGES, PRICES, AND EMPLOYMENT UNDER THE CLASSICO-KEYNESIAN ASSUMPTION

Under our new assumptions, "it would . . . be impossible to increase employment by increasing expenditures in terms of

---

[18] Keynes, *General Theory*, p. 291.

[19] *Ibid.*, p. 303.

[20] A notable exception is Hans Neisser's article, "Realism and Speculation in Employment Programs," in *International Postwar Problems*, vol. 2, no. 4, October 1945, pp. 517-32; see also Neisser's "The New Economics of Spending: A Theoretical Analysis," in *Econometrica*, vol. 12, nos. 3 and 4, July-October 1944, pp. 237-55. Otherwise volumes upon volumes have been written in the last decade on achieving full employment by increasing investment, without mentioning the possibility of compensating wage rises, or, for that matter, the importance of the absolute height of the wage level.

[21] See Howard S. Ellis, "Monetary Policy and Investment," in *American Economic Review*, vol. 30, no. 1, March 1940, Supplement, Part II, pp. 31-32.

money." [22] Increased investment will give rise to higher prices and wages rather than to increased employment. To follow Keynes, "the crude quantity theory of money . . . is fully satisfied; for output does not alter and prices rise in exact proportion to the quantity of MV." [23]

This means, incidentally, that cyclical movements will be characterized by the "apparent asymmetry" mentioned above. The cycle, while remaining a price-and-employment phenomenon during the downswing, will have become a pure price phenomenon in the upswing, the intercyclical trend of employment being downward.

Some additional remarks, however, seem warranted. For one thing, it may be doubted whether prices would always rise under the impact of higher demand. Under the assumption of perfect competition (in Joan Robinson's terminology) prices move upward in accordance with the increasing marginal costs, or, all other things being equal, in accordance with the decreasing marginal productivity of labor. If the marginal productivity of labor were not to decline and if the supply curve of labor were to run absolutely horizontally, prices would not need to rise. Higher demand would spend itself in higher output. But an entirely horizontal supply curve is excluded by the assumption of perfect competition and limited labor supply, as expressly acknowledged by Keynes.[24] It is true that marginal productivity could diminish very slowly and the labor supply be very elastic. In such a case, prices would not increase very substantially. But however small the price increase, the corresponding wage increase would always be sufficient to cancel the margin out of which entrepreneurs must pay the same wage for labor of decreased productivity.

It is possible that even under the system of perfect competition prices would not move up at all. This would be the case if the productivity of labor increased simultaneously with rising wages to such an extent that the newly employed units would not be less productive than the former marginal units. It can be safely assumed, however, that wages tend to move up with increasing marginal productivity of labor. This assumption is in conformity

[22] Keynes, *General Theory*, p. 284.   [24] *Ibid.*, p. 299.
[23] *Ibid.*, p. 289.

not only with everyday experience but also with the opinions of all contemporary literature, especially that on postwar full employment, which takes it for granted that an increase in the productivity of labor—and, for that matter, of capital too—must be used to raise wages.[25]

When, and in so far as, conditions of imperfect competition prevail, higher demand need not lead to higher prices. The monopolists or quasi monopolists may prefer to hold prices down if the demand is sufficiently elastic and if they can gain more by higher sales than by higher prices. If this happens in a relatively small sector, the general price level will hardly be affected. In large sectors of the economy, demand curves of high and of low elasticity must balance each other, for if all demand curves were of an elastic structure there would not be enough money to pay for the output. Therefore, even under the assumption that competition is overwhelmingly imperfect, prices must be expected to move upward with increased demand.

During a depression, output can fall in many industries in such a way that the optimum combination of variables and fixed costs at the lowest average cost no longer prevails. In a subsequent recovery, output can therefore be increased with no increase, or even a decline, in average costs—a very important case of imperfect competition. But for the price system of the economy, as a whole, this is irrelevant as long as *any* new plants are erected, because the marginal costs of the new plants are decisive for prices and wages. What happens during recovery is that losses in the under-utilized industries are converted into profits, or smaller profits into larger ones. We shall return to the question of these profits later.

Finally, it is sometimes argued that employment could be increased, not by lowering real wages but, on the contrary, by raising them, because an increase in real wages would lead to a change in the income distribution in favor of labor. This change in turn would imply a higher propensity to consume in the community; workers are supposed to spend more from 100 dollars of wages than employers do from 100 dollars of profits. Under the conditions

[25] See Alvin H. Hansen, "The Postwar Re-employment Problem," in *International Postwar Problems*, vol. 1, no. 1 (December 1943), pp. 31-40.

here assumed, however, the higher demand and higher prices that would follow from the higher propensity to consume would, in turn, lead to higher wages, because under our assumption wages move up with prices. So again there would be no margin left for the employment of less productive labor. Indeed, the margin would have become even smaller because of the original wage increase. For it would be highly unrealistic to assume—as is sometimes done—that a shift of income from the few (saving) entrepreneurs to the masses of (spending) workers could—except under very peculiar conditions—compensate the inflation of wages of the working masses.[26]

Labor's Claim on Increased Capital Profits

Without extra profits, out of which the less productive labor could be paid, employment could never increase. As mentioned above, however, these extra profits need not originate in the wage-lag. They may have their origin in the real or expected increase of the marginal productivity of capital, the same increase that induces to higher investment. It is on such extra profits that classic, non-monetary, long-term analysis relies when it concludes that inventions, which increase profits on capital, and savings, which lower the cost of capital, create employment. And it is on such profits from the use of capital that certain recent business-cycle theories—e.g., the "acceleration principle"—seem to rely. I myself have relied on them in my earlier writings.[27]

There is no doubt that increased marginal productivity of capital can furnish profit margins out of which less productive labor can be paid, especially if no part of the resulting profits goes to the lender of the investible funds, because the supply curve of these funds runs horizontally. (For all practical purposes, we can assume this is so in these days of "easy money policy.")[28]

All this presupposes, however, that profits from increased mar-

---

[26] On this question see Chapter 15, "The Investment Gap," pages 192-193.
[27] See note 14.
[28] The justification and the implications of the assumption of a practically stabilized interest rate are treated in Chapter 13, "Anachronism of the Liquidity Preference Concept," pp. 162-163.

ginal productivity of capital are not claimed by labor. Without discussing here to what extent labor is successful in satisfying these claims, we believe that, in view of prevailing trends, no analysis is realistic unless it examines what will happen if wages move upward as profits on capital increase. We proceed, therefore, by introducing the radical assumption that labor does succeed in obtaining the profits from increased marginal productivity of capital.

It is true that this assumption is somewhat vague, just as the claims of labor on these profits are vague. There seems to be agreement that entrepreneurs should pay wages according "to their profits" or "their ability to pay," but it is not at all clear whose "ability to pay" is meant. Is it the ability of the intramarginal entrepreneur who has succeeded in obtaining increased profits from his capital by his monopolistic or quasi-monopolistic position? Is it the ability of an entrepreneur who gains from full utilization of formerly under-utilized fixed equipment, as mentioned above? Such intramarginal profits could, of course, be claimed by intramarginal labor without any disadvantage to employment. Or is it simply the ability of any entrepreneur to derive profits from the more productive combination of capital and labor?

We exclude the first two possibilities from our discussion. Despite the fact that in recent labor disputes with large quasi-monopolistic corporations the "ability to pay" argument has played a major role, wages cannot be fixed according to the monopolist's ability to pay as long as the same wages are paid for the same quantity and quality of labor by other entrepreneurs. We concentrate our analysis on the question of what happens when labor claims the profits of increased productivity of capital.

The consequences are obviously more far-reaching than in the case cited above, in which labor claimed only the additional profits from falling real wages and from an increasing marginal productivity of labor, and left the profits that stimulate entrepreneurs to higher investments undisturbed. Here labor's claim cuts into these profits, producing a curtailing reactive effect on investment.

The effect of a rising marginal productivity of capital and of simultaneously rising wages cannot easily be described in the usual ways, because more than one independent variable is involved.

Higher productivity of capital affects investment, prices, and employment. Higher wages also affect investment, prices, and employment, but in the opposite direction and in different degrees. The matter becomes even more complicated because higher wages do not merely cancel out productivity of capital but also lead to a substitution of capital for labor.

The accompanying graph may give a rough idea of the results to which the interplay of the various forces can lead. It attempts to represent the various possible changes in capital productivity and in wages; it is not intended to reflect changes through time. We have entered in the graph on the horizontal axis (between A and B) rises in the marginal productivity of capital from 1 to 10 per cent under the condition that labor acquiesces in leaving these profits to the entrepreneur. Then (from B on) we have entered on the horizontal axis labor's claim to the profits from 0 up to 120 per cent. The vertical co-ordinate represents the quantitative changes that occur in the situations provided for on the horizontal.

Curve I is supposed to show the changes in investment (in the sense of monetary expenditures), curve II the changes in prices, and curve III the changes in employment. The area above the horizontal is considered the area of inflation of prices as well as of employment. The area below the horizontal is considered the area of deflation of prices and employment. Needless to say, our curves are entirely arbitrary and have only illustrative value.

We can visualize the following situations:

1. In the circumstance that labor agrees to leave the profits to the entrepreneur (A-B), investment (I) rises to a smaller or larger degree according to whether productivity of capital increases to a smaller or larger degree. Prices (II) and employment (III) also rise. But because capital becomes less expensive in comparison with its marginal productivity, while wages do not change comparatively, employment rises somewhat less than prices, and labor is to some extent replaced by capital. The higher demand spends itself partly on price and partly on employment, and the structure of the economy becomes somewhat more "capital intensive."

Generally speaking, the pattern that develops is that of an *inflationary employment increase*. It differs from the traditional

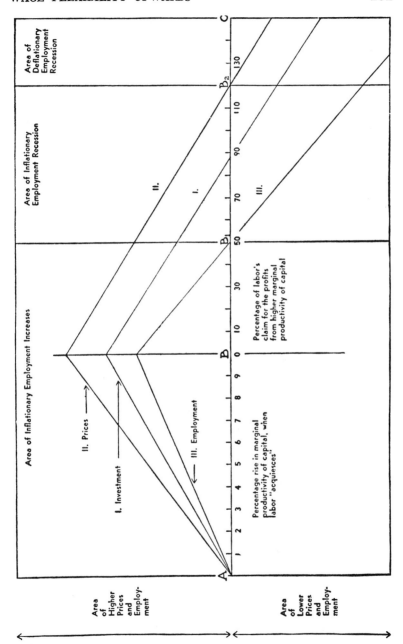

pattern of an inflationary boom only in that price inflation is now stronger, and employment inflation weaker, than in the past. This happens because real-wage lowering, which formerly diminished the compensation of labor in comparison with its marginal productivity, is absent.

2. Under the condition that labor claims smaller or greater parts of the profits from increased capital productivity (B-C), investment (I) declines, or rather, it rises less than formerly assumed, because the curtailment of profits works as a deterrent to investment; prices (II) and employment (III) also decline, or rather rise to a lesser degree. Employment is curtailed more than prices because labor becomes even more expensive than capital in relation to productivity. Again the demand spends itself more and more on prices and less and less on output, and again the structure of the economy becomes more "capitalistic." But until a certain point (B_1) is reached, employment does not fall below the level it had reached before the productivity of capital increased.

Up to point B_1 there is still some price and employment increase, but at that point there is only price inflation, and no employment increase. This is the point up to which labor can participate in the increased productivity of capital without outpricing itself and creating unemployment. The historical rise of the living standard of the masses, through increased productivity of capital, must, in general, have taken place according to this pattern.

3. After point B_1 is reached, the increasing claims of labor, while still leaving some possibility for an increase in investment, reduce employment to a lower level than the original. Prices continue to decline, but less than employment. The result is a combination of price inflation and employment recession, a situation that could be termed *low employment inflation*, or better, *inflationary employment recession.* This concept of an inflationary employment recession seems to be unknown to modern literature, and the possible occurrence of such a phenomenon is hardly mentioned. We believe, nevertheless, that the concept is of substantial, *practical*, and theoretical importance.

There is still to be considered the situation in which labor goes further with its claims, until investment shrinks to such an extent that not only employment and investment but prices, too, are below their original level. This is the point (B_2) where price inflation turns into price deflation. It is the traditional pattern of a *deflationary employment recession* that develops, with the difference, however, that the deflation affects employment much more than prices and with the further difference that it is the high cost of labor and not the high cost of capital—in comparison with productivity—that starts the decline. The cause-and-effect relationship is no longer (to paraphrase a well-known vulgar-Keynesian formula) "idle money, idle men" but "idle men, idle money."

Illustrative Examples

For illustration of the results of the various combinations of changes in capital profits and wages we refer to the following examples:

1. *Inflationary employment increases.* Though it may seem paradoxical, in the light of all the regulations that prevailed, the best recent example of an inflationary employment increase is furnished by the later part of the war boom. Investment, in the broadest sense, increased substantially in the expectation of high profits on war contracts; wages, meanwhile, were more or less stabilized by government decree. This means that the economy remained for the entire time within the "Keynesian range" or the "reaction-free period," with the result that there was extremely high employment. It is true that to a certain degree the war boom was due to an illusion on the part of labor as well as on the part of entrepreneurs. Labor failed to notice the lowering of its real wages because under the system of price ceilings goods eventually became scarce rather than expensive. On the other hand, labor accumulated, in the form of savings, that part of wages that it could not spend, as did the entrepreneurs with that part of their profits that remained after excess profit taxation. If one considers, however, that these savings have their counterpart in an enormously increased public debt—which, after all, is the debt of everyone in the community—one realizes that, on the whole, entrepreneurs

invested and/or labor worked for a compensation which was much less than they imagined. So the war boom was really created by the illusion or the hope that if anyone had to foot the bill, it would be the other fellow.[29] Nevertheless, so long as the "illusion effect" lasted, an inflationary prosperity developed. Money spent itself in higher output, and, where price ceilings were not established or could not be enforced, in higher prices.

2. *Inflationary employment recession.* A drastic example of this phenomenon was furnished in Europe during the hyperinflations after World War I. Since the budgets of many countries were hopelessly unbalanced, entrepreneurs expected huge inflation profits from nothing but building up inventories. The high profit expectations from this specific use of capital led to ever higher investment. As long as wages were fixed only after a certain time-lag, or not at all, in accordance with the declining purchasing power of money, labor remained extremely cheap. It was possible to employ even the most unproductive units, and consequently there was not only full employment, but even overemployment. As time passed, however, the masses learned to see through the money illusion and claimed increasing parts of the inflation profits. Finally, so-called "sliding wage scales" (*Gleitlöhne*) or "valorized wage rates" (*wertbeständige Löhne*) were introduced. Wages were paid at very short intervals, sometimes daily, according to a cost-of-living index. The result was an inflationary employment recession in many respects similar to that described above. Employment began to fall, and at certain times and places unemployment reached sizable proportions. Money inflation, however, went on despite this curtailment of inflation profits by the introduction of sliding wage scales; for the credit demand of the most important "entrepreneur"—the government—was insensitive to such profit reductions, or, for that matter, to the high interest it had to pay on its borrowings. Governmental obligations from past and current expenditures had to be met at any price. So "investments" of the government (curve I of our graph) remained high. Prices (curve II)

[29] See Chapter 6, "Compensating Reactions to Compensatory Spending."

went even higher, whereas employment (curve III) declined. It was the time when entrepreneurs no longer cared for production, but only for buying and reselling, that is, speculation. Money spent itself on ever higher prices and on ever lower output.

The stabilization of the currency through stabilization loans, high taxation, and the like, put an end to the government's deficit spending. Expenditures declined. The stabilization crisis—a deflationary employment recession—developed.

3. *Deflationary employment recession.* Besides the case just mentioned, such a phenomenon was clearly beginning to develop in the United States after World War II when prices remained fixed while wages were allowed to rise. When the ability of industry to absorb the high wages through increased productivity did not materialize to the extent anticipated, many enterprises, and particularly the small ones, were threatened with losses that would have made them close down. It was under the threat of a deflationary employment recession that the O.P.A. raised or abolished ceilings, whereupon prices advanced. This, incidentally, led to the popular belief that wage increases are inflationary, and not deflationary as we have contended. But what led to inflation in this instance was the fact that government agencies allowed prices to rise and that the consumer was able to pay the higher prices. The O.P.A., it is true, was forced to its actions by the preceding wage increase. *Within a system of given price and profit expectations,* however, wage increases must lead to deflationary employment recessions.

It is not at all improbable that the next major depression in this country will develop according to the pattern of the deflationary employment recession described above. This would mean that it would not be an interruption of the demand by liquidity preferences in the widest sense, accompanied by the traditional monetary and credit stringency, but the reluctance of marginal entrepreneurs to pay wages in excess of the marginal productivity of labor that would start the contraction process and give the developing depression its peculiar character.

CONSEQUENCES OF THE NEW ASSUMPTIONS

The new assumptions lead to a number of theoretical and practical consequences that differ in essential respects from traditional views.

For one thing, there is the matter of "analysis in terms of effective demand." "The division of the determinants of the economic system into the two groups of given factors and independent variables is, of course, quite arbitrary from any absolute standpoint. The division must be made entirely on the basis of experience, so as to correspond on the one hand to the factors in which the changes seem to be so slow or so little relevant as to have only a small and comparatively negligible short-term influence. . . ." [30] Clearly, the "effective demand analysis" is an outgrowth of the assumption that changes in the supply price of labor are "so slow or so little relevant as to have only a small and comparatively negligible short-term influence." But if changes in the supply price of labor are no longer slow and of little relevance in comparison with the changes in demand, the approach no longer makes sense. It is no longer appropriate to base an employment theory on a system in which wages are fixed, in which the credit volume is an independent variable, and employment the dependent variable.

It is not necessary to decide whether an analysis in terms of effective demand alone was justified ten years ago.[31] Today, an analysis in terms of effective *demand* that is not supplemented by analysis in terms of effective *supply*, especially of labor, is not justified in any circumstances.[32] It seems both illogical and certain to lead to false conclusions if one indulges (as is so often done) in elaborate estimates of employment at *various levels of effective demand,* from private or public spending, without making the corresponding estimates of the employment that is created by the same effective demand at *various wage levels.*

A second matter for consideration is that the devices to combat

[30] Keynes, *General Theory,* p. 247.

[31] See Chapter 6, p. 62.

[32] See the corresponding remark by D. McC. Wright in "The Future of Keynesian Economics," in *American Economic Review,* vol. 35, no. 2 (June 1945), p. 299.

unemployment known as "government deficit spending," "compensatory spending," or "functional finance" are clearly an outgrowth of the idea that in the general case more investment leads to more employment. If our analysis is correct, this will be true only under special conditions. Thus, before applying government spending one has to study carefully to what extent the wage situation has caused the unemployment, and whether and to what extent wages can be held inflexible in an upward direction. Unless this is done, government spending, apart from all fiscal difficulties, will only lead to price inflation. The indiscriminate creation of purchasing power every time private demand slows down for whatever reason or whenever full employment is not achieved, as advocated by the proponents of "functional finance," is indeed "like almost every important discovery . . . extremely simple." [33] It is, in fact, not only extremely simple but also an extreme oversimplification of very complicated problems. And if another proponent of "functional finance" wishes to "persuade people that inflation is impossible as long as there is serious unemployment, for under those circumstances a rise in money demands leads to a rise in output and employment, not to a rise in prices," [34] we should like to take the opposite position: people—economists and laymen alike—should be persuaded that even with serious unemployment the rise in money demand may, under today's conditions, lead to a rise in prices rather than to a rise in output or employment.[35] The widely held belief in an a priori parallelism of investment and employment is not justified.

[33] Abba P. Lerner, "Functional Finance and the Federal Debt," in *Social Research*, vol. 10, February, 1943, p. 39.

[34] Kenneth E. Boulding, *The Economics of Peace*, New York, 1945, p. 215.

[35] W. H. Beveridge, in his *Full Employment in a Free Society*, London, 1944, demands strict control of the labor supply. This is probably nothing but the tacit acknowledgment of the changes in the labor supply we have described. Yet the restoration of a free labor market remains as an alternative—and a desirable one, at least as long as we wish to live in a truly free economy, rather than in Beveridge's pseudo-free economy.

12. The Purchasing Power Theory—Sense and Nonsense *

When the average businessman thinks about wage problems and a wage policy, as he often must do nowadays, he cannot help being unhappy. On the one hand labor unions and government officials tell him that high wages are essential to maintain demand—and thereby employment—in the American economy; that to avoid or combat depression, wages should go up and/or prices down. On the other hand the businessman—while he is fully aware of the importance of the demand side—knows from experience what rising wages mean for his business. Higher wages do not trouble him much as long as he can be pretty sure that he can raise prices to cover his higher costs. But the average firm—especially the smaller firm—usually compares its wage outlays with existing prices, which it hopes will not recede. It knows that rising wages, unless offset by a rather slow process of improved productivity, can force it out of business.

In this confusing situation, what shall the businessman believe? Shall he follow the so-called purchasing power theory, in which wages are alleged to be the dominant means of maintaining demand? Or shall he rely on his own experience, which has taught him that production can be undertaken only if and when costs do not outrun prices?

* English version of an article published in the *Neue Zürcher Zeitung*, August 2, 1947.

AN OLD PROBLEM

Perhaps our businessman can find some consolation in realizing that what faces him has been the dilemma of economic science for hundreds of years. One theory, best known as Jean-Baptiste Say's "Law of the Markets," holds that no one should bother about demand, since each product creates its own demand; workers, entrepreneurs, and capitalists receive in the form of wages, profits, and interest so much money that they can always buy the entire output. Hence wages are of concern only as cost factors, not as demand factors.

An even older theory, usually called the purchasing power theory, denies this self-creation of demand. One can produce only if demand for consumption or production purposes is sufficient. It all depends, therefore, on the maintenance of demand. Neglecting more or less the importance of wages as cost factors, the purchasing power theory stresses their importance as a means of sustaining demand. It is consequently inclined to favor higher wages as a means of combating unemployment.

One can say without exaggeration that the history of economics has been the history of the over- and underestimation of the importance of the demand side in comparison with the cost side of the economy. The Mercantilists of the sixteenth and seventeenth centuries were adherents of the purchasing power theory and, incidentally, of monetary manipulation as a means of creating employment. The English Classicists of the eighteenth and nineteenth centuries were strongly opposed to the purchasing power theory and policy. In our century the importance of the demand side was clearly underrated when Britain tried to return to the gold standard after World War I, and when during the Great Depression she stuck much too long to the old parity—in both cases with disastrous effects on her economy. Later, under the influence of certain experiences and of the work of J. M. Keynes and his followers, the pendulum swung to the other extreme.

The demand side is now stressed again to such a degree, especially by the younger generation of economists, that one can almost speak of a purchasing power "myth"; and history seems to be repeating itself in that the adherents of the "myth" seem convinced that they have found an entirely new and revolutionary theory and a panacea for solving most economic disturbances. Apparently they fail to realize that what seems to them modern and progressive is, viewed historically, really antiquated and regressive. For not only has the purchasing power theory—including the oversaving and underinvestment theories—been advanced over and over again (though perhaps not in so complicated a form as by Keynes); but as early as 1742 it was recognized by David Hume and most recently by the so-called neoclassical school in continental Europe that the truth lies not in a one-sided purchasing power theory but in a synthesis of this theory and the classical approach.

THE CASE OF LACKING DEMAND

Let us return to the dilemma of the average businessman. If he has any analytical talents he will soon recognize—and better than many theoreticians today—that difficulties in his business are caused either by lack of demand or by something else.

First we examine the predicaments caused by lack of demand. Our businessman is only too well acquainted with them. He had an especially terrible experience after the crash of 1929. Before the crash, he had been accustomed to being able to sell his products in increasing quantities and/or at increasing prices. During more than eight years of prosperity he proceeded on an ever-expanding scale to enlarge existing and construct new plants and to pile up inventories; each new investment seemed entirely without risk and to assure profit. And he was equally lavish in granting ever higher prices to other entrepreneurs from whom he bought raw materials and half-finished products, and ever higher wages to his employees for their work. But one day he awoke to find that the whole situation had utterly changed overnight; the demand that had held up so many years suddenly collapsed, and with it prosperity and the psychology of prosperity.

What has happened is a repetition on an economywise scale of what happens on the stock market at the end of a boom. When the last bulls have bought, nobody is left on whom the bulls can unload their overbought inventories and their overcostly products.

Depression begins, with all its consequences. Nobody wants to buy any more; just as during prosperity everybody awaited an increase in prices and expanding demand, everybody now fears further dwindling of demand and sinking prices. As the French say, "La hausse amène la hausse"—only now "La baisse amène la baisse." A cumulative psychological process known as secondary deflation starts. Everybody suffers losses, especially those who have invested in new plants calculated for an output at boom rather than at depression levels.

Depressions are part of the so-called business cycles, known since the industrialization of Europe began. Despite all efforts to stabilize the economy they will continue to recur from time to time as long as the economy remains free in the sense that the governing forces are the people's decisions and the optimism or the pessimism with which they judge the prospects of the future.

Obviously, a depression does not end until fear of vanishing demand is dispelled and hope of recovering demand returns. Our businessman as a member of the economic community postpones buying and investing until that time.

The Case of High Costs

A quite different situation is no less familiar to our businessman. At any phase of the business cycle and especially when prices have remained on a relatively low level for a certain period without declining, it is not the price-and-demand factor that may hinder our businessman from engaging workers and buying raw material or machines. He may refrain because he considers his costs out of proportion to the prices he can expect. A good example of such a case is the building situation right now. Demand for new housing is assured at a level of rents well above those fixed by the O.P.A. Nevertheless, dwellings are not being built because, compared with such a level of rents and the corresponding prices of houses, costs are too high. This means essentially that wage rates are too high; for the material used for building consists partly of labor and only partly of raw material. Of course, the stoppage in building and the resulting unemployment and the underconstruction of houses is not a market phenomenon in the strict sense of the word. If

wage rates were adjusted downwards, underemployment and underconstruction would disappear and, incidentally, aggregate wages
would increase. It is just because this is not happening, owing to
rigidities and monopolistic manipulation of the labor market, that
unemployment and underconstruction persist.

Wages as *demand factors* obviously have nothing to do with these
disturbances. Wages are causative exclusively as *cost factors*. The
fact that they determine demand also is irrelevant. The economy
contracts merely because costs are too high. In this case, therefore, the classical approach, which considers wages as cost factors, is
correct. The main consequence is that wages can never, without
creating unemployment, be pushed above a level corresponding to
the productivity of workers who still wish employment.

Unemployment caused by too high wage costs should be called
"stabilized" or "voluntary" unemployment. No tampering with demand, no inflationary measure can alter such unemployment for
any length of time.

THE UNDERINVESTMENT DISTURBANCE OF DEMAND

As we have seen, two sorts of economic disturbance must be distinguished. For cyclical declines, a purchasing power theoretical
approach seems warranted; but in the case of voluntary or stabilized unemployment and underactivity the purchasing power
theoretical approach is obviously nonsense and the classical approach valid.

This combination of the classical and the purchasing power ap-
proaches represents roughly the synthesis theory achieved in continental Europe during the 'twenties. Distinguishing sharply between cyclical and stabilized unemployment, it refused to recognize
the demand side as relevant to the maintenance of full employment, except when a cyclical decline in prices, caused by fear of a
further decline in prices, was concerned.

However, during the 'thirties the situation changed. Every time
in history that a deflationary process has for any reason lasted very
long, the theory has been put forward that the depression is not
merely a reaction to a boom, but is the expression of an entirely
novel phenomenon—the lack of new investment opportunities. It

was contended that owing to the maturity and stagnation of the economy, savings could no longer be absorbed by new investments, and that the resulting "investment gap" created lack of demand of a structural and secular character. My father, who was a banker, told me at the end of the nineteenth century that he feared he would have to give up his business because his main source of income—interest—would soon disappear since nobody seemed to need to borrow money any longer. Yet seldom have investment opportunities been so high as they were during the next few decades!

Similar pessimistic forecasts were made promptly during and after the great depression of the 'thirties. The oversaving underinvestment theories of Keynes and his followers appeared, though such theories had been voiced and subsequently refuted over and over again. Once more—and this time really and irrevocably—the end of capitalistic expansion was assumed to have come. Once more the economy was supposed to be so saturated with capital that not even at the lowest interest rates could opportunities for investment be found—with the resulting "investment gap" and "insufficiency of demand." Once more a theory born of a special situation appeared to its adherents to have eternal validity. And once more, while the whole community of economists indulges in elaborating further niceties of the theory, the factual situation has, unnoticed by them, already changed and the "new" theory become obsolete. For not deflation but inflation, not lack of demand but high and rigid costs within a basically inflationary situation—these seem to have become the features of our time.

In this atomic age, when investments have reached such proportions that the means of private investors seem insufficient, there is no need to trouble much about the oversaving underinvestment theory. Indeed, the very mention of it seems a joke. One remark, however, may be warranted. The "stagnation theory" assumes that entrepreneurs decline to use their own or borrowed capital because investment would yield a profit incommensurate with the interest lost or paid. However, observation shows that only too many entrepreneurs have ample opportunity to use capital profitably if two conditions are fulfilled:

  a. Costs—not of capital, but of labor—are not too high.

  b. Prices of finished products do not fall during the production period.

It would be difficult to find an entrepreneur who does not engage in productive activities if these conditions are fulfilled. Of course wages may seem too high only in a broader sense: the use of labor may be too risky or costly for reasons other than the absolute height of the wage rate. When the entrepreneur fears that the government (by taxes) or labor unions (by organized action) are going to take away his profits, leaving him only the chance of losses, he will in the same way desist from productive activity. But this has nothing to do with "lacking investment opportunities" caused by a "saturation of the economy with capital."

SOME CONCLUSIONS FOR THE PRESENT SITUATION

Some people think that the American economy is headed for a recession of more or less serious proportions. To ward it off, lower prices and higher wages are advocated. If our analysis is correct, such a policy will hardly achieve its purpose.

First, it is unrealistic to pretend that all prices in the United States are fixed arbitrarily by monopolists. There are still free markets, especially for raw materials and foodstuffs, where prices are particularly high—not in spite of insufficient but because of very great demand. To force prices down on these free markets is neither possible nor necessary as long as demand—not least on the part of the government agencies—is great. Under the pressure of demand, prices will remain high. When demand slackens, prices will decline and there will be no problem of the unadjustment of prices to demand.

Prices that are fixed by monopolists or quasi-monopolists would also probably decline as demand receded, even if no outside influence were brought to bear. However, no objections can be raised to a policy that tries to hasten the adjustment.

But how about wages? According to classical theory, wages too have to be adjusted downward when prices decline. Perhaps for monopolies, where wages can still be paid out of profits, this process is avoidable. Many other enterprises, however, do not have enough of a margin, and these will die if squeezed between low prices and high wages.

If at this juncture the general wage level is pushed upward in accordance with the purchasing power theoretical approach described above, there is no doubt about what will happen. The wage earners who remain employed will of course have more to spend if their wages are raised. However, the aggregate purchasing power of the economy cannot be pushed up through the raising of wage rates by political action. Wages will act as cost factors, no matter what is done. The further rise of the already very high break-even points in many industries will bring about a contraction because more and more enterprises will be forced out of business, and unemployment will ensue. If we are really heading for deflation, not inflation—which was the government theory only a short time ago—demand must be supported by radical tax relief measures and ultimately by public works. Both would enhance the aggregate purchasing power of the economy without raising costs. But the raising of wage rates—as against aggregate wages by employing more people—will always be the worst method of increasing purchasing power; for there is no way of evading the fact that wages are the most important cost factor of enterprise. Should a policy of wage-raising really be pursued and the purchasing power theory get the upper hand once more, the recession we may be facing would have a good chance of developing into a serious and protracted depression.

13. Anachronism of the Liquidity Preference Concept *

It is the contention of this chapter that the concept of liquidity preference is not applicable under present conditions. In part, it has always been superfluous; moreover, the aspects to which it was once appropriate have lost practical importance through institutional changes that have taken place in the last decade.

The Present Concept of Liquidity Preference

As is well known, liquidity preference was conceived within the framework of the theory of interest. At some times it has been considered more important than at others.

a. In classical theory the liquidity preference concept, or something equivalent to it, is, generally speaking, not mentioned. The interest rate keeps the supply of money saved in balance with the demand for money to invest. The concept of hoarding or the possibility of hoarding plays no major role. The theory of interest was monistic, "pure." [1]

b. However, it had always been observed that the credit market supply was at times influenced by demand for credit that did not originate in the normal desire for capital, i.e., purchasing power for productive purposes; that a special "money or cash demand" existed.

---

* Appeared first in Kyklos, *International Review for Social Sciences*, 1947, 3.
[1] *Cf.* Gottfried Haberler, *Prosperity and Depression*, 1941, p. 195.

As a result of this observation, neoclassical theorists developed, in the so-called "loanable fund" theories of interest, "dualistic" theories of credit demand: money was demanded not only to be spent but also to be hoarded, and supplied not only because saved but also because dishoarded [2]—or incidentally, of course, because created by banks. These theories thus achieved a synthesis of what can be called "purely monetary" and of "pure" theories of credit demand and supply.[3]

c. This dualistic theory prevailed in continental European and Anglo-Saxon literature until Keynes replaced it by a monistic, purely "money demand" theory.

According to Keynes' liquidity preference theory, interest is paid for the "desire to hold wealth in the form of cash" and received as "the reward for parting with cash" against some instrument of saving.[4] It is "the reward for not hoarding," not "the reward for not spending."[5] In other words, the owner of a savings account receives interest because he does not *hoard,* not because he does not spend money; and he loses interest because he hoards money, not because he spends it. The demand for cash comes from the desire to transform savings accounts into cash. It is denied that money is demanded in order to be spent, not to be hoarded. In short, the switching from savings accounts into cash for hoarding, not the withdrawal of savings accounts for spending, is considered the only possibility. At least on the surface, this is a "monistic" theory of cash demand for hoarding purposes.

Keynes' liquidity preference theory has often been criticized with much acuteness. It has been demonstrated that a monistic

[2] *Ibid.,* p. 196.

[3] My own work on the subject goes back to 1918, when I published an article entitled *"Der Gegenstand des Geld- und Kapitalmarktes in der modernen Wirtschaft: ein Beitrag zur Theorie des Bankgeschäfts,"* in *Archiv für Sozialwissenschaft und Sozialpolitik,* 1925, vol. 51, p. 289; and *"Zur Frage des sogenannten Vertrauens in die Währung,"* in *Archiv für Sozialwissenschaft und Sozialpolitik,* 1925, vol. 52, p. 289. My "dualistic" theory was finally formulated in my *Volkswirtschaftliche Theorie des Bankkredits,* 3rd edition, 1930, p. 53 ff.

[4] J. M. Keynes, *The General Theory of Employment, Interest, and Money,* New York, 1936, p. 167.

[5] *Ibid.,* p. 174.

theory, neglecting the influence of saving and borrowing for consumption or production purposes on the interest rate, must necessarily be one-sided and unrealistic.[6]

My own main objection is that his theory is not consistent even as a "hoarding theory of interest," and does not explain what it purports to explain, namely, that interest is paid for keeping liquidity, and interest is received for parting with it.

1. Cash is defined not only as actual cash but may include "money-time deposits with banks and, occasionally, even such instruments as treasury bills, and it is as a rule co-extensive with bank deposits."[7] As one can earn interest on all such investments, one receives interest for holding liquidity, not for parting with it.[8] This interest may, it is true, be lower than interest paid on longer-term investments; but in times of money stringency short-term interest rates can be, and have been, higher than long-term; so that for holding liquidity, one not only receives interest, but even higher interest than illiquid investments would yield.

2. Keynes gives four motives for wanting cash: the Income motive, the Business motive, the Precautionary motive, and the Speculative motive.[9] All are clearly taken from the arsenal of the classical "pure" interest theory: anyone who holds cash for the purposes mentioned obviously holds it with the intention of spending it, either at regular intervals or speculatively sooner or later than is usual.

If individuals obtain cash or checking accounts for these purposes they have to pay interest, not for hoarding the money but for keeping it to be spent sooner or later. So in reality, interest is paid for spending, not for hoarding money.[10]

---

[6] Cf. Jacob Viner, "Mr. Keynes and the Causes of Unemployment," in Quarterly Journal of Economics, 1936-37, p. 152. D. H. Robertson, "Alternative Theories of the Rate of Interest," in Economic Journal, vol. 47, 1937, p. 431, and "Mr. Keynes and the Rate of Interest," in Essays in Monetary Theory, 1940, p. 1 ff. For a good summarization of the criticism of Keynes' liquidity preference theory see George Halm, Monetary Theory, 1942, pp. 72-73 and 220-23.

[7] Keynes, op. cit., p. 167, footnote 1.   [9] Keynes, op. cit., pp. 195-96.
[8] Cf. Halm, op. cit., p. 221.   [10] Cf. Halm, op. cit., p. 72.

3. The liquidity preference concept is so widened that it is supposed to be effective not only when somebody hoards or does not spend money because he wishes to retain cash, but also when he does not spend money for quite other reasons. It has thus become a negative rather than a positive concept. It suggests that hoarding, for instance because of low profits on an investment, is due to a special demand for liquidity, not to the simple fact that profits for the time being are expected to be lower than lost interest.

The general objection to Keynes' theory, however, is that it is monistic, not dualistic. "Such loose phrases as that interest is not the reward of non-spending but the reward for not hoarding seem to argue a curious inhibition against visualizing more than two margins at once." [11]

d. Since Keynes issued his *General Theory,* the neoclassical dualistic theory seems to have made a comeback—again, very generally speaking. It is recognized that money is wanted for spending as well as for hoarding. As a consequence of this dualistic approach, the interplay of the credit demand for productive purposes and for holding liquidity—which is considered to decline as interest rates rise—has a major role in contemporary writing on interest rates.

However, the concept of liquidity preference is much broader than the neoclassical concept of money demand. The demand is directed towards bank accounts and short-term investments as well as cash.

e. We shall try to prove that the concept of liquidity preference is superfluous and confusing when it goes beyond the neoclassical concept of money or cash demand. Money demand, too, has become an obsolete concept because of certain changes in currency systems. For all practical purposes, the classical monistic "pure" theory of interest is necessary and also adequate to explain interest rates in a modern economy.

THE CRITERION OF LIQUIDITY PREFERENCE

Within the Keynesian system the liquidity preference concept is introduced to explain why, under certain conditions, the supply of

---

[11] D. H. Robertson, *loc. cit., Economic Journal.*

credit available for ordinary demand is curtailed by an extraordinary demand. This special demand is supposed to absorb a part of the available cash; therefore some other demand is left unsatisfied. Liquidity preference is, as has been correctly stated,[12] a sort of "death trap" for savings in that it raises (by withholding the hoarded money from the credit markets) the interest rate above the level that assures (within a given demand schedule for credits) a given level of purchasing power. In other words, liquidity preference is supposed to explain what before Keynes was simply called "deflationary pressure from the credit supply side."

Deflationary pressure from the credit supply side is present—

1. If, *ceteris paribus,* effective demand, MV, declines, i.e., when there is deflation;

2. If the decline is due to the withholding of purchasing power from the credit markets by creditors who keep their funds in cash or relatively liquid rather than illiquid forms, thereby curtailing the supply of credit and raising interest rates above those that would otherwise prevail.

Let us now examine to what degree the liquidity preference concept, as generally used nowadays, fulfills these conditions and to what degree it belongs to quite different theoretical categories. The concept covers four kinds of liquidity preference, each of which coincides with a different situation in the money and capital markets: interest rates are low on short- and long-term, on first- and lower-grade investments; or they are low on short- and long-term investments but not on lower-grade investments; or they are low only on short-term money; or finally, they may be high on short-term money too.

LIQUIDITY PREFERENCE OF THE ENTREPRENEUR: LIQUIDITY PREFERENCE AS THE INVERSE OF INVESTMENT PREFERENCE

The liquidity preference of the entrepreneur is, directly at least, not at all due to a curtailment of the credit supply. If MV dwindles, it is because demand for credit is weak.

[12] Robertson, "Some Notes on Mr. Keynes' *General Theory of Employment,*" in *Quarterly Journal of Economics,* vol. 5, 1937, p. 173.

If an entrepreneur holds cash or checking accounts for *specula-tive or precautionary* reasons and does not spend them within a normal period, he undoubtedly exercises a deflationary influence on MV.   However, what causes the money to become idle is not a special liquidity preference of the entrepreneur.   It is the simple consequence of the fact that for the time being profits on produc-tive investments are deemed smaller than interest received for hold-ing bank accounts, the zero interest on cash, or incidentally, the in-terest that would have to be paid for borrowing money.   When the entrepreneur borrows from the bank, the marginal efficiency of capital is acknowledged to be solely responsible for the credit de-mand schedule at various interest rate levels.[13]   But there is not the slightest difference between borrowing from a bank and from oneself.   The liquidity preference is fully accounted for by the demand schedule for capital, which compares the utility of various amounts of capital with the utility of corresponding amounts of cash or bank accounts.   To speak of a special liquidity preference as a motive for refraining from productive investments is double count-ing, and as illogical as it is to speak of a special hunger preference of somebody who does not want to eat.   Liquidity preference is merely the inverse of the preference to invest.   The accumulation of cash or of bank accounts is just an expression of a weakening demand for credit—a downward shifting of the credit demand curve.   It is not *caused* by a special liquidity preference, nor does it *cause* deflation.   It is the consequence and reflection of what used to be called self-deflation.

It could be argued that the entrepreneur who accumulates cash or bank accounts curtails the supply of money that could serve as a source of credit for others and thus exercises indirectly a defla-tionary pressure.   We shall revert below to the question whether and under what conditions that might happen.

Liquidity preference of entrepreneurs is usually accompanied by low short- *and* long-term interest rates, high bond prices, and ample offering of bank credits.   This combination appears at the very end of a cyclical depression when inventories have been liquidated

[13] Keynes, *op. cit.*, p. 135.

under the impact of deflation. Banks have become liquid and are ready to grant new credit, whereas entrepreneurs are reluctant to apply for credit because they fear losses from further declining prices for their products. Credits are low and the economy remains in a state of underactivity.

To explain this situation, the concept of a "low marginal efficiency of capital," or its expectation, is fully adequate, and the liquidity preference concept is entirely unnecessary.

Liquidity Preference of Creditors: Liquidity Preference as an Expression of the Risk Factor

Just before the cyclical phase mentioned above is reached, short- and long-term interest rates are usually low, government and AAA bonds high, but venture capital, either directly or by means of the stock market and bank credits, is scarce; and what little is available is very costly. There is a margin between the "pure" interest rate, which is low, and the interest rate that comprises the risk premium, which is high. Though clearly arising because the flow of investible funds reaches only first risk investments and is prevented from reaching investments with higher risks, this situation too is often considered to be caused by liquidity preferences, this time of creditors or banks.

If banks are reluctant to grant new credits, it is because they fear their funds will be newly "frozen" and lost in case of enforced liquidation, not because they have "no money" or the money has disappeared in a "death trap." They have all the money they need either in their safes or as reserves in the central banks. What they desire to retain is not cash—in fact they try to get rid of it whenever they see a half-way safe or profitable investment opportunity— but their own bank liquidity in the private economic sense of the word. In this limited sense, I myself, twenty-six years before Keynes, considered interest as the reward for parting with liquidity.[14]

[14] Hahn, *Volkswirtschaftliche Theorie des Bankkredits*, 1st edition, p. 102: "If the amount of credits given by the banks is dependent on their private liquidity, the interest rate, i.e., the price that has to be paid for the credit, is

Incidentally it should be noted that the stringency of bank credit at this juncture is caused not only by a curtailing of supply but also by an increase of demand for credit. A new demand for credit, called in German *"Durchhaltekredite,"* appears. In a cyclical crisis, goods become unsalable at the prevailing price level. Producers are at first reluctant to incur losses by liquidating their accumulating inventories at lower prices. Instead they allow their inventories to pile up. Lacking money to pay current production expenditures, they have to apply to the banks for additional credit. Although this credit demand gets its impulse from the fact that buyers withhold their purchasing power from the markets for fear of falling prices, the ensuing credit stringency is caused not only by a dwindling supply of bank credit but also by the increased credit demand for the purpose of postponing the liquidation of abnormally high inventories. There is a genuine new credit demand.

The behavior of creditors that creates the situation characterized by low interest rates for first-class investments and high interest rates for lower-grade investments, as just described, is really not due to a liquidity preference at all. The situation is caused by the blocking of the flow between the pure money and capital markets and the investment markets, not by a deflationary pressure from the money side. Therefore the liquidity preference concept has no *raison d'être* as a special category; what it tries to explain is entirely covered by the concept of the *risk of the lender*.[15] It can also be interpreted as the lowering of the demand schedules of professional lenders who consider that only the interest rates at which they borrow themselves, not the risk premium, are covered by the high interest rates on the investment markets.

This margin between the pure and what has been called the gross interest rate, caused principally by the nonfunctioning of the

merely the reward for the loss of liquidity caused by the granting of the credit." Keynes uses almost exactly the same words (*General Theory*, p. 167): "The mere definition of the rate of interest tells us in so many words that the rate of interest is the reward for parting with liquidity for a specified period." Keynes stressed later the importance of the "liquidity of banks" (*Economic Journal*, vol. 47, 1937, p. 660).

[15] Mentioned by Keynes, *General Theory*, p. 144.

banking system, undoubtedly tends to narrow. Such a nonfunctioning is not likely to be tolerated in the future. Organizations—many
of which are already in existence—will grant the credit banks will
be reluctant to give, or the governments will guarantee such credit
so that the banks will no longer be concerned about their liquidity.[16]
It is a matter of opinion how far this development can be considered
to have gone already.

Liquidity Preference of the Arbitrageur Who Arbitrages Between Money and Capital Markets

Having considered the case where the *pure* interest rate is low on
money as well as on capital markets, we now examine the case
where short-term interests are low, but long-term interests, even
yields on government bonds, are high.

Arising in a cyclical phase somewhat before the one previously
described, this is the situation that plays such an important role in
Keynes' liquidity preference theory.[17] He considers it a case of
the liquidity preference of owners of bank accounts or of banks that
are bullish on interest rates because they fear an aggravation of
the crisis.[18]

Again there seems to be no special reason to retain a special concept of liquidity preference of the owner of bank accounts or cash.
What really causes the margin between long- and short-term money
is that the arbitrageurs between money and capital markets, who
usually borrow from the banks on short-term and buy long-term
bonds (the banks themselves can also be arbitrageurs in this sense),
hesitate when they consider that they would lose more on the price
of the bonds than they would gain from the interest rate margin.
The banks in particular hesitate to use their money-creating power
to buy long-term bonds. Therefore, what is called liquidity pref-

---

[16] This is why I cannot place the same emphasis on the risk factor as
H. C. Wallich does in his interesting article, "Changing Significance of the
Interest Rate," *American Economic Review,* 1946, p. 76, where, as far as pure
interest rates are concerned, conclusions similar to mine are drawn.

[17] Keynes, *op. cit.,* pp. 168 ff. and pp. 202 ff.

[18] That rising interest rates during a boom have nothing to do with liquidity
preference in any sense but are due to higher profit expectations has been
correctly observed by Jacob Viner, *loc. cit.*

erence is again merely the inverse expression of a low investment preference of the professional investor in long-term securities. Incidentally, this margin, too, clearly tends to disappear so that the importance of the phenomenon in practice, and therefore also in theory, must be considered as decreasing. The reasons are two-fold:

First, the prevailing easy-money policy has greatly reduced the risk that short-term interest rates will be allowed to rise. Secondly, the power the Federal Reserve System now has to buy long-term government bonds—which it will use, if for no other reasons than fiscal—puts the long-term interest rate, formerly solely dependent on the arbitrage between money and capital markets, almost as directly under its control as the short-term interest rate.

LIQUIDITY PREFERENCE THAT CREATES HIGH SHORT-TERM INTEREST RATES: LIQUIDITY PREFERENCE IDENTICAL WITH CASH PREFERENCE

Undoubtedly at times the money markets were very tight and short-term rates very high. Then there was real deflationary pressure from the money side. We contend, however, that these situations cannot be explained by liquidity preference in the usual way if bank accounts and short-term investments as well as cash are considered objects of the preference. We must distinguish between *liquidity preference for cash, in the narrowest sense, on the one hand, and for bank accounts, short-term investments, etc., on the other.*

The liquidity preference that could influence the supply for money and exercise a deflationary pressure from the money side on the basic short-term money rates *can only be a preference for cash, never for other investments.* To prove this, we have only to examine the demand and supply for purchasing power in an economy without currency. The procedure is the one I followed in my first article on money market problems, quoted above.[19]

[19] Mr. Hawtrey followed the same procedure in Chapter I, "Credit Without Money," in his *Currency and Credit*, 1919. Incidentally, the procedure leads inevitably to the statement that investments and savings are necessarily equal. In a "world with only credit," as soon as a credit has been granted and the

A. *Liquidity Preference in a Money-free Economy.* In an economy in which there can be no demand for or supply of cash, the demand for loans is obviously identical with the demand for and supply of sight deposits (checking accounts) in banks. As the ability of banks to create such accounts autonomously by granting credit furnishes the marginal supply of such credit, we can say that the supply of credit is dependent upon the ability of the banks to create credit through creating debtor and creditor accounts.

In such a situation money cannot be kept from the credit market because no money exists; there is no "death trap" for money. And as far as sight deposits are concerned, they are never withdrawn. The fact that they are "held" means that they have been loaned—through the bank as intermediary—to a debtor of the bank. The persons who hold them for liquidity reasons thereby satisfy their liquidity preference.[20] No hoarding can raise the interest on short-term money markets. The money might not spill over to capital markets, it is true, but liquidity preference can never create high interest rates on the *money* markets as long as bank accounts or money market instruments, not cash, are hoarded.

Again it could be argued that deflation would ensue if banks were unable or unwilling to grant new credit which would compensate a decreasing V through an increasing M; also that legal reserve requirements on the one hand and liquidity fears on the other could set a limit to such granting of new credit.

However, as far as liquidity fears (as described on p. 152) are concerned, they could never prevent the banks from buying first-class securities in any amount they wished, and thus from lowering the supply price of credit to any desired level. Moreover, refer-

credited amount spent for productive purposes, new deposit accounts are created. I formulated the theorem of the equality of investment and saving as early as 1920 with the statement that savings are either always invested or nonexistent (*Volkswirtschaftliche Theorie des Bankkredits*, 1st ed., p. 153). Keynes expressed the same idea in his *General Theory:* "No one can save without acquiring an asset, whether it be cash or a debt or capital goods" (p. 81), and "in the new situation someone does choose to hold the additional money" (p. 83).

[20] As clearly recognized by Viner, *loc. cit.*, p. 155.

ence to legal reserve requirements is clearly out of place in a "money-free" economy. If a certain percentage of bank accounts have to be covered by balances with central banks, holding the former amounts to holding, indirectly, the latter or the cash that can be freely obtained against the accounts.[21]   Therefore, if bank accounts for which a coverage is required are hoarded instead of spent, this is really the case of hoarding real cash discussed below under B.

For continental Europe, where reserve requirements were unknown and private banks were not dependent upon the central banks for credit expansion, as long as the public did not convert its deposits into cash, reference to reserve requirements would, of course, be entirely out of place.   Even in countries such as the United States, where coverage requirements exist, they could be of practical importance only at the beginning of a depression when, as described above, credit demand increases.   In the later stages of a depression, after bank balances have contracted, the excess of reserves is so large that every credit demanded can be granted.

B. *Cash Preference in the Past.*   What has led and theoretically in the future could lead to a deflationary pressure from the credit supply side is merely a demand for cash—a cash preference, we may call it.   It is the pre-Keynesian concept of money demand to which we thus return and which, in the opinion of this author, should never have been given up.

What are the reasons for such a money demand?   Obviously it could never appear in a "money-free" economy, where the demands for purchasing power in the form of bank accounts and for loanable funds are always identical.   Only when two kinds of purchasing power—bank deposits and cash—co-exist and are to a certain extent interchangeable can there be a demand for money outside of and not satisfied by bank deposits.

The customary assumption seems to be that to hold cash, instead of either holding a bank account or spending the cash, gives a cer-

---

[21] Accounts with the Reichsbank were therefore called *"Giralgeld"* by German writers and considered as money rather than as bank accounts.

tain pleasure or convenience that declines with the amounts involved. All sorts of supply and demand curves attempt to show the interaction of the demands for money to hoard and for money to spend at various levels of interest rates. However, this type of analysis, while logically perfect, cannot describe realistically how the demand for money affects the supply of credit. It fails also to clarify how far the liquidity preference concept, even in the narrowest sense of "money demand," *is still of actual importance at present and will be so in the future.* To do this, we must recognize that there are several varieties of money demand and that they are governed on the supply as well as on the demand side by quite different laws. The following varieties must be distinguished: [22]

a. *Extraordinary Money Demand.*[23] The most outstanding examples of extraordinary money demand occurred during the famous bank crises of 1847, 1857, and 1866 in England. The public, fearing for the safety of deposits, sought to turn them into legal tender. Because there was not enough money to transform the billions of bank deposits into real money, a terrific deflationary process ensued. Each crisis led to the suspension of the Peel Act. As soon as the Bank of England was permitted to issue as many bills as it wanted, the demand for cash subsided. Similar crises have occurred in the United States, the most recent in 1933.

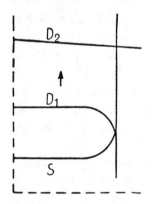

During such bank crises the money demand curve runs very high, almost horizontally, i.e., it is virtually independent of the interest rate. The public is prepared to pay very high interest rates for practically unlimited amounts. The supply curve, on the other hand, after a certain point runs nearly vertically. As more money is not available at higher rates, there is a real and terrific deflationary pressure from the money side.

[22] The distinctions are those made in my *Volkswirtschaftliche Theorie des Bankkredits,* 3d ed., p. 54 ff.
[23] *Ibid.,* p. 66.

b. A special case of the "extraordinary money demand" is the extraordinary demand for gold or foreign exchange,[24] which arises when not only "bank money" but also legal tender is suspect; so that a flight from the domestic currency ensues. The demand curve runs from the right to the left at very high levels, but not horizontally. The higher the interest rates, the more they are considered to offset the losses from currency depreciation. The supply curve, too, moves up to higher levels.

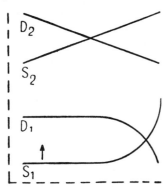

Under modern conditions, an extraordinary gold or foreign exchange demand usually leads to either the devaluation of the currency or a system of currency restrictions—witness the money disturbances of the 'thirties. Confidence in money at the former parity is not restored because readjustments of the basic disequilibria are not to be expected in a world of rigid costs.

c. *Ordinary Money Demand.*[25] We distinguish five varieties:

1. The demand arising because people are paying cash rather than by check.

2. The demand arising from a concentration of needs for cash at certain times.

In addition to these two, which, for obvious reasons, I have called technical,[26] there are three cases of nontechnical, "economic," money demand:

3. The demand arising when bank accounts grow with prices and/or output. Obviously, the percentage that has to be paid in cash must keep pace with the growth of bank accounts.

4. The demand arising from the higher turnover of bank accounts. More money is demanded because the cash usually brought to the banks in between payments has to remain longer outside the banks, thereby curtailing the money supply.

[24] *Ibid.,* p. 70.   [26] *Ibid.,* p. 78 ff.
[25] *Ibid.,* p. 74.

5. The demand arising when banks grant more credit to compensate for a decreasing V—as described above. It is partly satisfied by the influx of money to the banks when the velocity of turnover of bank accounts slows down and people keep their cash reserves in banks. However, to the extent that people keep their reserves at home, thus really hoarding, the banks need new cash to grant new credit, of which a certain percentage must be paid out in real cash. If money demands 3 and 4 can be called *inflationary,* the money demand described here can be called *antideflationary.* This demand for additional money arises because people "hoard" rather than "save." It is the only case where the "death trap" really works and the hoarding theory of interest is justified.

The main reason for differentiating these five varieties of money demand is that the satisfaction of each has quite different results. Satisfying money demands 1 and 2 is economically neutral, leading to neither credit expansion nor money inflation. Satisfying money demands 3 and 4 leads to inflation by enabling either credits to expand or the velocity of purchasing power to accelerate. By meeting or not meeting this inflationary money demand, monetary authorities can endeavor to stabilize the price level. Satisfying money demand 5 leads to an increase of credit, but not to inflation, because the increase of M offsets a previous decrease of V. Satisfying this kind of antideflationary money demand also is economically neutral.

It has become customary to consider all sorts of money demand as inversely dependent upon interest rates. The higher the interest rates, it is assumed, the less the propensity to pay cash and to hoard instead of to save, because the "quasi profit" of cash is seen to decline gradually.[27] However, the effect of the interest rate has been in the past and certainly is for the present and future very much overrated. To be realistic, one must consider the demand curve for cash as running at a high level almost horizontally from the left to the right at first, then very soon almost vertically down-

[27] I contrasted the "Quasi-Zinsgenuss" of the cash-holder to the receipt of interest by the holder of bank accounts in my article cited above (*Archiv für Sozialwissenschaft,* 1925, Vol. 52, p. 304).

wards. In the past when money was offered only at relatively high rates, the horizontal branch may perhaps have been cut by the supply curve, but to-day when money is offered at very low rates, only the vertical part, which reflects very inelastic demand, is cut by the supply curve. Therefore, even if the

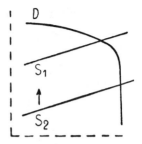

supply curve moves further down—in other words, if interest rates decline further—no more money is actually used.

Without doubt we are now experiencing the development of a new sort of technical money demand: black market operations and

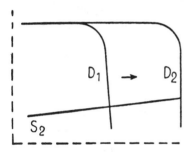

the possibility of tax evasion have tremendously increased the desire to pay large amounts in cash instead of by check. The demand curve for money therefore runs a long distance almost horizontally, i.e., for the additional demand not lower but nearly the same interest rates are offered. This demand, however, is satisfied at low interest rates because of the prevailing elasticity of the money supply.

EFFECTS OF MONEY DEMAND ON INTEREST RATES IN THE FUTURE

From the above I think it is evident that the future influence of liquidity preference, even in the denatured form of cash preference, on interest rates will be very limited, if it does not disappear entirely. Indeed, its influence may well be so small that theory could afford to ignore the existence of liquidity or cash preference and revert to the classical monistic "pure" interest theories.

a. *Extraordinary Money Demand.* There is no doubt that if a bank crisis occurs in the future the central banks of every country will immediately supply the banking system with money to meet the extraordinary money demand.

b. *Extraordinary Demand for Gold and Foreign Exchange.* Despite some illusions nourished during the Bretton Woods discussions, but fading more and more, interest rates will not be allowed to rise because of an external drain on foreign exchange, especially not if it is caused by capital flight. Devaluation and currency restrictions will always be preferred to the traditional play of the gold standard. Deflations from so-called external drains will not be tolerated, and the so-called external discount policy will be a thing of the past.

c. *Technical Money Demand.* Technical money demand, likewise, will no longer be able to bring about deflation. People may use or hoard as much money as they want. The supply will always be adequate. It is inconceivable that money scarcity due to changing habits of payment will be tolerated in the future.

d. *Economic Money Demand.* We must distinguish between inflationary money demands 3 and 4 and the antideflationary money demand 5.

1. The antideflationary money demand represents, as shown above, the real and only "death trap" situation. However, the "death trap" cannot cause money stringency in the future. Central banks will always offer enough cash to the banking system to enable "compensating" new credit to be created. As has been repeatedly stated,[28] any demand for money arising from increased liquidity preference can easily be met by issuing new money. It not only can be, but actually will be. And if this is true for a cyclical increase in liquidity preference, it must be even more true for a secular increase,[29] which Keynes seems to have had in mind in the first place. Governmental liquidity production will always outrun the liquidity preference of the public. There is no longer room for the assumption of the inverse dependence of the size of hoards on interest rates that Keynesians emphasize so much. Their assumption ignores the disappearance of the gold standard and its replacement by an entirely elastic currency throughout the world. The

[28] *Cf.* Howard S. Ellis, "Monetary Policy and Investment," *American Economic Review,* Vol. XXX, No. 1, March 1940, Supplement, p. 29; and Gottfried Haberler, "The Interest Rate and Capital Formation," *Capital Formation and its Elements,* National Industrial Conference Board, New York, 1939, pp. 126-27.

[29] As quite correctly stated by Ellis, *loc. cit.,* and Jakob Viner, *loc. cit.,* pp. 152 to 160.

quantity of money issued is no longer governed by considerations of legal limitations; rather these legal limitations are always modified as soon as other considerations seem to suggest increases in the quantity of money.

2. By controlling the inflationary money demand, central banks can, at least theoretically, control inflation and practice the so-called internal discount policy.

From all we have said it is clear that this part of "economic money demand" is identical with the "pure" credit demand. Cash, in a certain proportion to noncash forms of purchasing power, is demanded if and when funds for consumption or production purposes are wanted.

The problem of whether and at what interest rate central banks will be prepared to satisfy the economic money demand is the same as the problem of whether the easy-money policy which stabilizes interest rates for all practical purposes will be maintained. The relative merits of interest rate flexibility and stability are still being discussed. If any general statement can be ventured at this moment, it is that the overwhelming opinion seems inclined to sacrifice interest rate flexibility for interest rate stability. The internal discount policy, designed to combat inflation of domestic prices, will likewise hardly be applied in the future. Price fixing, rationing, and other measures will be preferred to the natural means, namely, a restrictive discount policy.[30] Among the many reasons the chief one, aside from fiscal considerations, is that easy money is thought to incite and perpetuate investments. In the writer's opinion, it does so only under very special conditions.

SOME CONSEQUENCES OF CHANGES IN MONEY DEMAND

Keynes' General Theory of Employment as presented in his *General Theory*, Chapter 18, rests essentially upon the choice of the independent and dependent variables of his system. Among his independent variables the most important is the rate of interest,[31] which is dependent upon the state of liquidity preference and on

[30] See Chapter 7.
[31] Keynes, *op. cit.*, p. 245.

the quantity of money; [32] his dependent variables are the volume of employment and national income. [33]   We have tried to show that interest rates are stabilized, liquidity preferences frustrated, and the quantity of money always created in accordance with prices and output which, in turn, are dependent upon quite different independent variables.   Consequently, Keynes' choice of independent variables seems so unrealistic that his Employment Theory is deprived of its usefulness as a tool of analysis.

Even more important than these theoretical effects of the changes in money demand are the implifications for the economy itself:

Deflationary pressure from the money side is not likely in the future.   Neither the *extraordinary* money nor the *extraordinary* foreign exchange demand of money crises will be allowed to repeat themselves.   Nor will deflations from an increase in "technical money" demand or from an "antideflationary" money demand, i.e., from liquidity preference proper, be allowed—undoubtedly a favorable development.

On the other hand, the adoption of an apparently permanent easy money policy has not only caused the disappearance of a "death trap" for credits, but has eliminated the possibility of stabilizing business activity through interest rate manipulation.   Since very low interest rates cannot be reduced further, the stabilizing effect of interest rate reduction in a depression is destroyed; and if a ceiling is put upon interest rates, the stabilizing effect of high interest rates during a boom cannot be counted upon either.

This means that our modern credit system, while protected against autonomous deflations from the credit *supply* side, has become very sensitive to changes on the *demand* side.   Low demand and deflationary tendencies and high demand and inflationary tendencies will no longer be mitigated by compensating interest rate movements. [34]

[32] *Ibid.*, p. 246.

[33] *Ibid.*, p. 245.

[34] To what extent the elasticity of money supply is now considered a matter of course is shown by the introduction of the so-called Acceleration Principle as an explanation of business cycles.   The requirement of large capital expenditures within a relatively short period, for an increase in the production of

If our analysis is correct, the pattern of future business cycles will differ greatly from that of past. Without trying to predict this future pattern, the following brief remarks may be ventured:

1. The beginning of a depression will no longer be characterized by high interest rates. The specific features of a monetary and banking crisis will be absent. The market for long-term government bonds may remain strong. There need not be anything like a general crisis of credit and confidence. Such symptoms were virtually absent already from the recession of 1938.

The unnecessary and exaggerated liquidations under the impact of deflations will not be repeated. On the other hand, too high inventories built up during the boom will not be immediately liquidated; the liquidation process will be protracted.

2. The depression, while less severe in the absence of real deflationary pressure, may be prolonged because the stimulating effect of declining interest rates is absent.

3. During prosperity the rising demand for credit will no longer be counteracted by the increasing cost of the supply. Easy money will postpone the end of the boom, but by no means indefinitely. If not curtailed by other changes detrimental to investment, e.g., too high wages, taxes, etc., overspeculation will go further than usual.

The paradoxical result of all this is that the business cycle will not be more stabilized in the future than it has in the past, in spite of all endeavors. There will be no more deflations from the credit supply side; however, this advantage will be offset by the stabilization of interest rates, which has destroyed a potentially strong anti-cyclical measure.[35]

consumer goods, has always been recognized. It is one of the cornerstones of Spiethoff's Overproduction Theory. Later monetary business-cycle theorists did well to reject Spiethoff's theory. They argued that what led to the overproportional capital expenditure was not so much the extraordinary demand as a too low discount rate which failed to curtail the credit supply sufficiently to guarantee an equal distribution of capital expenditures over time. If the old Spiethoff theory can today be presented in a new form without arousing objections, it is only because interest rates are practically stabilized and the credit supply perfectly elastic, so that a concentrated increase of demand causes a concentrated increase of expenditures for the production of capital goods.

[35] See Chapter 7.

14. The Economics of Illusion*

Quite briefly the essence of the late Lord Keynes' work *The General Theory of Employment, Interest, and Money* is: employment fluctuates with the intensity of effective demand, which depends, given a certain propensity to consume, upon the amount of investment—the spending of purchasing power for the purpose of adding to capital equipment. Investment in turn fluctuates—productivity of capital remaining the same—with the interest rate at which loanable funds are offered. Therefore, employment can be created by reducing the interest rate, provided entrepreneurs are willing to pay any interest at all; if they are not, the state must take over their investment activity, directing into circulation the purchasing power that private entrepreneurs would otherwise spend. An easy-money policy and—if that does not suffice—government deficit spending—monetary measures in a wider sense—can guarantee full employment.

Obviously an adherent of the pre-Keynesian approach would call this whole line of thinking an illusion. But it is perhaps less obvious that it represents not only illusionary economics but an "economics of illusion" in a very specific sense. For it presupposes an economy whose members do not see through the changes brought about by monetary or fiscal manipulation—or, as some might say, the

* Lecture delivered at the Studiengesellschaft für Wirtschaftspolitik, Zürich, Switzerland, September 12, 1947. An abridged version was published in German in the *Neue Zürcher Zeitung* (Sept. 19-21, 1947). The last section was published in English in *The Commercial and Financial Chronicle*, Dec. 18, 1947, under the title "Easy-Money Policy—the End of an Illusion."

swindle. Above all, it presupposes that people are blinded by the idea that the value of money is stable—by the "money illusion," as Irving Fisher called it. In all this we are not saying anything new; fundamentally, we are merely stating the approach of the classical economists.

The Classical Economists and the Money Illusion

It is usual nowadays to characterize classical economists as antiquated halfwits whose "teaching is misleading and disastrous if we apply it to the facts of experience." [1] This characterization could perhaps be applied more justly to Keynes' own theory. It is certainly not just when applied to the classical economists, who were familiar with the effects of manipulations that increase the supply of money. They were well aware that booms can be provoked and prolonged by inflation. Their vehement protests were founded on very extensive experience and acquaintance with the monetary depreciation, debasement of coins, and bank-note experiments of the Mercantilist and post-Mercantilist periods.

No classical economist denies that, in the first stage of an inflation, prosperity spreads as if by magic. Yet this prosperity is unreal; nowhere is it depicted more brilliantly than in the second part of Goethe's *Faust*. Prices rise faster than costs and profit margins are widened, rendering new enterprises profitable. For the following reasons, however, the stimulus soon loses its force:

On the one hand, prices break after a certain time unless new doses of the inflation poison are injected (and if they are, the experiment ends with the destruction of the currency). A rise in prices leads entrepreneurs to expect further rises. Consequently, they make new investments and build inventories, which in turn operate to boost prices further. The moment the stimulus of rising prices is exhausted, the cumulative boom spiral reverses its direction. Since there is no new stratum of buyers on whom the bulls can unload, the downward movement gains momentum. The English economist, A. C. Pigou, gives a penetrating description of the process in his *Industrial Fluctuations* (London, 1927). In an

[1] Keynes, *General Theory*, p. 3.

economy dependent largely upon exports, prices collapse even earlier: under the impact of the rising domestic price level, the balance of payments deteriorates, and the outflowing gold causes a deflationary process within the country, as David Ricardo described clearly in his 1810 pamphlet, *The High Price of Bullion.*

On the other hand, costs adjust themselves to the higher prices. The new enterprises become undermined from the cost side and the boom collapses for this reason: [2]

Interest rates cannot be held down in the long run, for interest rates rise because higher prices demand greater amounts of credit.[3]

If larger amounts of credit are created through the progressive increase of money, i.e., by the printing press, the process ends in a hopeless depreciation of the currency, in terms of both domestic goods and foreign exchange.

Wages, which have lagged behind prices, ultimately catch up, for workers care more about their real than their nominal wages. As Adam Smith remarked long ago: "Though the wages of the workmen are commonly paid to him in money, his real revenue, like that of all other men, consists, not in money, but in the money's worth, not in the metal pieces, but in what can be got for them." [4]

Unemployment, therefore, cannot be alleviated by monetary measures. It is caused by what today goes under the name of basic maladjustments in the cost structure. These must be corrected by voluntary adjustments of production factors. Production factors cannot be forced into curtailing their demands by a reduction in the real value of the money unit, i.e., by deceit or trickery.

THE GREAT DEPRESSION AND THE GREAT REFLATION

The classical economists gathered their experience during and after inflationary periods, and their teachings reflect their reaction to inflation. The present generation of economists gathered its

[2] David Hume, *Essay on Bank and Paper Money* (1752), in *A Select Collection of Scarce and Valuable Tracts and other Publications on Paper Currency and Banking,* edited by McCulloch, 1862.

[3] David Ricardo, *The High Price of Bullion,* 4th ed., London, 1811, pp. 35-37.

[4] Adam Smith, *An Inquiry into the Nature and Causes of the Wealth of Nations,* 8th ed., London, 1796, I, 440.

experience during the Great Depression of 1929-30, and its opinion reflects its reaction to the Depression and a swinging over of the pendulum to the preclassical, Mercantilist approach which greatly overestimated the beneficial effects of inflation. This is not to say that the reaction was not in part justified. The hyper-classicism of those who in the early 'thirties sabotaged every attempt at reflation, of whom many today are the most zealous and extreme proponents of monetary and budgetary manipulation, was undoubtedly theoretically untenable and practically disastrous. In most countries the hoarding of foreign exchange and of gold from fear of devaluation, and in the United States the hoarding of money from fear of further price reductions, deepened the Depression more and more. Wider and wider circles of the economy were ruined by deflation, until finally only the strongest enterprises survived, or those that were protected by moratoriums or subsidies. Unemployment increased. But hardly was the pressure from the money side—in most countries after the devaluation of the currency or the introduction of currency restrictions—mitigated (not because of the intelligence of the responsible persons but under the impact of the loss of foreign exchange) when suddenly the proverbial life on the ruins bloomed. The effects of the Depression vanished over night and strong recovery set in: in England after the devaluation; in the United States after numerous injections of credit; in the gold standard countries of that time—France, Holland, and Switzerland—after their devaluations, which occurred much too late; in Germany after the nonsensical Brüning-Luther deflation policy was given up and the Nazis had started their work-creation and spending measures. No wonder that faith in monetary manipulation through what one may call the Great Reflation (in contrast to the Great Depression) was strongly reinforced. The public and the experts deduced, *post hoc ergo propter hoc* and undoubtedly with some justification, the force of monetary reflation in overcoming crises.

LIMITATIONS ON AND POSSIBILITIES OF CREATING EMPLOYMENT BY INCREASING INVESTMENT

Does the experience of the Great Reflation refute the theory of the classical economists? Does it contradict what we said about the collapse of the price level and inflation on the one hand and the adjustment of costs upward on the other? We think not. Indeed we believe that it substantiates classical theory. The Great Depression showed that the limitations—and within the limitations the possibilities—of creating employment through investment and/or alleviation from the money side are in fact exactly those the classical economists described.

The rise in prices and employment after 1932 was, especially in the United States, succeeded by a severe though short depression in 1937. Once more the classical economists were vindicated—Boom was followed by Bust.

The easy-money policy initiated in 1932 was a factor in raising the price level generally, or at least was not an impediment. The extent of the price rise is striking when one looks on the depression of 1937-38 as merely an interruption and views the entire period since 1932 as a unit. Prices are everywhere higher than they were in 1932, and in some countries, many times higher—a clear expression of the old quantity theory that the effect of a greater amount of money practically exhausts itself by inflating prices.

The year 1936 was a real boom year as far as prices and many other indices are concerned, but, in contrast to earlier boom years, it did not lead to full employment. Several million were unemployed, even at the peak of the cycle—a phenomenon for which many explanations were given, among which the "classical" is the most plausible. The rapid upward adjustment of costs, especially wages, shortened the lag that in former cycles had made possible the employment of less productive labor.

Yet for five full years after 1932 the economy undoubtedly showed distinct signs of recovery. During this period, therefore, not all the circumstances that according to the classical economists nullify the effects of monetary changes can have been present. An analysis of the Great Reflation shows why and reveals the prerequisites of what the classicists called the "transition" period.

The price level obviously cannot break unless prices have risen. In the first stage of an inflation, prices either do not rise at all or rise only slightly because of their traditional stickiness. A sort of voluntary price ceiling and rationing system keeps them in line.

During the first years of both world wars a similar system, enforced by law, offset the effects of lax methods of war financing.

When an economy is emerging from a deep depression, wide sectors still function under the law of decreasing costs. Greater profits are reaped through faster turnover until the point of optimum utilization of equipment is reached. Up to that point, turnover alone, not prices, tends to rise substantially and the danger of price breaks remains at a minimum.

The danger of a reaction is caused not by a rise in prices but by the expectation of further rises engendered by a rise in prices. At the beginning of a cyclical upswing, however, the psychological environment is still deflationary. When the price rise eventually comes, it therefore has at first merely an antideflationary effect, not an inflationary one. Instead of inducing the illusion of further rises in prices, it only dispels the illusion of further declines in prices.

Despite rising prices, costs do not adjust themselves upward so long as the "money illusion" is effective, i.e., so long as the public, and especially labor, thinks that what is happening is a chance and temporary rise of prices coming from the side of goods, not of money, and that it is not due to depreciation of the currency. In our inflation-conscious times, however, when everyone—certainly every union leader—seems to carry a living-standard index curve in his pocket, the money illusion can hardly fool anyone for long. The chief assumption of Keynes' employment theory—namely, that the workers demand in "the general case" maintenance of their nominal wages, not of their real wages—is therefore entirely unrealistic today.

Even if workers realize that their hourly real wages are declining, they nevertheless may not demand higher wage rates at the beginning of recovery. First, because the rise in weekly wages, through increased employment, offsets the decline in hourly real wage. Second, because after the rise in real wages during the depression, the moral justification for wage increases appears slight. Third, unions cannot expect that their demands will be heeded when there is unemployment. However, this period of acquiescence, too, tends to become shorter. The idea inherent in the so-called purchasing power theory—that high wages stimulate recovery—has in many important quarters replaced the more correct idea that high wages curtail employment.

Long-term wage agreements, as well as long-term rent and loan contracts, can, for purely technical or juridical reasons, prevent the adjustment of costs to the changing value of the currency, though for a certain time only.

The Alleged Permanency of the Money Illusion—the Beginning of the Great Illusion

The effects of monetary manipulations thus last until the impact of the manipulation on prices, then the repercussion of prices on costs, are felt; in other words, as long as the economy is in what I have called the "reaction-free period." All this is in accordance with the approach of the neoclassicists, who derived their monetary business-cycle theories from the knowledge of the mechanism of the transition period—without, however, making the mistake of deriving from it a general theory of employment.

What the neoclassicists reproach Keynes and his followers with is that they have succumbed to this error. By assuming that the special conditions of the transition period are always present, they have formulated a theory of employment that is unrealistic and confusing, if not illogical, and that has thrown economic science back, if not into, then surely to the brink of, a purely Mercantilistic preclassical approach. Keynes himself, it is true, was cautious in his formulations. His responsibility lies solely in claiming that the assumptions of his theory were present in "the general case." But most of his followers, and above all the vulgar-Keynesian writers, forget that the replacement of the wage-theory of employment by an inflation- or reflation-theory of employment is justified only as a theory of the recovery phase, never as a general theory. Within the framework of a business-cycle theory it makes sense to regard certain factors, especially costs, as lagging behind others. If large groups of the population did not retain faith in the traditional value of money longer than other groups, there would be neither stability of economic life nor cyclical changes in employment. Prices would, so to speak, get out of hand from one moment to the next; and not being able to rely on even moderately stable costs, no entrepreneur would venture to expand production. However, to assume that when the value of money is consciously and willfully manipulated, the members of the economy will be bluffed for any length of time and will allow dupes to be made of themselves is an illusion.

To what economic-political illusions has this economics of illusion led?

THE ILLUSION OF DEVALUATION

The attempt to alleviate depressions by devaluating the domestic currency in relation to gold or foreign currency has been made again and again throughout history.

Devaluation of the currency is a trick by which, in countries dependent upon foreign trade, the domestic price level can be pushed upward by raising the supply price of imports and the demand price of exports. The immediate consequence is that a rigid and overpriced cost level is rendered cheap and bearable in terms of domestic as well as world market prices. The devaluation doubtless has the advantage, before deflation, that it favors debtors, who are already sorely tried, and prevents the revolution-creating effect of too drastic an "adjustment downwards"—a fact overlooked by certain hyper-classicists during the Great Depression.

Devaluation obviously can have the desired effect only if made in the reaction-free period. An emergency measure, it can be applied only once and under special circumstances. In "the general case" it cannot work, as the classicists have demonstrated time and again, for as costs adjust themselves upward, the facilitation of production is canceled. Furthermore, there is of course always the danger that foreign countries too will devaluate in competition for the temporary advantages in foreign trade. Then prices on world markets decline in terms of gold but do not rise in terms of the domestic cost level—the only thing that counts.

Incidentally, it seems as if the illusion of devaluation had been replaced by something that might be called the "illusion of non-devaluation"—the illusion that in the long run devaluation can be avoided though no attempt is made to halt domestic inflation. Our times labor under the illusion that unwarranted foreign exchange rates can be maintained permanently. Devaluations are therefore improbable even if they are warranted by internal inflation. Even more improbable is a "preceding" devaluation, one not forced by the cost structure but undertaken for the sake of foreign trade advantages. It was just this sort of devaluation that seemed to the proponents of Bretton Woods so especially menacing—without reason, since the devaluations of the 'thirties were nowhere, except in the United States, "preceding" devaluations.

THE ILLUSION OF AN EASY-MONEY POLICY AND DEFICIT SPENDING

We must distinguish whether these measures are taken in order to combat unemployment, or for other—especially fiscal—reasons.

THE FIGHT AGAINST UNEMPLOYMENT

When a depression is so far advanced that most of the exaggerations of the preceding boom have been liquidated, an easy-money policy can help to shorten the depression and to ward off the so-called secondary deflation, which is mainly psychological.

But further benefits are often attributed to an easy-money policy. It is thought that even after the economy has reached the recovery stage, employment can be stepped up by lowering interest rates. However, employment is either not increased at all or increased only for a time. In the last analysis, employment depends upon the relation between wages and prices. Outside the "reaction-free period," wages rise as money declines in value. To assume, as some Keynesians do, that prevailing unemployment hinders the upward adjustment of wages is erroneous. It should do so, but does not because of the power of trade unions.

Lower interest rates, to be sure, facilitate production. But only for a time. Lower interest rates mean higher profits, which awaken the envy of labor. Many a wage increase has been won with the slogan that an increase in corporation profits should be used to raise wages. As far as labor absorbs the profit margin resulting from lower interest rates, employment does not grow but declines. Because labor—not only in the large enterprises but also in the small and marginal—has become more expensive and capital cheaper, the economy adopts more capitalistic and labor-saving methods. Moreover, lowering interest rates is a one-time stimulus: it cannot be repeated, for negligible rates cannot be reduced further.

Lowering interest rates during a boom can at best prolong the boom for a certain time—but the price is a still worse collapse when it comes. For the reduction does not take place in a "reaction-free" period but in a period overripe for reaction. In this period the public's illusion that the boom will go on forever breaks down. No monetary manipulation—at least, not one made within the framework of a free capitalist economy—can save the illusion. Investments decline irresistibly. Keynes' idea that low interest rates are a remedy for booms [5] is therefore strange, to say the least.

About the complex question of deficit spending, on which the literature has continuously been growing, we confine ourselves to the following brief remarks:

Budgetary deficits as such need not lead to catastrophe, but they harbor certain dangers—whether the deficits are involuntary, as in France today, or voluntary, as in the United States in the 'thirties.

Underlying the deficit spending idea is the recognition that the pessimism prevalent during depressions and its cumulative effects can be mitigated or even dissipated if the state proceeds to invest in place of private entrepreneurs who are reluctant to invest. The idea is old. It has always found expression in most financial textbooks in the recommendation that the government should concentrate its investments in depressions and exercise restraint during prosperity.

As far as the much advertised "functional finance" is identical with this recommendation, it is appropriate but not new, despite the claims of its advocates. However, something more far-reaching is usually understood by functional finance—a fiscal policy according to which the government must support demand by compensatory spending whenever unemployment develops. In other places I have taken a stand against the crude, naïve approach that is the basis for recommending such a policy. Here I mention only the objections that follow directly upon what I have said above about an easy-money policy in inflationary times.

a. The support of demand in depressions after the exaggerations of the boom have been somewhat corrected is not only allowable but advisable.

[5] Keynes, *op. cit.*, p. 322.

b. Outside of this situation deficit spending cannot lessen unemployment owing to structural conditions, especially high wages, or to laws inimical to enterprise. It would have to be continued indefinitely. The higher price level that would render production feasible under a given cost situation would have to be supported by ever new governmental spending, because part of the purchasing power would always be seeping away through savings. Permanent governmental deficits, however, mean of course cumulative governmental indebtedness, which in turn leads eventually to bankruptcy or inflation, or both. It is wrong to assume, as some do, that the public will absorb any amount of government bonds. They fail to recognize that, from a certain moment on, new bonds can be placed only on very disadvantageous terms, and ultimately not at all—with the result of genuine inflation.

The idea behind functional finance has quite logically led to the claim that the state can and must guarantee full employment. The claim is incomprehensible for an economy that is still so far free that the state controls neither prices nor wages. Shall full employment be guaranteed at every (even the most senseless) wage level that trade unions, believing in the purchasing power theory, contrive to attain? Unless a state controls the amount and price of labor in a totalitarian way, it cannot guarantee full employment, any more than a physician who is not in a position to keep his patient from drinking to excess can guarantee him health.

If deficit spending is used to prolong a boom that is ripe for collapse, as has also been proposed, the consequences for the finances of the government will be still more disastrous. Unless the real maladjustments are corrected, not only will the financial position of the state be ruined but in a relatively short time the entire structure of the economy will be altered. The economy will become overwhelmingly socialist or state-capitalist—just what the proponents of functional finance allegedly want to prevent. For the state would have to replace "compensatorily" all the many enterprises that can operate only during a boom because they do not adjust their costs, especially wages, to the changed conditions.

But the idea of deficit spending is illusionary in a specific sense also: the desired effects can happen only if and as long as the members of the economy are unaware of the nature and effect of the budgetary manipulation.

The ability of the state to invest, and to this end to lend and spend, when private enterprise does not dare, is not due to any supernatural force or quality. It comes about merely because, unlike the private entrepreneur, the state can distribute the deficits among the members of the community. Even if the deficits are at first lent by the members and not taken from them by taxation, the members remain liable and must some day pay at least the interest on them, unless the government debt is allowed to mount indefinitely. A community that takes into account governmental investment but not the resulting debt would be just as short-sighted as is a community that regards an increase of war loans in the hands of individuals as an increase of wealth for the community, or a private enterprise that enters its assets but not its liabilities on its books. The businessman, especially the investor, is well aware of these matters, as is evident from his attitude toward an increasing public debt—his fear of declining profit margins because of the threat of higher taxes.

In the long run the entrepreneur responds to deficit spending by compensating reactions; with the result that private investment in general declines as government investment increases. As soon as prospective taxes are calculated as present costs, private enterprise becomes unprofitable and is given up.

Nevertheless, deficit spending can for a time and under certain conditions create employment. There must be the illusion that the community is not liable; or that the other fellow will pay the bill—as is usual in war booms; or that by the time the taxes have to be paid boom conditions will prevail and profits will be so high that the tax burden can be disregarded in current cost calculations. This third approach would be sensible. However, it is clear that all these conditions can be present only under special circumstances and only for a limited time.

FISCAL REASONS FOR AN EASY-MONEY POLICY AND DEFICIT SPENDING

Antideflationary measures to combat unemployment will hardly be of practical importance in the near future. With the exception perhaps of the United States, where from time to time the imminence of deflation is discussed, it is generally admitted that the world is in the midst of an inflationary boom. Where there *is* unemployment, it is not attributed, even by the most extreme Keynesians, to lack of demand.

In an inflationary world, deficit spending and an easy-money policy have other reasons. Deficit spending is resorted to simply because of inability to balance the budget. It is purely involuntary. An easy-money policy is advocated because it seems to make possible a speedy reduction of the interest and debt burden of the government and the balancing of the budget without imposing higher taxes. Sometimes it is urged also as a command of social justice. The latter argument is of course based upon pure illusion. Small savers pay the bill directly or indirectly via savings banks and insurance companies, whereas large capitalists, who are interested chiefly in equities, harvest the profits from refunding operations.

Undesirable Concomitants

An easy-money policy is, however, illusionary in inflationary times mainly because of its undesirable concomitants.

When demand for credit is strong, interest rates will not long remain low unless the quantity of money is increased. The inevitability of this increase is exactly why the classicists warned so persistently against keeping interest rates artificially low.

In inflationary periods an increase in the quantity of money immediately affects prices. The inflation in most European countries today is due to a lax credit policy—as far as it is not due merely to a lax fiscal policy in the past and present. The illusion persists that one can go into the water of such an inflationary policy without getting wet by inflation.

The illusion—or rather its breakdown—that an increase in the quantity of money does not inevitably lead to inflation sows a bumper crop of new illusions, as is only too evident now in England.

The first illusion it creates is that, contrary to the experience of centuries, the groups of the population that most need protection can be protected from the consequences of inflation by price ceilings rather than by correction of the basic monetary mistakes. The result is black markets.

The second illusion is that price ceilings will not affect the quantity and kind of production. As ought to be self-evident, and as was confirmed by our experience under the O.P.A., an economy squeezed between rising costs and fixed prices cannot function. When maximum prices are set, especially on mass consumption goods, unessential and luxury goods are made instead. Production also declines absolutely with the rise in costs and wages.

Another illusion is that money can in the long run fulfill its function of stimulating production if a rationing system has deprived it of its unlimited purchasing power. When goods are rationed, more money means not more goods, but at best more savings. And savings are hardly desirable when people are starving, are therefore more concerned about the present than the future, and in addition fear that their savings will become worthless. If more money does not mean that people can buy more goods, they will work as little as possible, thereby reducing production still further. These interrelations are even more obvious in Germany than in England. The entire German economy seems to be collapsing chiefly because the currency has been degraded to a sort of supplement to ration coupons.

Astonished, a bit horrified at what they have perpetrated, yet happy over the prospect of new fields for their activity, the planners demand more and more regulation of production, as well as of investment, until finally everything, including job allocation, is regulated by the government. The "Road to Serfdom" is thereby followed to its end, not least for industrial workers, in whose name and for whose protection an easy-money policy was advocated.

The planners do not see that everything that has happened is due to a fundamental illusion: that scarcity of capital in a poor country can be glossed over by low discount rates. Poverty of nations, as of individuals, should manifest itself by a scarcity of money. There must not be as much—and as cheap—money available as is desired, and poverty only begins on the markets for goods. Under a reasonable monetary policy, there must be goods for every quantity of money. Scarcity must show itself in money. We do not wish to imply here that a sound monetary policy would solve all problems in needy Europe. Though certainly not a sufficient condition of recovery, it is however an essential one. Nor do we wish to say that it would be easy to raise discount rates substantially in a country accustomed to the poison of cheap money. Many difficulties, especially those connected with the nonconsolidation of the debt, with the banking situation, and with the budget, must first be overcome. Furthermore, a rise in discount rates alone would hardly be effective, though it would be much more effective than many contemporary theoreticians assume. Therefore, an energetic interest policy would probably have to be supplemented by measures aimed at absorbing and removing the pent-up inflationary forces—perhaps on the lines of the Belgian model. In other words, there would have to be a thorough monetary reform if the traditional means, the interest rate policy, did not suffice to render purchasing power, which was provisorily dormant during the war, permanently dormant. In any case, without rendering money scarce, the sole alternative to a progressive depreciation of the currency is a totalitarian economy regulated to the utmost.

Inflation, of course, also has repercussions outside the domestic prices. It leads to raising prices of the foreign exchange of countries whose monetary policy is more conservative—or which, because of their advantageous economic position, need not be conservative. If the foreign exchange rate is stabilized, inflation leads on the one hand to black markets for gold and foreign exchange, and on the other to a strongly passive balance of trade and payments with sound-currency countries. Gold and foreign exchange flow partly directly into these countries, partly indirectly via those third countries from which one has imported and to which one, in ignorance of the situation, has promised convertibility of one's own currency into "hard" currency. All allegedly superfluous payments to foreign countries are soon suspended and the currency is no longer convertible.

Illusions About International Effect of Inflation

From this situation arises a further illusion—the illusion of the "God-made passivity of the balance of trade," as I called it almost thirty years ago when I endeavored to fight the great German inflation. I tried to prove that the destruction of the mark was due simply to domestic inflation, not to disturbances in the balance of trade or payments. If President Havenstein and the others then in charge of the Reichsbank did not understand the argument and gave inflation a free rein, they can perhaps be pardoned because no tradition of monetary theory existed in Germany. But a similar excuse cannot be made for Great Britain today. Her most outstanding economist, David Ricardo, tried to make clear one hundred and thirty years ago—after the Napoleonic Wars—that it was not lack of goods or a compulsory passive balance of trade that induced the outflow of gold (as the directors of the Bank of England thought), but simply the fact that gold or foreign exchange was the sole cheap export. Ricardo compared the attempt to replenish the deficits in the balance of payments by buying or borrowing gold or foreign exchange from abroad with pouring water into the hole-riddled jar of the Danaïds.[6]

"THE SCARCE DOLLAR"

A sort of subdivision of the illusion of the "God-made passivity of the balance of trade" is the illusion—and the slogan—of the "scarce dollar." It is understandable that debtor countries should use it, but not that creditor countries should take it seriously. In the last analysis, the dollar is scarce in England while many other currencies, especially of the pound area, are abundant because it is easy to export to soft-currency countries and difficult to import from them. And it is difficult to import not because their production apparatus was destroyed in the war. Neither Canada nor Australia was bombed or invaded. The differences in the possibilities of foreign trade with the hard- and soft-currency countries arise solely because the price of the hard currency is too low in terms of domestic currency, so that imports are unduly facilitated and exports impeded. This remains true although official prices of goods in soft-currency countries are sometimes no higher than

[6] On the tremendous effect of the domestic monetary policy on the balance of payments, see also Chapter 4, "Capital Is Made at Home," p. 34.

in hard-currency countries, since at these prices goods are often unavailable.

To say that foreign exchange is scarce means to view economic phenomena in isolation rather than in the framework of causal conditions. Foreign currencies will always, and obviously, become scarce if the natural means of regulating demand for them—discount and credit policy—are not applied. Also, a scarcity of foreign currency should express itself in scarcity of domestic money.

SACRIFICES NEEDED

A stringent monetary and fiscal policy entails sacrifices for the population. Taxes must be raised and wages and profits must be low enough to bear the greater interest burden. If for social and political reasons such sacrifices cannot be asked of the people, recourse must be had to foreign aid through taking loans or gifts. In the interests of truth, however, one should not speak of dollar scarcity until one has tried to increase the supply of and decrease the demand for domestic capital through higher interest rates in order to avoid the alleged crisis of the balance of payments, which is in reality merely an inflation crisis. Under a reasonable monetary policy, scarcity of capital or of goods need not lead to inflation or currency restrictions.

ILLUSION OF NONDEVALUATION

From the illusion of the scarce dollar, and from the failure to recognize its real causes, follows the illusion that devaluation can be avoided. It is undoubtedly correct that, for the reasons mentioned above, devaluation alone would not be of any benefit. Unless supplemented by monetary reform, it would have to be resorted to over and over again. Moreover, theoretically, there is always the alternative of a very incisive deflationary policy which would go beyond forestalling future inflation. Such a policy is, however, practically out of the question for other reasons.

It must be admitted that the "illusion of nondevaluation" is nourished by the Bretton Woods Organization, which reinforces still further the strong tendency of our time to conceal rather than remove inflations. The International Monetary Fund is based on the illusion that nineteenth-century currency stability can be achieved, even approximately or for a time, in this twentieth-century world, a world in which the will and the ability to adjust domestic factors, which have become rigid according to the exchange rate, are no longer present.

A currency can be stabilized only when there is sovereignty in credit and fiscal matters, and above all, in the wage policy of a country. The International Monetary Fund has no sovereignty in individual countries and, as matters stand, can have none. Its potentialities are confined to certain "technicalities," especially in the realm of short-term equalization of the balance of payments, which in normal times are superfluous, and in times of insecurity, like today, are unimportant to the point of ridiculousness. Stabilization begins at home. On the other hand, the International Monetary Fund creates a psychological atmosphere that prevents exchange rates from reaching a level corresponding to their purchasing power and eternalizes currency restrictions—just the thing the Fund was set up to prevent. In this atmosphere, attention is distracted from the one really essential matter: sound credit and fiscal policies in the individual countries.

THE PUSH TO BILATERALISM

In any case, the result of Bretton Woods has so far been that official (unfortunately, not unofficial) exchange rates are stabilized, but foreign trade is reduced through this very stabilization and, worse yet, pushed more strongly in the direction of bilateralism. If, nevertheless, the endeavor to stabilize currencies is not given up, but is supposed to be adopted by further organizations to be founded, the reason is probably that—as is so often the case—what was originally the means to the end, has become the end itself.

Meanwhile what had to happen happened. If the foreign value of currencies is fixed at a level much above the level that would correspond to its domestic purchasing power and to the entire economic situation of the country, the only solution is an ever stricter regulation of all foreign trade. Through a complicated system of licenses, luxury articles—nonessential but much sought after in the inflationary environment, such as films and tobacco—must be kept out. There must also be a general transition to a strict reciprocity under which only as much is bought from each country as is sold to it. This system, which means of course the end of multilateral trade and of world free trade—so much desired especially by the United States—is familiar. It was the system of the so-called New Plan of Schacht. Introduced when Germany's balance of payments was deteriorating rapidly in the wake of the National Socialist spending policy, it was combined with a compulsory system of export subsidies and import excises designed to compensate for the fact that the external value of the mark had been fixed much too high. The system functioned well for years, but it must not be forgotten that it functioned within a totalitarian state in which free communication with foreign countries was forbidden and sending capital abroad was subject to the death penalty.

The most tragic—or tragicomic—illusion, the inevitable consequence of all other illusions, is that the world must now split, as far as foreign commerce is concerned, into two parts: the world of hard- and the world of soft-currency countries. It is as if the countries of these two worlds were in a kind of natural community determined by their economic conditions or by their lot in the war. But did Argentina and Sweden, which were typical war-profiteer countries, suffer from the war, or has something changed in their economic position? Or are they hurt by being caught between the pincers of agricultural and industrial prices?—of which the impact, incidentally, is very much overrated. Certainly not. The community of soft-currency countries is not a community of economic conditions but a community of lax monetary and fiscal policies, a community of ignorance about monetary theory, of inexperience with monetary policy, and of political doctrinaire stubbornness.

15. The Investment Gap[*]

Critics of Keynesian economic theory or policy do not usually stress its logical inconsistency. In their opinion what is wrong is that the underlying factual assumptions are unrealistic or, more specifically, correct only in very special cases. Their charge is similar to that of Keynes against classical theory: that its assumptions are in general not "those of the economic society in which we actually live, with the result that its teaching is misleading and disastrous if we attempt to apply it to the facts of experience."[1]

The miracles the Keynesian system works can be attributed to the data taken as dependent and independent variables and as fixed, plus certain assumptions concerning the shape of important functions, especially the consumption, money supply, and investment functions. Change these assumptions to what non-Keynesians consider more realistic terms and the classical or neoclassical theory reappears like an old picture when the layers of paint laid on by successive generations are removed.

In a certain sense the Keynesian factual assumptions were never correct; in another, they have been invalidated through changes of the last decade. It is not pure chance that "modern employment theory sheds little light"[2] on the practical problems of today, which are essentially problems of wage-price relationships and—at least for the time being—of overabundant, not of deficient demand. But with the lag peculiar to economics, publications based upon the Keynesian approach are more frequent than ever.[3]

[*] Appeared first in *Schweizerische Zeitschrift für Volkswirtschaft und Statistik,* 1948.

[1] Keynes, *The General Theory,* p. 3.

[2] Sumner H. Slichter, *Review of Economic Statistics,* 1947, p. 140.

[3] That Keynesianism and its success are due to a certain historical constellation becomes clear when one reads reactions from outside the Anglo-American

In Chapter 11, "Wage Flexibility Upwards," I tried to show that Keynes' wage assumptions, so essential to his investment theory of employment, must be considered unrealistic and/or anachronistic. In Chapter 13, "Anachronism of the Liquidity Preference Concept," I tried to do the same for the assumptions underlying the liquidity preference concept. In the present chapter I examine the assumptions underlying the so-called "investment gap approach," especially those concerning the consumption and the investment-demand functions.

Anyone familiar with Keynes' theory will agree that if these three cornerstones—the assumptions concerning the behavior of people in matters of wage demands, liquidity preference, and consumption—were removed, nothing would remain of his system except a formal construction inadequate to describe and explain reality. And the far-reaching conclusions for economic theory as well as policy derived by those who think along Keynesian lines would have to be revised in many respects.

The Basic Difference Between the Classical and the Keynesian Attitude

The investment gap approach is responsible for the emphasis modern theory lays upon consumption as the prerequisite for production. And it is responsible, too, for the attitude of our times, so favorable to spending and so unfavorable to saving—an attitude fundamentally different from the classical, which always deemed saving a virtue.

For the classical economists the problem of filling "the gap" [4] between saving and investment did not exist. Interest rates were supposed to keep saving and investment always in balance. Keynes, on the other hand, believes that increased savings are not neces-

---

deflation-fearing realm. We quote at random: "An entire world separates us from the conceptions of modern economics which, influenced by *Keynes,* considers that full employment is threatened mainly by the lag of investment behind saving. How far this theory is valid for the English economy is not for us to decide. As far as present German conditions are concerned, it sounds like a bad joke." (Translated from *Der Wirtschafts-Spiegel,* Wiesbaden, Oct. 1, 1947, p. 365.)

[4] Keynes, *op. cit.,* p. 98.

sarily absorbed by investment in the wake of falling interest rates. If they are not absorbed, the balancing of saving and investment takes place through a decline in saving in the wake of a decline in employment to what can be called a "poverty equilibrium": "There must be sufficient unemployment to keep us so poor that our consumption falls short of our income by not more than the equivalent of the physical provision for future consumption which it pays to produce today." [5] The result is that the economy remains "in a chronic condition of sub-normal activity for a considerable period without any marked tendency either towards recovery or towards complete collapse." [6] Thus, if investment is not increased, expansion of employment is hindered unless consumption keeps pace with production. In short, saving regulates employment.

Keynes' assumptions in this as in other important problems cannot help being unrealistic because, in trying to establish a "general" theory, he makes statements concerning the behavior of men in general, whether in short- or long-term situations, under dynamic or static conditions. His purpose is to overcome what he considers one of the weakest points in prevailing theory—the inconsistency between general and business-cycle theory. But men's reactions to more income vary with circumstances; therefore a "combination theory" which attempts to cover all cases really covers none.

Dividing Keynes' combination theory into its components and distinguishing short- and long-term equilibrium situations on the one hand and dynamic and static conditions on the other, we shall discuss in turn: "general" short-run equilibrium; cyclical movements; and long-run equilibrium.[7]

We shall try to prove that—

a. An investment gap approach is not applicable in the case of general short-term equilibrium because the consumption (or saving) function does not have the form Keynes assumed;

[5] *Ibid.*, p. 105.
[6] *Ibid.*, p. 249.
[7] See my *Volkswirtschaftliche Theorie des Bankkredits*, 3d ed. In the first two editions I sought to give a "general" theory of the effects of credit expansion; in the third edition I differentiated sharply between static and dynamic situations.

b. Cyclical depressions are neither induced nor aggravated by unabsorbable savings; something quite different, what we call "waiting," is at work;

c. In long-term equilibrium an investment gap, while conceivable under special conditions, could at best explain a progressive decline in employment, never stagnation, i.e., a long-lasting low level of economic activity.

The "Psychological Law" and Its Implications Within Keynes' System

Keynes makes the relation between an increase in income and in consumption or saving the basis of his entire system. Calling it a "psychological law," he gives it two forms: a stronger and a weaker.

In its weaker form the law states that when income increases, consumption also increases but somewhat less; i.e., marginal consumption never equals marginal income:

The fundamental psychological law, upon which we are entitled to depend with great confidence both *a priori* from our knowledge of human nature and from the detailed facts of experience, is that men are disposed, as a rule and on the average, to increase their consumption as their income increases, but not by as much as the increase in their income.[8]

In its stronger form the law states that marginal consumption not only never equals marginal income but that the "marginal propensity to consume falls off steadily as we approach full employment."[9]

Both statements are meant as "general" statements. They are supposed to apply to all sorts of increases in income, whether due to cyclical and other short-term changes or to improvements in productivity and other long-term changes. This is obvious if from nothing else than his remark: "We have short periods in view, as in the case of the so-called cyclical fluctuations of employment";[10] and by his further remark that the psychological law is valid "apart from short-period changes"[11] though not for "far-reaching social changes or . . . the slow effects of secular progress."[12]

[8] Keynes, *op. cit.*, p. 96.
[9] *Ibid.*, p. 127.
[10] *Ibid.*, p. 97.

[11] *Ibid.*, p. 97.
[12] *Ibid.*, p. 109.

What is the significance of the psychological law in Keynes' system?

a. It serves to establish an unemployment equilibrium. Given a certain amount of investment and a consumption function that obeys the psychological law, employment is, so to speak, squeezed down by the lack of demand due to the deficiency of consumption (or increase in saving) that would follow higher employment: "the insufficiency of effective demand will inhibit the process of production." [13]   For if "entrepreneurs were to increase employment as a whole, their proceeds will necessarily fall short of their supply price." [14]   Therefore "the increased employment will prove unprofitable unless there is an increase in investment to fill the gap." [15]

To establish this employment equilibrium, the psychological law in its weaker form suffices.

b. It serves to explain at least in part why prosperity does not last. As income increases during prosperity, saving increases. If a demand deficit is to be prevented, the current rate of investment must rise. However, it becomes increasingly difficult to find new investment opportunities. This line of thinking places Keynes distinctly in the ranks of the oversaving or underinvestment business-cycle theorists. It is expressed in various passages of his *General Theory*, though (as we shall see) contradicted in others. It is given its most striking formulation when it is used to explain the crash of 1929:

It became almost hopeless to find still more new investment on a sufficient scale to provide for such new saving as a wealthy community in full employment would be disposed to set aside. This factor alone was probably sufficient to cause a slump.[16]

c. It serves to explain why allegedly modern economies must remain in a state of chronic underemployment in the long run: "to fill the gap between net income and consumption, presents a problem which is increasingly difficult as capital increases." [17]

For the second and third purposes, too, the psychological law in

[13] *Ibid.*, p. 31.   [16] *Ibid.*, p. 100.
[14] *Ibid.*, p. 261.   [17] *Ibid.*, p. 105.
[15] *Ibid.*, p. 98.

its weaker form suffices. If saving in the current production period is to be by only the slightest degree larger than in the preceding period, the rate of investment must rise; otherwise, income cannot increase. However, investment would obviously have to increase much more if the psychological law in its stronger form were valid. On the other hand, in the long run, an investment gap from the investment side could threaten even if there were no psychological law whatsoever. Even if saving, while remaining positive, does not increase at all, a continuous addition to the capital stock could in time lead to a saturation of the economy with capital and thus to a downward shift of the investment curve.

Our main problem remains, however: is there a "psychological law"? And if there is, can it have the effects attributed to it in Keynesian theory? The answer depends largely upon how the increase in income comes about:

a. Aggregate real income can increase if entrepreneurs engage former unemployed workers because, for instance, wage demands have been lowered. This is the case Keynes treats in his Chapter 19 ("Changes in Money-Wages").[18]

b. Income can increase in the wake of and through the peculiar mechanism of the credit expansion characteristic of cyclical upswings.

c. Aggregate real income can increase by reason of the greater productivity of labor brought about either by technical progress or the use of more capital. This is essentially a long-run increase.

"GENERAL" SHORT-RUN EQUILIBRIUM: INCOME RISES WHEN EMPLOYMENT INCREASES AFTER WAGES HAVE BEEN REDUCED

Keynes' presupposition in the case of short-run equilibrium is that a deflation threatening in the wake of higher employment would prevent any improvement in the rate of unemployment. But this need not be the case. Suppose wage demands are reduced 10 per cent, and aggregate income—through increased employment—is raised 20 per cent. If half of the 20 per cent is saved, prices will be deflated 10 per cent on the average. Thus the effect

[18] *Ibid.*, pp. 261 ff.

of the decline in the supply price of labor would be nullified and an increase in employment indeed prevented. However, if less than half is saved, employment would increase despite the deflation of the price level.

We shall not discuss here the possibility of a deflationary employment increase.[19] Instead we will concentrate on the question whether an increase in employment can lead to deflation.

"In general," people tend to use part of an increase in income to provide for the future. No psychological law is necessary to explain this behavior. Under modern conditions people, except the very poor, always devote part of their income to the future, if only in the form of life, old-age, or sickness insurance. Furthermore, it has often been verified empirically that the saving-income ratio is usually higher in rich than in poor families.

However, the increment to income from an increase in employment induced by lower wages—the case Keynes really has in mind in Chapter 19—cannot be called a "general" case. It is a very special case. Only if violence is done to the facts can the psychological law be considered to work here. It has in this special case never been verified statistically, and probably never can be. For most increases in employment are cyclical and not due to a spontaneous decline in wages; and when wages do decline spontaneously, the effects could hardly be separated from those of simultaneous cyclical developments.

Moreover, probability points against the working of the psychological law in this special case. For here the addition to the income of the community comes from the income of the former unemployed—according to Keynes: "not all the *additional employment* will be required to satisfy the needs of additional consumption." [20] If any general rule on the behavior of the newly employed—formerly unemployed—can be established, it is that they probably spend *all* their earnings. And even if they saved, the saving would be of negligible significance. For all practical purposes the curve

[19] For the opposite phenomenon, "inflationary employment recession," see Chapter 11, p. 132.

[20] Keynes, *op. cit.*, p. 97 (italics mine).

of spending and the curve of income coincide if the increase in aggregate income is due to new employment.

To state the contrary and to use the statement as a basis for a *general* theory of employment seems therefore entirely unrealistic.

Nor can it be assumed that the newly employed increase aggregate saving because they stop dissaving. Usually the unemployed live on the earnings of members of their family or on unemployment relief, which in turn is financed by taxes on the income of other members of the community, not on their capital.

But it might be objected: suppose the unemployed have been supported by public deficit spending, i.e., by spending the savings of the community. Then such dissaving would decline as unemployment declined. However, this objection would merely introduce governmental anti-depression measures into the argument. When governmental deficit spending stops, deflation may follow. But such deflation does not occur because people are inclined to save parts of their income in accordance with the psychological law. It occurs because the government ceases to spend the savings of the community.

It has furthermore been argued: if employment increases after wages have been reduced, the income of entrepreneurs increases, and of this new income a part will be saved. This is not the case Keynes had in mind when he established the relationship between increased income and saving. For, as a simple graph would show, such new income of entrepreneurs does not mean an *additional* income to the community. It merely means that the distribution of income has been altered. Profits have increased at the expense of wages. Such redistribution of income might of course lead to more aggregate saving, but it need not.

Under present conditions saving would probably even decline, not increase because income would be shifted from lower to higher tax brackets. This may be otherwise, but never so generally and so automatically that it warrants the establishment of a law according to which increase of employment through wage lowering must lead to deflation via increase in saving. But even if aggregate saving would increase: to assume that the deflation threatened by the saving of the relatively few entrepreneurs could nullify the effect of the preceding deflation of the wages of the working masses—except under very peculiar circumstances—betrays a lack of sense of proportion.

The whole Keynesian "formal analysis" suffers furthermore from the inconsistency that it takes into account the effect of wage lowering and employment increase on saving but not on investment decisions, which are not in the slightest less probable. Every businessman expects in fact—and not without reason—that in an otherwise neutral atmosphere wage lowering leads to an inflationary boom via increased investment rather than to a deflationary depression via increased saving. For the newly employed workers have to be equipped with tools and machines and—very often forgotten—have to be paid, which fact alone creates a new demand for credits. If therefore the news would spread that the unions had lowered their wage demands, a boom on the stock market and not a slump would develop. This is one of the chief reasons why Keynesianism appears so very unrealistic to businessmen. The theorist will object that an equilibrium analysis must take into consideration all reasonable reactions, not just one. By failing to do so one can indeed demonstrate the possibility of equilibria that are most amazing to classical thinking. But they are no real equilibria in any correct sense of the word, not even short-term equilibria, but at best transitory situations.

What then limits employment if not a deflationary pressure from an investment gap? In "general" or "formal" analysis the answer can only be the answer of the classical economists: employment is dependent solely upon the wage level and the marginal productivity of labor.

A Digression: Prices and Employment in an Economy with a Perfectly Elastic Money Supply

Of course the problem remains whether an increase in employment will not be hindered by a scarcity of funds to meet the bigger payroll, especially when the demand for labor is very elastic, so that a slight decline in wage rates leads to a big increase in employment. Formerly, this impediment to employment was extensively discussed in connection with the "neutral money" problem.

However, if meeting a bigger payroll, and thereby an increase in employment, is hindered by an undersupply of money, the reason is clearly not an excess but rather a deficit of investible funds. Furthermore, the problem would not be how to pay for the products of the newly employed, but how to pay their wages. Obviously, this problem does not exist as long as the supply of money is almost perfectly elastic at a very low interest rate level. As this is written (March 1948), the trouble is that entrepreneurs, if their credit is good, *can* obtain all the additional money they need for bigger payrolls at practically the same low interest cost—not that they cannot obtain it.

Parenthetically it may be added: the quantity of money plays, as is well known, an important role in Keynes' system as an independent variable. It is held responsible for certain changes in investment and employment. If the money-supply curve remains unchanged as the result of deliberate government policy, the quantity of money of course ceases to be an independent variable. And if the supply curve has become not only stable but also almost horizontal, the supply of money being almost perfectly elastic, the quantity of money can hardly be considered useful any longer as a fixed datum in any equilibrium analysis.

Indeed, the problem now is not how to meet payrolls inflated by full employment, but how to prevent payrolls—and the price level—from inflating indefinitely. What then puts a ceiling on prices and wages when money is not scarce? What keeps them from skyrocketing? It is sometimes argued that wages and prices cannot rise indefinitely because the purchasing power to buy the products at higher than prevailing prices would be lacking. The flaw in this argument is that high wages create in the aggregate sufficient purchasing power to absorb at least the price increases due to them.

Now, if no wage increase need ever lead to the situation so feared by Keynes—where the proceeds from production fall short of the outlays—why do entrepreneurs not grant every demand for an increase in wages? A "circular analysis," reckoning with a limited money supply, can give no answer after the money supply has become perfectly elastic. Obviously, it would also be a vicious circle to assume that the prices entrepreneurs expect for their products act as a ceiling on wage increases. For the prices themselves are a function of the demand created by the wage increases. The answer can be given only by "chain analysis," according to which entrepreneurs reckon with the price pattern of the past, which they consider stable as long as optimistic or pessimistic expectations do not suggest markups or markdowns.

Our assumptions concerning the elasticity of the money supply may not seem entirely warranted. In fact, there are signs that the prevailing easy-money policy cannot be maintained indefinitely. It nevertheless seems more useful to base an analysis on a state of affairs in which the money supply is perfectly elastic than to continue to assume that the economy will constantly be disturbed by a scarcity of money.[21]

CYCLICAL MOVEMENTS

A. Can increases in saving due to rising income (shifts *along* the income curve) lead to depression?

Undoubtedly during cyclical upswings saving increases, not only absolutely, not only proportionately to the increase in income, but even more than proportionately. However, there seems no proof and not even a probability that "the marginal propensity to consume falls off steadily as we approach full employment."[22] Saving is apparently greatest at the beginning and the middle of an upswing.

The special case of high saving during cyclical upswings evidently impressed Keynes so much that he felt impelled to formulate his general psychological law. In fact, everything he says about income and saving fits this case, the case of "prosperity saving," as we should like to call it.[23] But is prosperity saving due to an increase in income by reason of higher employment? It may be conceded that over a longer period the newly employed too begin to

[21] See Chapter 13, "Anachronism of the Liquidity Preference Concept."

[22] Keynes, *op. cit.*, p. 127.

[23] I drew attention to "prosperity saving" in the third edition of my *Volkswirtschaftliche Theorie des Bankkredits*. A statistical verification was attempted in my *"Zur Frage des volkswirtschaftlichen Erkenntnisinhalts der Bankbilanzziffern,"* in *Vierteljahreshefte zur Konjunkturforschung*, I, 1926, Erg.-Heft 4; reprinted in *Geld und Kredit*. Neue Folge, Tübingen, 1929.

save. Yet if Keynes is right, wages tend to lag behind prices during a boom. According to the psychological law, however, declining real wages would mean decreased saving. On the average, saving would scarcely increase.

The windfall profits that accrue during an inflationary boom offer a better explanation. Unless taxes are too progressive, the savings of profiteers overcompensate the decline in the savings of the victims of inflation. Such savings have correctly been called "secondary" or "induced" savings.[24]

The paramount reason for "prosperity saving," however, seems to be that the monetary expansion is not recognized as such at the beginning or even in the middle of an upswing, by either buyers or sellers. People are not prepared to compete for the goods on hand by bidding prices up. Buyers prefer to wait in the hope that goods will soon be plentiful at the old prices. On the other hand, sellers do not mark up their prices because they hope they will be able to replace their inventories at the old price. In other words, at the beginning of an upswing and far into prosperity a sort of voluntary rationing and price-ceiling system prevails. Although goods are available in only limited amounts, their prices are not raised. In wartime this system is enforced by laws and regulations. It is in large degree responsible for the huge amounts of "war savings." What happens during a war boom in this respect is nothing but a replica of an ordinary boom on a gigantic scale.

So the increase in saving during an upswing has nothing to do with the stickiness of spending habits, i.e., with the reluctance of people to spend all their increased income on current consumption. It has to do with the stickiness of price expectations. Prosperity saving is, in other words, caused essentially by inflation that is not recognized as such. One might therefore call it "inflationary saving."

But whatever its origin, prosperity saving can never explain how a boom can end for lack of sufficient investment opportunities; certainly not, if one subscribes to Keynes' general statements about the relations between investment, income, and saving.[25] According

---

[24] Fritz Machlup, *Review of Economic Statistics,* 1943, pp. 26-39.
[25] Keynes, *op. cit.,* p. 184.

to these the increase in saving during an upswing is due to increased income, which in turn is due to increased investment typical of prosperity. What is really the consequence of investment can never be the cause of a deficiency in it. Investment is always sufficient to absorb the saving it creates. And because investment financed by credit expansion brings on inflation which in turn leads to saving, such saving is not a deflationary force but a force that at best can dampen the inflationary force of investment financed by additional credit.

Thus the form of a curve showing the propensity to consume at various income levels during an upswing is relevant only for the degree of the inflation caused by the increased investment. If the propensity to consume is high, investment will have strong inflationary effects. If the propensity to consume is low and therefore saving is high, the effects of investment will be less inflationary. But the form of the consumption function can never be of any importance for the capacity of investment to absorb saving. Abundance of saving cannot explain the deficit in investment at the beginning of a depression. Even in the last minute of the boom saving is absorbed by the very investment that brought it into existence.

Under one condition alone could investment create saving it could not absorb: if the increased income led to a *decrease* in consumption. In this case investment would be impossible, because a resulting saving would not only hinder inflation but cause deflation. Such a form of consumption curve, however, is highly improbable.

The situation prevailing at the end of an upswing shows in fact that saving, increasing during and by reason of the upswing, has nothing at all to do with terminating it. For until the downward shift in investment and consumption causing the turn really sets in, the situation is characterized by inflation and/or high interest rates; there is neither deflation nor an abundance of new saving such as a "wealthy community in full employment would be disposed to set aside." [26] In any case, the turning cannot be caused by savings

26 *Ibid.*, p. 100.

increased by "shifts *along* the curve." Nor is, incidentally, the turning from depression to recovery caused by such shifts along the curve. Depression ends not because savings decrease during the downswing in the wake of decreasing income, but because from incomes no longer decreasing a greater portion is spent: after an exhaustion of inventories, a change in the psychological situation or—familiar to every stock market speculator—a growth of cash balances in relation to the price level.

In conceding that the form of the consumption function is relevant for the inflationary effects of new investment, we do not wish to imply that the consumption function, though perhaps stable in the long run, remains stable during the cyclical upswing and that it is determinable in advance—an assumption underlying the so-called multiplier concept. To what degree money is spent or saved during an upswing, and what forces are at work at every stage, is just the question business-cycle theorists try to solve. To this end they analyze the dynamic process of the upswing and the resulting changes in profit expectations. The "multiplier" concept, however, is either a *truism*—in stating that money not saved is spent until it is finally saved; or it is a *petitio principii*—in implying that a constant portion is saved or spent. The problem is: how big will the various portions be? What will happen during a certain period after the government has spent a billion dollars on public works? What will be the various consumption quotas? The answer can never be given in advance. For the function of production and consumption is never stable over time in a dynamic world. They depend on innumerable data responsible for the successive reinvestment and consumption decisions of the individuals. Therefore the multiplier which seemingly gives the answer as to the effects of governmental or other investments on future income and employment, in reality only reformulates the question.

B. Can spontaneous increases in saving or decreases in investment (shifts of the curves) lead to depression?

1. *Increases in saving.*

In the main parts of his *General Theory* Keynes considers an increase in saving induced by an increase in income as the cause of subnormal activity. On the other hand, he seems to think that cyclical depressions are due to a spontaneous increase in saving and/or a spontaneous decrease in investment. The reason he gives for the 1929 crash in the passage quoted [26] could be interpreted in this way.

An increase in saving proper cannot, however, lead to anything resembling the typical pattern of crises and depressions, except in very special cases:

a. If an increase in saving (in the usual sense of the word) were causative, the boom would peter out, not end suddenly.

b. During a crisis and in the first phases of a depression, interest rates rise. Investment demand, especially for financing unsalable inventories, is high. There is no "oversaving"; rather there is "undersaving," as certain business-cycle theorists contend. Deflation is brought on not by an oversupply of investible funds, but by "liquidity preference," i.e., a curtailment of the supply of funds from the "money side." Incidentally, such a deflation will, as I tried to show in Chapter 13, hardly occur in the future because of the institutional changes of the last decade.

c. Some time after the break, a new sort of deflation develops—the so-called "self-deflation" accompanied by low interest rates. But this self-deflation is not brought about by an increase in saving in the usual sense of the word. For:

If more is saved—investment schedules remaining the same—interest rates will fall, uncovering new investment opportunities. This fall will not be hindered by the disappearance of money into hoards [27] or into central banks—provided the discount rates are not kept "unnaturally" high, which would of course represent an independent cause of deflation. Not until interest rates have reached zero (or what creditors consider a minimum rate to compensate the inconvenience and risk of lending) can deflation ensue. But a reduction to such a level is highly improbable unless something else happens to depress interest rates.

2. *Decrease in investment.*

In the well-known passage in Chapter 22 ("Notes on the Trade Cycle") Keynes attributes the depression to a breakdown of "opti-

[26] *Ibid.*, p. 100.
[27] In Chapter 13 I have tried to show that, under present conditions, demand for money to hoard is not stimulated by a reduction in interest rates.

mistic expectations as to the future yield of capital-goods sufficiently strong to offset their growing abundance and their rising
costs of production and, probably, a rise in the rate of interest
also." [28]

Here Keynes is clearly an adherent of the old oversaving underinvestment—via overinvestment—theories. For, according to these
theories, during prosperity so much capital equipment is built up
that finally all investment opportunities are exhausted, the investment curve shifts downwards and deflation and depression ensue.

Keynes, as far as I can see, added nothing to this approach, as
presented, for instance, by Spiethoff. So what neoclassic monetary
theorists, especially the Wicksellians, objected to still stands. Ac-
knowledging that shifts in the propensity to invest may occur from
time to time they considered the elasticity of money supply or the
fact that interest rates were alternately too low and too high in
comparison to the "natural" rate as the ultimate reason for fluctuations in investment and thus for inflation and deflation.[29] A downward shift of investment following a former upward shift would
in fact—under the assumption of "neutral" money—lead only to a
lower interest rate, not to deflation; for new investment opportunities would be uncovered through the "neutralizing" downward
shift of the supply schedule for investible funds.

3. *Simultaneous decrease in consumption and investment.*

Whether an autonomous decrease in investment brought about
by earlier overinvestment would have provided the sufficient or
even necessary condition to bring about depressions of the type
known until now can, however, be doubted. I personally think
that another sort of decrease in investment has been far more important in originating crises and depressions, namely, the decrease
in investment happening simultaneously and as a consequence of a
decrease in consumption.

The statement that depressions are brought about by simultane-
ous decreases in consumption and investment is quite in line with
Keynes' ideas, as expressed in another passage of his "Notes on the
Trade Cycle" (Chapter 22). Here he attributes lack of demand to

[28] Keynes, *op. cit.*, p. 315.
[29] Concerning the so-called "acceleration principle," *cf.* footnote 34, p. 164.

simultaneous declines in the propensity to consume and to invest. Not quite consistently with his general approach, he considers the breakdown of consumer demand to be *"induced"* by a breakdown in demand by investors rather than the other way around: "Unfortunately a serious fall in the marginal productivity of capital also tends to affect adversely the propensity to consume." [30] But wherever the movement starts, at a cyclical peak the propensity to consume is supposed to diminish, the propensity to save to increase.

Keynes states furthermore that "overinvestment" has two meanings:

> It may refer to investments which are destined to disappoint the expectations which prompted them or for which there is no use in conditions of severe unemployment, or it may indicate a state of affairs where every kind of capital-goods is so abundant that there is no new investment which is expected, even in conditions of full employment, to earn in the course of its life more than its replacement cost.

And he concludes: "Overinvestment" in the second sense of the word is not "a normal characteristic of the boom." [31]

People may be "overbought," but never "overinvested." It seems advisable to make this basic difference between overbuying and overinvesting quite clear.

Obviously the yield on capital can increase for two reasons:

i. The marginal utility of capital increases because of technological progress;

ii. Prices rise during the production period or—in the case of speculative investment in inventories—during the period of speculation.

Now it may be that during the upswing investment turns out to have been temporarily "accelerated" because people have been enabled by elasticity of money supply to cluster their investments in the present instead of spreading them evenly over time.[32] But, as explained above, such temporary "overinvestment" need lead subsequently only to low interest rates, not to a demand deficit, and surely not to a deficit that appears suddenly.

[30] Keynes, *op. cit.*, p. 319.
[31] *Ibid.*, p. 321.
[32] As Wicksellians would put it.

So expectations concerning the second alternative must be at work. Observation proves indeed that demand for investment has never subsided only because entrepreneurs became skeptical about the technical profitability of capital. It subsided because entrepreneurs became skeptical, too, about the demand for their products. To this extent, not a general pessimism about the yield of investments, but a very special pessimism, namely, about consumer demand, was at the root of the reluctance to invest. In any event, depression is not essentially due to too much investment. In fact, during a depression one invests in order to apply more capital to a unit of labor so as to reduce costs. Genuine *overinvestment* is not "a normal characteristic of a boom." Nor is, consequently, genuine oversaving: savings increasing from slow changes of consumption habits are always absorbed in an economy in which there is no "overinvestment."

This is sometimes denied because during a depression the prices of capital goods fall more than those of consumer goods. Likewise, stocks drop sharply under the impact of lower earnings and perhaps higher interest rates. But only the prices of capital goods frozen into a certain, hitherto optimum, combination with labor decline more than proportionately. If a factory is built to employ 10,000 workers, it obviously cannot be run at a profit if only 5,000 work. However, the prices of capital goods not already frozen in certain combinations with labor and produced currently do not decline overproportionately; and the entrepreneur who has the courage to build a plant during a depression does not have to pay any more on the average than if he bought consumer goods. Existing under-utilized equipment, in contrast, is marked down to the price at which the earnings, low because of "false combinations," are capitalized at the prevailing interest rate.

4. *Saving vs. Waiting.*

In crises and depressions consumption and derived investment decline. But is the decline in consumption really saving? We think it is not and that it should be clearly distinguished from genuine saving. The indiscriminate use of the term is at least partly responsible for the fact that Keynes and, even more, his followers attribute the end of prosperity to "saving." The decline in spending for consumption that occurs in crises and depressions should therefore be called by a special name, for instance, "waiting" (although in earlier literature "waiting" is sometimes used synonymously with saving). And the increase in spending that happens during a boom and is induced by the expectation of higher prices should be called "hurrying." That Keynes should treat "saving" and "waiting" as one and the same phenomenon, namely, as a deficient propensity to consume, is only natural. In a timeless analysis, which is not concerned with the sequence and causality of events, a reduction in consumption must appear to be of the same nature whether due to a desire to provide for the future, as in the case of genuine saving, or to hope or fear of price declines as in the case of "waiting." For while waiting, like saving, certainly reflects a declining propensity to consume, its concomitants, and consequently its causes, effects, and the remedies for it, are totally different. Before Keynes the two phenomena were clearly distinguished, and "waiting" was called "buyers' resistance" or "buyers' crisis" (the latter in German *Absatzstockung* or *Absatzkrise*) and, in line with common usage, never identified with saving. A return to this pre-Keynesian distinction seems warranted because saving and waiting differ in several ways: [33]

i. In motive. One saves out of prudence; one waits only because one hopes for or fears lower prices.

ii. In duration. Saving ends with the emergency for which one has saved; hence it may never end.

iii. In character. Waiting is a purely cyclical phenomenon. It happens at the end of a boom and during the downswing. It has its counterpart on the upswing in what may be called "hurrying." Waiting and hurrying do not happen in lieu of, but interplay with, saving and dissaving in certain phases of the cycle. At times, for instance at the height of a boom, hurrying may reduce or even overcompensate the demand-restricting power of increasing saving; at other times, for instance in a crisis, waiting may reduce or overcompensate the demand-stimulating power of declining saving.

[33] *Cf.* Chapter 8, "Is Saving a Virtue or a Sin?", p. 100.

This interplay of hurrying and saving on the one side, and waiting and dissaving on the other, could, incidentally, probably be verified statistically: waiting and hurrying would manifest themselves chiefly in fluctuations in the velocity of money; genuine saving would be reflected chiefly in an increase of savings accounts and certain securities.

iv. In the policies they may require. Waiting may have to be discouraged as harmful; saving may have to be encouraged as beneficial. This, by the way, would have been the attitude of neo-classical theorists. The modern attitude, in contrast, seems to be inimical to both, for it advocates a redistribution of income that tends to discourage not only waiting but also genuine saving.[34]

There remains of course the question why the consumption curve suddenly shifts downwards. It is the duty of business-cycle theorists to show the causes of the shift. After a lifetime of practical experience I personally, although not denying the importance of an autonomous decline in investment from which the movement may start, am inclined to attribute great importance to the simple fact of overbuying or overspeculation in the widest sense: during a boom people expect ever higher prices. But as at a certain moment there are no new layers of buyers on whom speculators can unload, prices stop rising. Now the speculators try to sell, but as the suddenly increased supply of goods is too large for normal demand, prices fall. Soon everyone postpones even normal purchases. Prices decline further, leading people to expect still lower prices. These facts were described over and over again by business-cycle theorists in the nineteenth century in order to explain depressions and crises. On them in this century A. C. Pigou built his famous theory of *Industrial Fluctuations*.[35]

[34] The interplay of "waiting" and "saving" during the German inflation was examined in "Zur Frage des sogenannten Vertrauens in die Währung," *Archiv für Sozialwissenschaft und Sozialpolitik*, Band 52 (1924), pp. 289 ff.

[35] The inadequacy of the Keynesian short-run equilibrium theory to explain business cycles has been at least implicitly acknowledged by those of his followers who have tried to "dynamize" his system—e.g., Harrod, Samuelson, Kalecki, Smithies, and Metzler. In building up such macrodynamic models, the liquidity preference concept has not played any role, but the consumption function has been retained and a number of additional assumptions have been introduced. These cannot be discussed here in detail. As far as I can see,

If our "waiting theory of depression" is correct, the following conclusions are warranted:

i. One should not worry about overinvestment—i.e., lack of opportunities for investment in crises or depressions. Entrepreneurs hesitate to produce because they fear losses no matter whether they produce in a more or a less "capitalistic" way. Such losses could be incurred in an economy that uses little capital as well as in a highly capitalistic economy. Cyclical depressions therefore cannot be attributed to an investment gap despite the somewhat confusing fact that interest rates drop sharply in the later phases of a depression. They fall not because of oversaving and underinvestment, but because people "wait" simultaneously to consume and to invest. The money they do not spend accumulates in the banks. The banks in turn lend on the money market, giving it the appearance of extreme easiness.

ii. The statement that "the remedy for a boom is not a higher rate of interest but a lower rate of interest" [36] cannot be correct. Investment declines not because interest rates are high in view of the marginal productivity of capital, but because people no longer expect higher prices. To reduce interest rates would therefore be entirely inappropriate. Low interest rates, far from opening new investment opportunities in a technical sense, would merely encourage the use of credit for speculation on higher prices. They would only prolong the boom and prepare the way for an even more severe decline.

iii. Keynesians who hold saving to be a vice and spending a virtue oversimplify the problems involved. While a sudden increase in genuine saving during a depression might accentuate the noxious effects of waiting, a thrifty economy is superior to a spendthrift economy because it assures a higher living standard, provided that in the long run there are no impediments to the flow of savings into investment. And while in a depression the income of lower brackets is obviously spent more freely than that of higher, wage increases, as advocated for instance by unions, remain the worst method of

none of these models can explain the *sudden* break characteristic of a crisis. They could at best explain a slow structural decline.

[36] Keynes, *op. cit.*, p. 322.

supporting demand. For whereas demand can be supported by many other means, wage increases unavoidably raise costs, thus leading to structural unemployment.

LONG-RUN EQUILIBRIUM

Keynes believes in the possibility of an investment gap also in the long run. This is evident from the passages already quoted [37] and from his remarks about the responsibility of the state "for directly organizing investment" in the future.[38] These remarks laid the foundation for the theory of the maturity and stagnation of our economy and of the inevitability of state capitalism.

The assumptions underlying Keynes' statements have not been verified statistically; indeed, considerable evidence of their incorrectness seems to be accumulating.

1. How large have savings averaged over a long period?

The great significance many writers attribute to the long-run effects of saving induces the feeling that they have somewhat lost their sense of proportion. One gets the impression that people work only in order to accumulate wealth. In reality investment—additions to capital stock—plays in the long run a rather small role in keeping an economy going. According to Simon Kuznets, only 6 to 7 per cent of national income went to net capital formation in 1919-1938.[39] Obviously it is much easier to find new investment opportunities for such a small percentage than for higher percentage of national income.

There also seems to be no proof that in the long run the saving-income ratio rises with income. This ratio has been constant as far as the secular trend, not the cycle, is concerned.[40] What may be correct for the case of an individual moving into a higher bracket seems to be quite wrong in—and should not be confounded with—the case of a whole community getting richer over time.

[37] *Ibid.*, pp. 97 and 109.
[38] *Ibid.*, p. 164.
[39] *National Income: A Summary of Findings* (National Bureau of Economic Research, 1946), p. 18.
[40] Arthur F. Burns, *Stepping Stones Towards the Future* (National Bureau of Economic Research, 27th Annual Report, 1947), p. 13.

Nevertheless, the absolute amount of saving undoubtedly increases when real income increases, as it has always done in the long run. Furthermore, with the simple passage of time capital accumulates even though the net increment to savings and investments during any one period may be very small.

2. Has there been a tendency toward an investment gap in the long run?

If saving and investment tend to get out of balance, deflation must ensue. No proof can be found that on the average the secular trend has been toward deflation. At some times, the propensity to invest has been stronger than the propensity to save; at other times, weaker. But the trend has always been toward a relative strengthening of the propensity to invest and toward inflation.

Keynes attributes the alleged trend toward deflation partly to hoarding. But, as has been shown frequently, and recently by me,[41] "liquidity preference" cannot curtail the supply of loanable funds in the long run.

Keynes offers an additional argument for the statement that "to fill the gap between net income and consumption, presents a problem which is increasingly difficult." [42] One might call it the "capital disinvestment" argument. Its premises are that consumption is "satisfied partly by objects produced currently and partly by objects produced previously, i.e., by disinvestment." [42] "Now all capital investment is destined to result, sooner or later, in capital disinvestment." [43] Therefore "new capital investment can only take place in excess of current capital disinvestment if *future* expenditure on consumption is expected to increase." [43] In this connection Keynes recalls *The Fable of the Bees:* "The gay of tomorrow are absolutely indispensable to provide a *raison d'être* for the grave of today." [44] The conclusion is correct but the premises are untenable. There is no reason why in the long run and in the aggregate, capital should ever be disinvested. As a matter of fact, economic progress has been achieved mainly by successive additions to capital stock. Only

---

[41] See Chapter 13.
[42] Keynes, p. 105.
[43] *Ibid.*
[44] *Ibid.*, p. 106.

during severe depressions, if at all, has disinvestment taken place. So the picture of an economy suffocating in its own fat because capital goods, transformed into consumer goods, constantly press on the markets for the latter, is based upon a factual error. The sole problem is to provide demand for consumer goods coming from current production, not from disinvestment. Whether the increased productivity resulting from capital accumulation leads to an over supply of goods is of course another problem. But in the long run it is not a problem at all because living standards tend to keep up with productivity.

The *long-run* investment argument has been presented by economists during history every time a *cyclical* depression lasted longer than was expected. It might well be that we shall not hear about it for quite a long time.

3. A long-term analysis with long-term assumptions.

The chief objections to Keynes' "Chronic underinvestment" theory is, however, that it is a long-run analysis based upon short-run assumptions—a fault arising from his endeavor to construct a "combination theory."

In the last analysis, underinvestment could threaten in the long run only if the demand price for capital fell to zero or to a point below which creditors were willing to lend. According to the "stagnation" school, this is supposed to happen because the saturation of the economy with capital exhausts investment opportunities and causes the investment curve to shift downward as time goes on.

Now suppose there were really a lack of opportunities. Could and would it inevitably cause an interruption in the flow of savings into investments? To assume this would assume that the productivity of capital is a fixed schedule, depending only upon the quantity of capital; in reality it is a function, too, of the amount of labor supplied at various wage rates. The newly employed labor—becoming profitable through reductions in wages, provided demand for labor is not too inelastic—will need new capital equipment. And this resulting increase in the demand for capital will be greater than the reduction in the demand for capital by enterprises with a strong

capital structure. As Keynes mentions as a possibility, a reduction
of money wages "will increase the marginal efficiency of capital"
and "the change will be favourable to investment." [45]

So the insufficient marginal productivity of capital can threaten a
secular investment gap under two assumptions only:

i. that wages are fixed;

ii. that unutilized capital equipment is so ample that demand for
capital would not be stimulated by lower wages.

These two assumptions are indeed introduced by Keynes in his
short-term analysis, where they might be tenable and realistic under
certain conditions. In long-term analysis, into which they are taken
over indiscriminately, they seem entirely out of place.

Obviously, stable wages cannot be presupposed outside cycle
analysis, at least under conditions of perfect competition. If the
labor market is competitive, unemployment tends to reduce wages.
Only labor monopolies could keep wages—and unemployment—
high.

Equally, demand for capital cannot be considered fixed, because
higher employment necessitates more capital equipment unless one
can rely on unused capacity. When an economy emerges from
depression, one can indeed rely on such unused capacity. But in
the long run there cannot be anything like unused capacity. Labor
and capital must be assumed to be combined in the optimal way
so that every increase in employment entails an addition to capital
equipment.

Hence one can never speak of an absolute absence of investment
opportunities as long as there is *voluntary* unemployment, unless
the demand for new capital in case of increased employment is
extremely inelastic. Outside of this very special and improbable
case, underinvestment—nonabsorption of savings—need never occur.
If there is nevertheless unemployment, it is not because demand
for capital is too low but because labor is too costly. It is caused
by a strike, so to speak, of labor, not of investors.

This, by the way, is quite in line with the Keynesian idea that a
slackening of population growth reduces the demand for capital.

[45] *Ibid.*, p. 263.

Obviously the effect must be the same whether the supply of labor is restricted by a decline in population or by the unwillingness of some to work at wage rates that would insure full employment.

4. The remaining case.

In one case, however, the nonabsorption of potential savings is at least theoretically possible: if everyone is employed at the beginning of a production period, a reduction in wages cannot lead to the absorption of either more workers or more capital. Therefore a very low demand for investment could produce deflation and unemployment.

But does this mean that a lack of investment opportunities can explain chronic depression and unemployment? Unemployment can be of two kinds. If it is brought about by low demand for products and deflation ensues, it is involuntary unemployment in Keynes' sense. If it is brought about by the high cost of labor, it is voluntary. Only the first kind can in any way be connected with an "investment gap." But there is no *a priori* presumption that this kind is present in cases of chronic depression. Unemployment is not synonymous with underinvestment, and not every unemployment can be charged to lack of investment, as so many do nowadays.

But even the "involuntary" unemployment brought about by deflation cannot explain a protracted *stagnation*. For involuntary unemployment is essentially short-run; it cannot last forever. If the quantity of money decreases by reason of deflation, wages must adjust themselves to the new, reduced quantity of money, just as they adjust themselves to inflation.

So while immediately after deflationary pressure has started, unemployment can be considered to be due to deflation, after a certain time the responsibility shifts. Long-run unemployment must be considered to be due to high wages. Nor could it be argued that a *new* investment gap would threaten if wages were reduced. For, as we have shown above, the employment of the former unemployed does not lead to such a gap. Nor in the long run would a reduction in wages provoke fear of a renewed deflation, as Keynes seems to think; [46] not even if all entrepreneurs were Keynesians. In non-Keynesians a reduction of wages inspires hope for higher prices through higher investment, anyway.

Of course if saving (*ex ante*) exceeded investment not once but in consecutive production periods, wages would never get adjusted. Wage declines would always lag behind deflation, causing genuine involuntary unemployment. But this would be a *dynamic* process with all the characteristics of a *cyclical depression,* not stagnation, which the investment gap is supposed to explain. Cyclical depression can, however, be explained much more realistically by the "waiting" approach. *Static* or *stabilized* unemployment is never a "low demand" unemployment, caused by entrepreneurs' fear that "the proceeds realized from the increased output will disappoint" them because the "proceeds will necessarily fall short of their supply price." [47] It is always high-cost unemployment.

Confused by Keynes' timeless and isolated analysis, many economists do not recognize sufficiently the essential difference between the two kinds of unemployment. Businessmen, on the contrary, know very well whether they are curtailing production because demand is low or because costs are rising. Curtailment for the former reason can lead to progressive deflation and involuntary unemployment. Curtailment of production when prices do not decline but remain at a low level for a long time—in other words, when there is a true long-term equilibrium—has nothing whatever to do with low demand. In this case there is only one reason for low employment as well as low investment: a wage level that is too high.

This statement, which is identical with the classical employment theory, must be qualified in only one respect. Wages can seem too high not only absolutely but also in relation to the general conditions under which production is carried on. Insecurity concerning continuity of production—a threat of strikes, for instance—can be as serious a deterrent to employment as exaggerated wage demands. What is of theoretical importance is that such facts are not, in the last analysis, impediments to investment. They menace profits not

[46] *Ibid.,* p. 263.
[47] *Ibid.,* p. 261.

on the use of more units of capital per unit of labor, but on the use of more units of labor per unit of capital.

There is no theoretical justification for discouraging saving and encouraging spending—as distinct from cyclical "hurrying" and waiting. Keynes is wrong in denying that "a decrease in spending will tend to lower the rate of interest" and increase investment.[48] He is also wrong in assuming that spending determines "the aggregate volume of employment." [49] And it is theoretically confusing and must lead to disastrous practical consequences if "a decreased readiness to spend" is regarded "as a factor which will, *ceteris paribus,* diminish employment" rather than "a factor which will, *ceteris paribus,* increase investment." [49]

In the general case—outside cyclical disturbances—Say's law is valid. Money is always spent on either consumption or investment. Therefore national income does not depend on "marginal productivity of capital, the propensity to consume, liquidity preference, and the amount of money," as Keynesians believe. In fact, I think that such a statement will appear very awkward in a not too distant future. Especially the idea that the amount of money determines national income may again be considered what it really is: a serious relapse to preclassical economies and a rationalization of inflationary policies.

National income, identical with production, depends—as common sense suggests—on the amount of labor it pays to employ. This fundamental fact should be the basis of every modern employment theory as it was the basis of the classical theory. The proposition that in general the flow of money is interrupted by saving and the economy more or less permanently threatened by deflation can only lead to paradoxical conclusions.

[48] *Ibid.,* p. 185.
[49] *Ibid.*

16. Continental European Pre-Keynesianism

In contrast to most of his followers, Keynes was well aware that his ideas were not entirely original. Every age has brought forth a crop of books on "easy money," having in common the thesis that economic disturbances, especially unemployment, are caused largely by monetary maladjustments and can be corrected by monetary measures. Keynes himself points out in his *General Theory* the merits of the Mercantilists.

When a young man I read with great interest a book called *The Gold Craze*,[1] written by an American living in Germany, which anticipated the arguments in favor of a domestic easy-money policy and of external devaluation. It was considered the product of a crank and went more or less unnoticed by economists.

Another precursor of Keynes was the "unduly neglected prophet, Silvio Gesell,"[2] the proponent of *Schwundgeld* (vanishing money). Gesell's book, *Die Verstaatlichung des Geldes* (1891), was well known in continental Europe, especially in Switzerland. But despite wide propaganda by clubs formed to spread his theories, it was not taken seriously either. The proposition that depressions could be postponed indefinitely by keeping money rolling through fear of its depreciation rather than by correcting maladjustments seemed too absurd.

Keynes could have discovered an even closer spiritual relative in his contemporary, Gottfried Feder, who promised full employment

[1] W. Lincoln Hausmann, *Der Goldwahn,* Berlin, 1905.
[2] Keynes, *General Theory,* p. 353.

213

through *Breaking the Slavery of Interest.*[3] The Nazis, before they came to power, used his theories in their campaign against democracy and the free enterprise system, but afterwards threw him out of his high office, recognizing that, if put into practice, his theories would immediately ruin the Reich's currency and credit.

Furthermore, my own *Volkswirtschaftliche Theorie des Bankkredits,* containing essential parts of Keynes' ideas, appeared as long ago as 1920. Influenced by it, a whole crop of easy-money books sprouted on the Continent. However, the counterarguments advanced during the next decade [4] were so convincing that in my third edition I modified my theory in essential respects.

As I think it rather important to show that the arguments against my theory apply also to Keynes', I have tried to demonstrate that the basic ideas of my *Volkswirtschaftliche Theorie des Bankkredits* were in substance, if not in form, very similar to those of his *General Theory.* To this end I have summarized what I consider essential and common to the two theories, supplementing each statement by quotations of some characteristic passages from the two books. Many other passages that show similarities can, incidentally, be found in the two books.

The Consumption Deficit

1. Employment and production are dependent upon demand, but demand is not automatically created by production or employment. A consumption deficit threatens when employment increases, because part of the larger income is saved (Keynes' "psychological law").

Hahn, p. 148:

"The smaller consumption has its origin in the psychological attitude of the member of the economy: a worker, an industrialist, a business man is not inclined to spend more just because he earns more. The conservatism inherent in all his social activities, and above all, in his living standard, keeps his consumption constant within certain limits. A man does not consume more simply because he produces more. He does not,

---

[3] *Das Manifest zur Brechung der Zinsknecktschaft des Geldes,* 1932.
[4] This literature was reviewed in the preface to the third edition, 1930.

to be sure, forego remuneration for his activity but he demands it in another form, namely, in the form of means for future spending. The desire for consumer goods to raise the current living standard is replaced by the desire for means of hoarding and saving to ensure the future living standard. As soon as their wants are covered to a certain extent, people begin to feel, so to speak, mercantilistic rather than physiocratic."

Keynes, p. 97:

"But, apart from short-period *changes* in the level of income, it is also obvious that a higher absolute level of income will tend, as a rule, to widen the gap between income and consumption. For the satisfaction of the immediate primary needs of a man and his family is usually a stronger motive than the motives towards accumulation, which only acquire effective sway when a margin of comfort has been attained. These reasons will lead, as a rule, to a greater *proportion* of income being saved as real income increases. But whether or not a greater proportion is saved, we take it as a fundamental psychological rule of any modern community that, when its real income is increased, it will not increase its consumption by an equal *absolute* amount, so that a greater absolute amount must be saved, unless a large and unusual change is occurring at the same time in other factors."

p. 98:

"This simple principle leads, it will be seen, to the same conclusion as before, namely, that employment can only increase *pari passu* with an increase in investment; unless, indeed, there is a change in the propensity to consume."

2. An increase in income leads to an absolute increase not only in saving but also in the proportion of the income saved, i.e., in the saving-income ratio (Keynes' "psychological law" in its stronger form [5]).

Hahn, pp. 153-54:

"Credit expansion accelerates as well as increases the building up of savings accounts. . . . Credit expansion not only builds bigger savings accounts but builds them faster."

Keynes, p. 127:

". . . the marginal propensity to consume falls off steadily as we approach full employment."

[5] See Chapter 15, "The Investment Gap."

THE INVESTMENT GAP

1. The consumption deficit can be harmful because the purchasing power withdrawn by saving does not necessarily come into the hands of entrepreneurs seeking funds to invest.

Hahn, p. 147:

"The argument that every production leads automatically to a corresponding consumption appears incorrect if the producers of consumer goods save their purchasing power and if the resulting purchasing power deficit is not always automatically made up by the granting of new credits by banks.

"If, concerning the reasons for depressions and crises, we return to Malthus' ideas, we see that the stagnation on the market for goods that occurs in the course of the boom phase of a business cycle is due to the fact that the purchasing power of working individuals, which normally comes back to the entrepreneur in the form of demand, no longer finds its way back to him. Checking accounts are transformed into savings accounts, are 'consolidated,' and no longer cause demand on the markets for goods."

Keynes, p. 165:

"But the notion that the rate of interest is the balancing factor which brings the demand for saving in the shape of new investment forthcoming at a given rate of interest into equality with the supply of saving which results at that rate of interest from the community's psychological propensity to save, breaks down as soon as we perceive that it is impossible to deduce the rate of interest merely from a knowledge of these two factors."

2. Certain preclassicists, especially Malthus, deserve praise because they saw much better than Ricardo and other classicists that savings can interrupt the flow of demand.

Hahn, p. 147, note 138:

"It is astonishing how clearly Malthus recognized these interrelations. His opponents argued that every saving automatically increases the demand for producer goods: against them Malthus asserted that their chief error lay in the assumption that accumulation automatically creates demand (*Principles of Political Economy*, Ch. 7, 3d par.). The same holds true today for those who, with the prevailing opinion, assume an absolute dependence of investment on saving."

Keynes, p. 362:

". . . in the later phase of Malthus the notion of the insufficiency of effective demand takes a definite place as a scientific explanation of unemployment."

p. 364:

". . . Ricardo, however, was stone-deaf to what Malthus was saying."

INTEREST AND LIQUIDITY

1. Savings are not automatically absorbed by investments because money is essential also as a means of liquidity. Interest must therefore be considered as the price for acquiring and the compensation for parting with liquidity. As lending money entails risks, interest can also be considered as a compensation for taking risks.

In discussing interest and liquidity, Keynes' argument is phrased almost exactly like mine, except that he attributes the supply of credit to the liquidity preference of individuals, whereas I attribute it to the liquidity preference of banks, for the simple reason that banks are the marginal lenders in an economy.

Hahn, p. 102:

"If the amount of the credit advanced by banks is dependent on their individual liquidity, interest, i.e., the price that has to be paid for the credit, is merely the reward for the loss of liquidity caused by the granting of the credit. From the viewpoint of the bank, interest is the reward for running the risk."

Keynes, pp. 166-67:

"It should be obvious that the rate of interest cannot be a return to saving or waiting as such. For if a man hoards his savings in cash, he earns no interest, though he saves just as much as before. On the contrary, the mere definition of the rate of interest tells us in so many words that the rate of interest is the reward for parting with liquidity for a specified period. For the rate of interest is, in itself, nothing more than the inverse proportion between a sum of money and what can be obtained for parting with control over the money in exchange for a debt for a stated period of time."

p. 182:

"The mistake originates from regarding interest as the reward for waiting as such, instead of as the reward for not-hoarding; just as the rates of return on loans or investments involving different degrees of risk, are quite properly regarded as the reward, not of waiting as such, but of running the risk. There is, in truth, no sharp line between these and the so called 'pure' rate of interest, all of them being the reward for running the risk of uncertainty of one kind or another. Only in the event of money being used solely for transactions and never as a store of value, would a different theory become appropriate."

2. Liquidity requirements are a highly subjective matter, depending upon confidence and speculation.

Hahn, pp. 59-60:

". . . the means of banks are determined by the latter's liquidity. The creation of claims against a bank leads in fact only to the one important consequence that its balance sheet is lengthened and its liquidity impaired.

"However, the actual state of liquidity or non-liquidity is merely a center around which the considerations of the individual bank manager oscillate. For opinions about liquidity are in highest degree subjective. With more or less strong confidence in the future, a higher or lower degree of liquidity will be deemed adequate. The supply of credit offered by banks, which, as shown above, constitutes fundamentally a supply of confidence, depends upon the strength of the prevailing confidence."

Keynes, pp. 196-97:

"In normal circumstances the amount of money required to satisfy the transactions-motive and the precautionary-motive is mainly a resultant of the general activity of the economic system and of the level of money-income. But it is by playing on the speculative-motive that monetary management (or, in the absence of management, chance changes in the quantity of money) is brought to bear on the economic system."

p. 148:

"The state of long-term expectation, upon which our decisions are based, does not solely depend, therefore, on the most probable forecast we can make. It also depends on the *confidence* with which we make this forecast—on how highly we rate the likelihood of our best forecast turning out quite wrong."

3. Interest rates are in large degree determined conventionally.

Hahn, p. 104:

"The owners of checking and deposit accounts owe their income to historical chance rather than economic necessity. Unlike every other payment in economic life, payment of interest does not serve to stimulate supply. For the owners of checking and deposit accounts would—as the example of England teaches—leave their funds, which they need as a means of payment, in banks even if interest were not paid."

Keynes, p. 203:

"It might be more accurate, perhaps, to say that the rate of interest is a highly conventional, rather than a highly psychological phenomenon."

4. The liquidity of even long-term investments can be improved by creating what I have called "indirect liquidity."

Hahn, pp. 94, 95, 96:

". . . a special technique of credit granting was gradually developed with the aim of lessening the dangers of the illiquidity inherent in investments. It makes investments, so to speak, artificially liquid by granting them what we would like to call an 'indirect liquidity.' . . . The illiquidity of the investment disappears as soon as the assets of the bank need no longer be turned into cash by withdrawal but can be liquidated by sale.

"The chief example of such an indirectly liquid investment is the ordinary commercial bill. . . . Other examples are all transactions that lead to the creation of stocks and bonds."

Keynes, pp. 150-51:

"Decisions to invest in private business of the old-fashioned type were, however, decisions largely irrevocable, not only for the community as a whole, but also for the individual. With the separation between ownership and management which prevails today and with the development of organized investment markets, a new factor of great importance has entered in, which sometimes facilitates investment but sometimes adds greatly to the instability of the system."

p. 153:

"Investments which are 'fixed' for the community are thus made 'liquid' for the individual."

INTEREST AND EMPLOYMENT

1. If lack of investment—caused by interest rates too high to guarantee that investments will absorb savings—makes for a deficiency of effective demand, and thereby unemployment, a reduction in interest rates must bring about employment. This is

contrary to the classicists' view; they thought that a reduction in interest rates leads at best to inflation.

Hahn, p. 132:

"Reducing interest rates . . . causes, as will be shown, also increase of production. Thus the argument of the quantity theorists must be wrong; namely, that the lower interest rates achieved by increasing the quantity of money could never raise industrial employment, because more goods could not be bought as prices would be higher."

Keynes, p. 292:

"If we reflect on what we are being taught and try to rationalise it, in the simpler discussions it seems that the elasticity of supply must have become zero and demand proportional to the quantity of money."

Hahn, pp. 140-41:

". . . the opinion of the quantity theorists, shared by nearly all interest, credit, and capital theorists, that money and credit expansion do not increase production, is not only inexact but entirely wrong. By altering distribution, every expansion of credit increases the quantity of goods. Credit creates goods out of the nothingness in which they would have remained unproduced."

p. 149, note 142:

"Herein lies a further reason why the quantity theory is to be considered merely a quite rough solution of the problem of the relation between the quantity of money and the prices of goods, and why the banking theory, which assumed the automatic elimination of additional and superfluous money, contained a correct kernel. . . . It shows too the validity of the assumption that the level of incomes determines the level of prices. It would be much more correct to say that the level of expenditures is the determinant."

Keynes, p. 375:

". . . the extent of effective saving is necessarily determined by the scale of investment and . . . the scale of investment is promoted by a *low* rate of interest, provided that we do not attempt to stimulate it in this way beyond the point which corresponds to full employment. Thus it is to our best advantage to reduce the rate of interest to that point relatively to the schedule of the marginal efficiency of capital at which there is full employment."

2. The reason a reduction in interest rates must bring about employment is that it alters the distribution of income in favor of

entrepreneurs, enabling them to use additional labor profitably despite its diminishing marginal productivity. The change in the income distribution takes place at the cost of the rentier class.

According to Keynes, the worker too bears a part of the cost, because he can buy less with his wages when prices rise following the credit expansion that takes place after interest rates are reduced. This argument is, to my mind, unrealistic.

Hahn, p. 137:

"As shown above, the expansion of credit has the consequence that through competition of enterprises, expanded in the wake of interest reductions, wages begin to rise. . . .

"To those who have been unwilling to work . . . the value of the wage now appears higher than the value of leisure. They change from 'marginal non-workers' to 'marginal workers' because the fundamental facts of their valuations have changed. The remuneration offered for work has become greater. And this is really the case and does not depend merely upon a kind of self-deception on the part of the worker due to the nominal increase in wages. To be sure, the increase in labor's earnings causes the prices of consumer goods to rise because of the larger demand. Nevertheless, the increase in wages is not only nominal but real; for the prices of goods always tend, because of the competition of entrepreneurs, to equal the costs. But as the latter have risen to compensate only for the additional outlays for wages, not for capital, the prices of goods have risen only to this degree, that is, less than wages. There thus remains a real increase in the remuneration paid labor which appears the more important for economic calculation the more one considers that compensation of other participants, although nominally still the same, has been devaluated through the rise in the prices of goods."

Keynes, p. 290:

"Since that part of his profit which the entrepreneur has to hand on to the rentier is fixed in terms of money, rising prices, even though unaccompanied by any change in output, will re-distribute incomes to the advantage of the entrepreneur and to the disadvantage of the rentier. . . ."

p. 8:

". . . The supply of labor is not a function of real wages."

p. 284:

". . . if the classical assumption does not hold good, it will be possible to increase employment by increasing expenditure in terms of money until real wages have fallen to equality with the marginal disutility of labor, at which point there will, by definition, be full employment."

3. The limit to increasing employment by reducing interest rates is reached when the labor supply cannot be augmented by further wage increases.

Hahn, p. 145:

"Credit expansion as a means of raising production and consumption, and thereby the well-being of the nation, is effective . . . up to the point where new credit is no longer able to induce new labor forces to enter production, when through wage increases the last reserves have been tapped."

Keynes, p. 289:

"Consequently, as effective demand increases, employment increases, though at a real wage equal to or less than the existing one, until a point comes at which there is no surplus of labour available at the then existing real wage; *i.e.* no more men (or hours of labour) available unless money-wages rise (from this point onwards) *faster* than prices. The next problem is to consider what will happen if, when this point has been reached, expenditure still continues to increase.

"Up to this point the decreasing return from applying more labour to a given capital equipment has been offset by the acquiescence of labour in a diminishing real wage. But after this point a unit of labour would require the inducement of the equivalent of an increased quantity of product, whereas the yield from applying a further unit would be a diminished quantity of product."

4. The net effect of an increase in effective demand following an expansion of credit is in general twofold: on prices, on the one hand; on production, on the other. For the unutilized reserves of workers give elasticity to modern economy.

Hahn, pp. 135-36:

". . . in the modern economy . . . the increase in the demand for goods and labor on the part of enterprises whose purchasing power has been augmented by an expansion in credit leads to a rise not only in prices but also in production, to prosperity. . . . One reason is the enormous progress in the techniques of production, especially in the greater use of machines. . . . The other reason is that the modern economy, as a result of this progress in techniques, possesses—in the persons of rentiers, women, and workers willing to work overtime—a tremendous reserve of unoccupied, half occupied, and workers who can be induced to work harder. From this labor reserve the relatively small amount of labor necessary to step up production can easily be won. The two factors together cause the phenomenon that can best be called the 'elasticity' of the modern economy."

Keynes, p. 285:

"Effective demand spends itself, partly in affecting output and partly in affecting price, according to this law."

p. 296:

". . . and the increase in effective demand will, generally speaking, spend itself partly in increasing the quantity of employment and partly in raising the level of prices. Thus instead of constant prices in conditions of unemployment, and of prices rising in proportion to the quantity of money in conditions of full employment, we have in fact a condition of prices rising gradually as employment increases."

GENERAL RECOMMENDATIONS TO COMBAT UNEMPLOYMENT

1. Technological progress tends to reduce prices directly or through the pressure it exerts on wages through labor-saving machinery. To counteract these undesirable by-effects of technological progress, credit expansion is recommended.

Hahn, pp. 139-40:

"In the modern economy, as far as credit is not expanded, a certain number of workers are thrown out of work each year because labor-saving methods of production are constantly being adopted. Furthermore, the urban population is still growing today in modern industrial countries. As the possibilities for work, as such, do not grow as fast as the population, a certain part of the addition to the population becomes unemployed. The excess supply of labor thus created tends to press on wages and thereby also on the prices of goods until, on the one hand, the supply of labor contracts through the elimination of those for whom the lower wages no longer seem an equivalent for leisure; in other words, until 'marginal workers' become 'marginal non-workers.' . . . Here credit expansion steps in as a corrective and an eminently social factor. It increases the demand for labor, thereby preventing the decline of wages and the prices of goods, and putting to work new strata of workers who, with static credit, would have to remain outside the production process. It thus prevents the raising of the capitalist's share that would otherwise follow from falling prices."

Keynes, p. 271:

"In the long period, on the other hand, we are still left with the choice between a policy of allowing prices to fall slowly with the progress of technique and equipment whilst keeping wages stable, or of allowing wages to rise slowly whilst keeping prices stable. On the whole my preference is for the latter alternative, on account of the fact that it is easier with an expectation of higher wages in future to keep the actual level of employment within a given range of full employment than with an expectation of lower wages in future, and on account also of the social advantages of gradually diminishing the burden of debt, the greater ease of adjustment from decaying to growing industries, and the psychological encouragement likely to be felt from a moderate tendency for money-wages to increase."

2. Employment can be increased either by lowering wages or by expanding credit. In the general case the latter is to be preferred. My statement was, however, much more cautious than Keynes'.

Hahn, p. 141:

"Every expansion of credit increases the quantity of goods. But whether for this reason an expansion of credit is always a boon for a country is not decided thereby. Moreover, whether expropriation of money owners and rentiers is not too high a price for a larger total output can be decided only from certain non-economic viewpoints. The problem, seemingly theoretical, is in reality political."

Keynes, p. 268:

"Having regard to human nature and our institutions, it can only be a foolish person who would prefer a flexible wage policy to a flexible money policy, unless he can point to advantages from the former which are not obtainable from the latter."

RECOMMENDATIONS TO COMBAT CYCLICAL DEPRESSIONS: AN EASY-MONEY POLICY AND GOVERNMENT SPENDING

1. As booms end when demand becomes deficient, new demand must be created. This can be done by making new investments profitable by lowering interest rates, i.e., through an easy-money policy.

Interest rates should be reduced at the top of the boom instead of raised in the traditional way long before the peak; by such a method the boom can be protracted indefinitely.

This is the statement I regret most and the one that aroused most opposition when my book was published.

Hahn, p. 150:

"Since production is hindered by the stagnation of consumption . . . is it possible to induce the entrepreneur to continue production even when he cannot sell goods, so that he produces for stock rather than for consumption?

"Such possibilities exist, at least in theory. One possibility is to grant larger and, above all, cheaper credit, the moment consumption begins to stagnate, so that entrepreneurs will be spurred to continue producing."

Keynes, p. 164:

". . . we are still entitled to return to the latter [i.e., the interest rate] as exercising, at any rate, in normal circumstances, a great, though not a decisive, influence on the rate of investment. Only experience, however, can show how far management of the rate of interest is capable of continuously stimulating the appropriate volume of investment."

p. 322:

"Thus the remedy for the boom is not a higher rate of interest but a lower rate of interest! For that may enable the so-called boom to last. The right remedy for the trade cycle is not to be found in abolishing booms and thus keeping us permanently in a semi-slump; but in abolishing slumps and thus keeping us permanently in a quasi-boom."

2. If, despite lower interest rates, demand is not created, the government must and can replace private demand by public spending.

Hahn, p. 151:

"The other way to continue production in an economy and have its results stored, despite lack of consumption, is to have the results of production that are ready for consumption taken over by a large scale buyer. This way, however, is open only if the buyer, who would of course need immense amounts of credit, enjoys the privilege of not having to pay interest. Otherwise he would be unable to 'hold' the goods.

"Such a privileged debtor exists in every economy in the person of the government. For although the state has to pay interest on its loans, it can transfer the burden to the taxpayer, so that it practically enjoys credit without charge; and, in any case, does not have to calculate the interest burden as a cost in the way an 'economic' subject must."

Hahn, p. 136, note 125:

"Had houses, means of transportation, and labor-saving machinery been built, with the same methods of financing, instead of war materials, the golden age would have dawned through the ensuing abundant satisfaction of every demand."

Keynes, p. 164:

"I expect to see the State, which is in a position to calculate the marginal efficiency of capital-goods on long views and on the basis of the general social advantage, taking an ever greater responsibility for directly organising investment; since it seems likely that the fluctuations in the market estimation of the marginal efficiency of different types of capital, calculated on the principles I have described above, will be too great to be offset by any practicable changes in the rate of interest."

RECEPTION AND INFLUENCE OF MY BOOK IN CONTINENTAL EUROPE

The reader may not feel that Keynes' and my theories coincide as closely as I feel they do. To me, the similarities evident in the above quotations are amazing, especially in view of the fact that my book was written sixteen years before Keynes', in another tongue, in another economic environment, and before the demand-supply-curve language was as entrenched as it is today. One is struck by the similarity of the gist of the two books. Consider, for example, that the *leitmotif* of Keynesianism—that it is better to produce nonsense than nothing—which led him to praise pyramid-building,[6] can be found in my book where it is expressed as follows: "The time that passes without production and is thus unused can never be recouped," and "The saying 'time is money' is applicable also to the wealth of nations." [7]

Incidentally I have never been able to understand why Keynes did not quote my work in his *General Theory* although there is no doubt he knew it, for he quotes me in the German translation of his *Treatise on Money* [8] when he refers to the approach of German scholars to the savings-investment problem.

As mentioned above, my theories were widely discussed in business and academic circles. A second edition of my *Volkswirt-*

[6] Keynes, *op. cit.*, p. 131.
[7] Hahn, *Volkswirtschaftliche Theorie des Bankkredits*, p. 148.
[8] Munich and Leipzig, 1932, p. 140, note 2.

schaftliche Theorie des Bankkredits had to be published in 1924, and a third in 1930. As in the case of Keynes' *General Theory,* opinions about my book went to extremes of approval and disapproval. Some critics, especially older men, dubbed it the height of scientific nonsense, cynicism, and carelessness; in short, just a bluff. The great economist and statistician Bortkiewicz, for example, was very hostile. Others, especially younger students, looked upon it as an entirely new discovery of immense theoretical and economic-political importance. To my followers—for instance to Hans Honegger, author of *Der schöpferische Kredit,* 1929—there seemed no limit to what credit and monetary expansion could achieve. When their publications came to my notice, I wrote, paraphrasing the exclamation from Schiller's *Wallenstein* that I quoted in an early chapter of this book: "God defend me from my friends; from my enemies, I can defend myself!" Compared with what some of Keynes' followers in this country advocate, however, these recommendations seem highly conservative and orthodox.

I am now of the opinion that my ideas, as expressed in the first and second editions of my book—and consequently also the corresponding ideas of Keynes—are bad economic theory, leading to fatal economic policy, mainly for the reasons developed in the preceding chapters in this book. To a certain degree I had already taken them into account in my third edition.

The development of money and credit theory on the Continent during the 'thirties might be summarized as follows: theory at first turned away from the classical concept of a more or less inelastic economy to a concept that emphasized strongly the possibility of stimulating production and avoiding depression by monetary manipulations. The pendulum had swung back to an almost preclassic Mercantilistic concept. However, after a short time the exaggerations were recognized and the pendulum swung back, though only part way. A sort of synthesis of classical and pre- and post-classical theory was reached: a synthesis that avoided the undeniable inadequacies of classical theories as well as the mistakes of Mercantilist, free-money, vanishing-money, easy-money theorists and monetary illusionists in general.

17. Concluding Remarks: Keynesianism—Progress or Retrogression?

KEYNESIANISM—AN INFLATION-DEFLATION THEORY OF EMPLOYMENT

In order to pass a general judgment on Keynesianism the term must be defined. This is not easy because Keynesianism has come to embrace many and varied ideas. For not only has Keynes himself made self-contradictory statements but his statements are often at variance with those of his followers, who again vary widely among themselves in their views. Therefore any general remark on Keynesianism will and can easily be met with the objection that one has misunderstood the master or picked out the views of the wrong disciples. It might nevertheless be possible to define it pretty distinctly by pointing to a certain basic approach common to all Keynesians, but totally uncommon to orthodox classical or neoclassical economists. This basic approach is best expressed in the formula that Keynesians themselves consider the essence of the new creed and which they repeat over and over again: "National income" (and/or employment) "depends upon the propensity to consume, the marginal efficiency of capital, the liquidity function and the amount of money. . . ." [1]

What is the meaning of this statement so amazing to classical economists who, of course, would expect the variables upon which

---

[1] Compare, for instance: Papers and Proceedings of the Sixtieth Annual Meeting of the American Economic Association, May 1948, page 272, and many other places.

employment depends to also include the wage level? Obviously these variables are meant to determine "effective demand" or, in monetary terms, the degree of inflation and deflation. And if they at the same time determine employment, we are faced with what is essentially an inflation-deflation theory of employment, and a one-sided one at that. For inflation and deflation are considered dependent solely upon *investment* and *consumption*. In reality, they are in the first instance dependent on future employment and thus inversely on the wage level. For what is spent on consumer or capital goods produced *this* week is the income of those employed in the *next*.

It is a peculiar picture of an economy from which this theory is abstracted. It is the picture of an economy in which output and employment are so tightly coupled with the amount of circulating money that they can only expand if the latter has been inflated. Moreover, because the new money is spent—after a short initial period—on output *and* prices, increases in employment and output are always more or less associated with price rises. And as the money inflation is supposed to be brought about by interest rate lowering or increase of efficiency of capital, the increased output is connected with an increase in investment. In the same way decreases in output and employment are coupled with money deflation, price declines and decrease of investment.

Compare with this the working of the economy as imagined by the neoclassicists. They knew that expansion and contraction of employment and output *could* be brought about in the way just described, and many of them thought that they *were* thus brought about in the course of the business cycle. But in general they considered changes in output and employment as independent of money inflation and deflation, from price inflation and deflation and from changes in investment. In their opinion, employment and output can increase without any increase in the amount of circulating *money*. This happens if wages are lowered within the framework of an inelastic money supply. Here an unchanged amount of money spends itself on a higher output, but on lower prices. And if the money supply is elastic, employment and output nevertheless can increase without *price* inflation provided wages are deflated. The increased amount of money spends itself solely on increased output. In both of these cases lower costs, especially wages, provide the increased profit margin for the employment of less efficient labor that in the Keynesian scheme is provided by price inflation. And, in both cases, output and employment increase also independently of any addition to investment and thus of changes in the capital structure of the economy.

AN ELEMENT OF IMPERFECT COMPETITION IN A SYSTEM OF PERFECT COMPETITION

In neoclassic economics, production can expand for all sorts of reasons in all sorts of ways. It can expand with prices rising, unchanged or even falling. It can expand with or without new investments. Everything depends on the absolute and relative costs of capital and labor. In Keynesian economics—as represented by the employment formula mentioned above—it can expand only through money inflation, price inflation and an increase in investment: it represents a very one-sided—a monistic—theory of employment.

What are the reasons for this one-sidedness? Why do Keynesian and classical economics differ so widely? I think the answer is easy. The absence of really *universal* perfect competition is responsible for the wonders of the Keynesian world. Through the assumption that wages are inflexible and unadjustable to the prevailing price situation, an important element of imperfect competition is introduced on one single market, namely, the labor market, in an alleged system of entirely free markets. In all other fields of the economy the market prices are supposed to be lowered under the impact of competition until supply and demand equalize. Every supplier of industrial products, of railroad traffic, of real estate, of commodities, is expected to lower the supply price of the goods he produces or the services he renders if he really wants to get rid of them. But such lowering of the price of labor is excluded by the assumption that labor will not tolerate the lowering of nominal, as distinct from real, wages. Once this assumption is made there is of course only one way to influence the size of employment and production: by inflation and deflation. And these in turn can never be induced by changes in wages. These consequences are indeed awkward. But they are quite plausible within a system in which on one important market, the labor market, supply prices are inflexible in nominal, but oddly not in real, terms. Here inflation is left as the only way out of an otherwise unadjustable situation.

Keynes' "Conceptual Apparatus"

The aim of this volume has been twofold. First, to show that Keynes' theory is one-sided, that an inflation-deflation theory of employment does not cover the "general cases." Second, to prove that his inflation-deflation theory of employment suffers in itself from inherent weaknesses. Neither do shifts in liquidity preference, the propensity to consume or the marginal productivity of capital lead necessarily to inflations or deflations; nor do inflations and deflations in turn lead to fluctuations in employment, except if and as long as wages are rigid.

If this is correct the usefulness of Keynes' so-called "conceptual apparatus" for the analysis of long-run, short-run and cyclical situations cannot be as great as is assumed nowadays even by "moderate Keynesians." I myself consider it in fact as very slight. My conclusions can be summarized as follows:

Long-run equilibria do not exist in the real world. They are fictions designed to depict the structure of an economy after such adjustments have taken place as can reasonably be expected under the assumption of free competition. Of paramount importance among such adjustments are the downward shifts of supply prices of the productive factors, labor and capital, which enable them to join or rejoin the production process. A long-run equilibrium theory of employment has therefore to assume that wage demands of those still wanting to work are lowered until demand and supply equalize and "involuntary" unemployment disappears. Just as supply on commodity markets cannot remain unabsorbed it seems unwarranted to assume that on the labor market, in the long run, supply can outgrow demand. A long-run equilibrium in which supply and demand for labor does not come into balance because of wage rigidity is a contradiction in terms. It could not serve the purposes for which it is constructed.

For *short-run situations*—for which it is meant in the first place, but by no means exclusively—Keynes' analysis suffers from the opposite defects. Short-term analysis is not concerned with fictions. It is meant as a tool to describe and explain reality. Reality is always dynamic. Periods of prosperity and depression alternate. Neutral static periods do not exist. Keynes' theory is essentially static. It treats the short-term equilibrium as an isolated phenomenon and examines the results of shifts in one variable, for instance, of income, assuming that other functions such as consumption or investment are "fairly stable." [2] But in dynamic reality stable functions are practically nonexistent. Every single equilibrium is, so to speak, only a snapshot out of a chain of equilibria. Changes in one link of the chain set the stage for overall changes that happen in the next and modify the effect of the impulse. The sequence, interaction and causality of all these changes, not one single shift in an otherwise static world, have to be explained. Therefore only a chain or sequence analysis, as distinct from Keynes' circular analysis, can be useful.

As an example of how misleading circular analysis turns out we may refer to the investment gap theorem so essential for Keynes' whole system: production cannot, *ceteris paribus*, be increased, because according to the so-called "psychological law" some part of the increased income is not spent so that deflation threatens. Applying even the crudest form of chain analysis we see immediately that the increased current income meets the output of the *preceding* period, which of course does not increase retroactively. Therefore prices would go up or, at least, inventories would decrease. Either would create optimistic expectations for the prices to be obtained for *current* production. In other words, shifts in the price expectations would counteract the effect of the "psychological law" even if it existed.

If this is a realistic description of a short-run equilibrium in a changing world—and I believe that every cyclical recovery proves it

[2] *Cf.* Keynes' *General Theory*, p. 95.

is—then an increase in income leads, *ceteris paribus*, to inflation, not deflation. The cornerstone of Keynes' really fantastic theory, according to which things must get worse just because they get better, is overthrown.

It is the aim of *business cycle theory* to explain why from time to time the economy moves away, periodically and rhythmically, from an equilibrium and why it tends to return to it only after a lag, and by a sudden sharp corrective reversal rather than by a slow adjustment process which might have no substantial effect on employment and production.

I cannot see that Keynes has added anything to previous endeavors to explain this riddle of the cycle. Nor do I think that his followers, in trying to "dynamize" his system, have added any new explanation. A huge literature and an immense display of ingenuity have achieved nothing but a distinct step backwards, for instance by blurring the difference between saving and "buyers' resistance." More confused than enriched, we will have to return repentantly to the answers of neoclassical monetary business cycle theorists. We may again decide whether we want to rely, for instance, on the importance of the clustering of investment demand (Professor Schumpeter), the errors in monetary policy (Wicksell and his school), or on optimistic and pessimistic mass psychology (Professor Pigou), the last being my own choice.

KEYNESIANISM AND APPLIED ECONOMICS

Can Keynesianism be considered useful when applied to practical problems? Has it improved our ability for correct diagnosis and prognosis of economic evils? I think that the answer must be negative. In the Keynesian world costs are more or less fixed, whereas prices fluctuate and have a tendency toward deflation. But this is not the situation today. Since the end of the great depression, with only the interruption of the short crisis of 1937-38, things have been different and will perhaps stay that way for quite a while. The demand situation is no longer deflationary, nor can the cost situation be considered anything like stable. Demand is stabilized or even inflationary and wages move up, without their traditional lag, but sometimes even faster than prices. Clearly in such a situation the Keynesian "inflation-deflation theory of employment" cannot be helpful. The classical employment theory that connects employment with the productivity of labor and the real wage level seems to focus the attention much better on the really important variable.

But after this boom a depression will come again. Will the younger generation, brought up under the influence of Keynes' ideas, be well equipped to diagnose the various reasons for the dwindling demand and the developing unemployment? I am afraid not. For Keynesianism has produced certain peculiarities in their thinking of which they themselves are hardly aware but by which they will be greatly handicapped. They originate in Keynes' employment theory being a one-sided, monistic theory which distracts the attention from some factors while putting the spotlight on others.

One of these peculiarities is the preoccupation of economists exclusively with questions of demand. Like salesmen of Fuller brushes, everybody seems to be trembling for fear that demand is not sufficient. The consequences are twofold. First, unemployment is always considered caused by insufficient demand although, after all, stabilized or structural or, in Keynes' words, "voluntary employment" is, or can also be, an important component of total unemployment in a depression. Second, it is forgotten that goods, in order to be sold, have to be produced plentifully and at low cost if the living standard of the nation is to be maintained or raised. In spite of the experience of the war and postwar period, economists seem not to be concerned about increasing production and employment by technical progress and greater use of capital, dependent on increased savings. I fear that a generation deluded by the belief that national income depends on spending for consumption and, even more grotesque, on the amount of circulating paper money, will have to learn the hard way that it can only be increased through work, thrift and technical progress.

A further peculiarity of contemporary economic thinking, again a consequence of Keynes' monistic theory, is what one would call the "estimate craze"; the abundance of estimates of future national income. Underlying all these estimates is the belief that future demand can be calculated in advance within certain limits. The demand for investment purposes especially is supposed to be calculable according to what business or government is expected to spend on investments. But first demand is not only created by spending for investment, but also by spending for employment, the last not at all identical with the former. Demand on the market for dresses could, for instance, be increased if more housemaids were employed—a possibility ignored by a theory concentrating on the demand-creating power of investments. Secondly, investment itself is not only dependent on the productivity of capital but also of labor. If an enlarged labor force has to be equipped, more has to be spent on investments. Nor is the wage level alone decisive. A change in the political atmosphere, too, can radically influence the size of investments. And finally, a small change in price expectations can alter the amount spent on investment, and on consumption, too, so radically that a potentially deflationary situation turns inflationary and vice versa, with the result that all forecasts turn out to be wrong.

The "peculiarities" mentioned are responsible for another peculiarity of our times: the standard for evaluation of economists, so different from the past. Today somebody is considered a good economist who can express more or less hypothetical statements on functional relationships in mathematical formulas or graphs. Previously somebody was considered a good economist who could evaluate and forecast the relative strength of the forces making for shifts of data in the future. Judgment, experience and common sense were believed more important than a formal education relying on methods appropriate in natural sciences but hardly in economics. For these deal with human beings with unpredictable reactions and not with machines with predictable movements. The forecasts on postwar deflation demonstrate the results of a technical overstatic approach—forecasts which, incidentally, seem to have done no harm to the forecasters in their own minds, nor in the minds of the public.

As far as mathematics in economics is concerned, I quote what

Keynes, certainly more competent in this matter than I, said in one of the few passages in his book with which I agree:

> It is a great fault of symbolic pseudo-mathematical methods of formalising a system of economic analysis, . . . that they expressly assume strict independence between the factors involved and lose all their cogency and authority if this hypothesis is disallowed; whereas, in ordinary discourse, where we are not blindly manipulating but know all the time what we are doing and what the words mean, we can keep "at the back of our heads" the necessary reserves and qualifications and the adjustments which we shall have to make later on, in a way in which we cannot keep complicated partial differentials "at the back" of several pages of algebra which assume that they all vanish. Too large a proportion of recent "mathematical" economics are mere concoctions, as imprecise as the initial assumptions they rest on, which allow the author to lose sight of the complexities and interdependencies of the real world in a maze of pretentious and unhelpful symbols.[3]

Full Employment Policy

Nowhere does the difference between Keynesian and pre-Keynesian economics show up stronger than in the matter of full employment policy.

Classical-neoclassical economists had not the ambition to "maintain full employment." Their idea was: every boom is followed by a depression during which the excesses of the boom have to be corrected and liquidated; the price level is bound to fall. Interference by interest rate manipulation or deficit spending can prevent the price level from falling too far below an "average" level, but never maintain it at boom level for any length of time. Costs, especially wages, have to adjust themselves to the new price level. Before this happens no real recovery is possible. Only an economy where costs have been adjusted to the new price level keeps going in a "natural way" without ever-renewed inflationary injections.

Keynes' full employment policy is more ambitious. It does not aim at restoring but at maintaining full employment. But this ambition is somewhat involuntary. For in his system full employment cannot be restored through wage adjustments. It can only

[3] *Ibid.*, pp. 297-98.

be *maintained* through price and demand support. Wages cannot be lowered in view of labor's resistance to lowering of money wages and in view of a threatening "oversaving deflation" which would overcompensate the effects of lowering of wages. There is only one way out: inflation or reflation by manipulating the interest rate downward and by government spending. If a man is taking a bath and the water in the tub is shallow he must lower his body to be covered. If he does not lower himself the only other way to be covered is to run more water into the bathtub.

We have tried in this volume, especially in Chapter 6, "Compensating Reactions to Compensatory Spending," to show that such "refilling of the bathtub" is practicable only in very special situations, for instance, during a depression, after the excesses of the previous boom are already well liquidated but never with a view to extending a dying boom. Otherwise, to go back to our metaphor, the water will soon flow out of the tub again or it may be impossible to cover the body at all. Therefore, not only must the opening of the faucets be well timed but also the body must already have been lowered quite a bit.

It is true that intervention can be too late and too weak. This was the mistake committed at the beginning of the thirties, at least in Europe. A deflationary monetary and fiscal policy was continued for much too long a period and reflationary measures, when finally introduced, were too timid.

Today the great danger lies in the opposite direction. Keynes himself has expressed the opinion that low interest rates are the means of prolonging a boom [4] and many of his followers think that government spending has to set in every time demand dwindles.[5] This has created an atmosphere that may well force an intervention at too early a moment and on too large a scale. But I doubt its success. Before the boom is liquidated to a certain extent and the price and demand situation, created through overspeculation, revised downwards, everything spent will prove to have been poured into a barrel without a bottom. Nothing else will be achieved but a waste of valuable ammunition. A short-

[4] Compare the quotation on p. 205.
[5] Compare the quotations on p. 137.

lived consumer-spending boom will soon collapse without having
revived the economy to a natural life but after having endangered
the credit and currency of the country.   Whether one wants it or
not, prices will go down in the next depression from their boom
level, as they have always done in depressions, and the only question is at *what* level the price decline can and should be arrested.
So, after all, wages will have to come down: the man in the bathtub will have to lower his body.

But will he do it?   I must confess that I doubt it and this situation frightens me.

I have once already lived through a period in which wages
should have been lowered but were not because of the arguments
of the purchasing power theory.   From 1927 on employment began
to decrease in Germany at a time when demand was still holding
up.   Entrepreneurs held that unemployment was the result of a
too rapid rise in wages and a subsequent replacement of labor by
capital.   Labor leaders rejected wage reduction in the face of
steadily mounting unemployment.   Their argument was, just as it
is today, that high wages are necessary to maintain a high level of
purchasing power.   Indeed the reasons advanced at that time in
dailies representing the views of labor were so identical with those
of today in this country, that I sometimes have the feeling of living
this period of my life over again.

As is well known, wage reductions were opposed in Germany
for years by the trade unions.   They even succeeded in obtaining
substantial wage increases at a time when the depression was
already clearly noticeable.   Only later, at the bottom of the depression, they consented to extensive wage reductions, then entirely useless in view of the very deflationary price policy of the
Brüning government.

In France the arguments of the purchasing power theory were
officially accepted by Leon Blum and his government before the
last war.   Wages were at that time raised in an already clearly
deflationary environment.   This was, in my opinion, one of the
chief reasons for the economic chaos which characterized the prewar Blum era.

But what was the position of economic science?   One is entitled to state that at that time in Europe the purchasing power theory was considered fundamentally wrong by an overwhelming majority of scholars. The first to warn against its fallacies was the late Professor Gustav Cassel in an article which appeared in 1927 and which aroused great interest all over the world. This article, "Selbstkritik! Die Sinnlosigkeit der deutschen Arbeitslosenpolitik" ("Self-criticism! The Senselessness of the German Unemployment Policy"), explained how senseless it was to keep the wages of the employed high and to pay subsidies out of the income of the employed to the unemployed, instead of letting the whole population work at adjusted wage rates.[6]

But the warning was not confined to orthodox economists. Professor Emil Lederer, a member of the Unabhanige Socialdemokratische Partei, who surely cannot be suspected of having been inimical to labor, in his book *Eine Untersuchung ueber die Armut der Nationen* (*An Enquiry into the Poverty of Nations*), 1927, says with reference to the effect of economically non-adjusted wage rates: "A sharp decline of the economy will be the consequence. The unemployment allowances cannot be paid any longer and the artificially erected wage system must collapse inevitably. A valorization of labor, what this policy would mean . . . , is just not possible for the long run."[7]

And as to scientific opinion outside Europe, I may be allowed to quote a few sentences of Professor Alvin Hansen, obviously written before he became a Hansenian:

"It is therefore not surprising that the theory should become widespread that higher wages are the cure for the restricted market and declining price level of the last decade. This theory is accepted, one might almost say, by nearly every one in the United States, not only by trade union leaders but also by leading business men, politicians, and journalistic economists. During the 1930 depression leaders of American public opinion in all walks of life were constantly urging that the surest basis for

[6] A summary of the response to this article in the scientific and political world in Germany can be found in my little booklet which appeared in 1930, *Ist Arbeitslosigkeit unvermeidlich?* (*Is Unemployment Inevitable?*).

[7] I refer furthermore to a pamphlet, "Rentabilitaetskrise (Veroeffentlichungen des Vereins deutscher Maschinen Bauanstalten, 1930)" which demonstrated statistically the parallelism between rising wages and unemployment.

a revival of prosperity was a maintenance of wages or even an increase in wages. This state of affairs indicates a confusion of thought for which, it must be admitted, professional economists are in part to blame." [8]

"You cannot raise the general level of prices by the simple process of raising wages. And it is an amazing fact that professional American economists have not come forward to point out the fallacy that lurks here." [9]

"We shall not succeed in solving the depression through the soothing and agreeable device of inflation. We shall come out of it only through hard work, and readjustments that are painful. There is no other alternative." [10]

If the downward adjustment of wages was opposed in the last depression in spite of a warning by economic science, resistance against adjustments will hardly be weaker now that economists too adhere so overwhelmingly to purchasing power theory. In the last analysis Keynes wrote his *General Theory* in order to find a way out of a situation which seemed to him hopeless if attacked in a traditional way. He felt that wages must be lowered in and after a depression but he advised lowering them in real terms because it seemed no longer possible to lower them in money terms. He has, as I once said, transformed the evil of a rigid wage system into the virtue of an inflationary employment theory. But by doing this and conceding that wages are unadjustable downwards he has of course rendered them even less adjustable than they already were.

It is a well-known sociological phenomenon that theories, even basically incorrect, if once accepted, can turn into an independent power which leads to the effect to which the original facts as such would never have led—thus seemingly proving the correctness of the original theory. The classic example for such an effect of a theory is Karl Marx' "Klassenkampf" conception (class struggle) which caused the development of class-consciousness rather than vice versa.

Perhaps we have to acquiesce in the fact that money wages have

[8] Alvin Harvey Hansen, *Economic Stabilization in an Unbalanced World*, New York, 1932, p. 279.

[9] *Ibid.*, p. 279.

[10] *Ibid.*, p. 378.

become unadjustable downwards and even have a tendency to increase during depressions—tragically not the least through the influence of a doctrine designed to protect the economy against such rigidities. But before acquiescing we should consider what an economy will look like which has again and again to be pulled out of a deflationary situation by government spending. Such an economy must necessarily undergo fundamental changes in its social structure. In the long run governmental deficit spending leads necessarily to a progressive socialization of enterprises. Taxation has, from a certain point on, to be increased in order that government spending does not ruin the currency and credit of the country. Through this more and more enterprises become unprofitable so that the government must again replace them in their function of providing employment.

It is beyond the topic of this volume to examine whether the development which leads from economic rigidities to ever more governmental spending and from there to Socialism, is inevitable. Undoubtedly other alternatives exist. One is to urge the regulation of the whole economic process by the government, based on the idea that it is better to have all factors fixed according to a unified and centralized plan than as a result of the struggle of different pressure groups. This is how a Fascist economy works.

The other possibility is to put the economic laws to work again and in that way to rebuild a free economy. I personally hope that this way is still open.

Appendices

As, in my opinion, the objections raised to my *Volkswirtschaft-liche Theorie des Bankkredits* can, with the same justification, be raised against Keynes' work, excerpts of two of these criticisms, namely, one by Professor Howard S. Ellis and one by Professor Gottfried von Haberler, are reprinted in the following pages. Both criticisms give a good summary of the contents of my book, thus enabling the reader to compare them with Keynes' work.

There is also reprinted in the following pages an article "The Gold Exchange Paradox" which I was reluctant to include in the main part of the book because it deals with a situation no longer existent. On the other hand, I thought it should be reprinted because certain conclusions arrived at in the article, namely, the incompatibility of internal inflation and external currency stabilization, can be applied to the problems of today.

There follows for readers interested in my earlier work a table of contents of my two books *Geld und Kredit* (1924) and *Geld und Kredit, Neue Folge* (1929).

Finally, I have added a list of those of my articles written after 1929 which have not been included in the present book because they are not of interest to the American reader of today. One of the articles mentioned, namely, "Deficit Spending and Private Enterprise," a lecture delivered at Harvard University and reprinted in the U. S. Chamber of Commerce *Bulletin* No. 8, has not been included in order to avoid certain repetitions.

I

Excerpt from Howard S. Ellis, *German Monetary Theory,
1905-1933*, Harvard University Press, 1934, 1937, Chapter
XVIII, "The Schumpeter-Hahn Type of Cycle Theory"
(pp. 327-34).

Hahn's Theory of Productive Credit

The enthusiastic popular reception accorded Hahn has already
been the occasion for comment; but *The Economic Theory of Bank
Credit* in particular enjoys such wide recognition that academic
economists, somewhat grudgingly,[1] have had to take cognizance of
its claims. Indeed, as Haberler remarks, there has grown up of late
a sort of separate Hahn literature; scarcely a work can be published
in the field of money and credit without a fairly exhaustive critique
of his doctrines.[2]

The necessary foundation for a theory of business cycles, says
Hahn, is a correct apprehension of the nature and functions of credit
in the economic process. In Germany the conventional view nowadays represents credit as a store of permanent or temporary savings
deposited with the banks by the public.[3] Classical economists
made no mistake in tracing down every credit to abstinence, at a
time when the volume of currency was definitely limited. Today
the quantity theory does indeed take account of elastic bank credit,
but the tradition is still preserved that credit originates in saving.
Not primary but created deposits are the basic phenomenon. No
longer are banks merely offices for borrowing and lending money,

[1] E.g., Friedrich A. Hayek, *Geldtheorie und Konjunkturtheorie,* Vienna, 1929,
p. 84.

[2] *Cf.* Gottfried Haberler's review, *Archiv* 56, p. 803. Hahn himself gives
three or four pages of references upon his doctrines in the third edition of his
opus, Tübingen, 1930, pp. xiv-xvi.

[3] L. Albert Hahn, *Volkswirtschaftliche Theorie des Bankkredits,* 1st ed.,
Tübingen, 1920, p. 6; 2nd ed., Tübingen, 1924, p. 6. Until the concluding
section, page references pertain to these two editions, which are identical.

but dealers in "credit" in the literal sense of "confidence"; and interest, from being at one time a payment for saving, has become a price paid for confidence.[4]

In the sphere of goods this change signifies that *"capital formation is not the consequence of saving but of the extension of credit."* [5] This follows from the logical primacy of demand over actual production, a primacy concealed by the temporal precedence of the latter before the former. The real prerequisite for the appearance of a capital good is effective entrepreneurial demand, which credit extension brings into being.[6] It is not asserted that lending itself actually produces goods, but that it induces an increase in production through a change in distribution. How this transpires will appear from consequences attending a bank rate lower than the expected yield of capital goods, arising either from an absolute reduction of the former while the latter remains constant, or from a rise of the latter with bank rates unchanged.[7]

Lower interest charges reduce costs to all entrepreneurs operating upon credit, not merely those to the producers of durable goods.[8] As a result all production expands, competition for labor and raw material grows more intense, and there appears at first that strictly inverse correlation of prices and discount rates described by the quantity theory. But in the modern industrial system, the introduction of labor-saving technique set over against a virtually constant volume of capital has resulted in an underlying tendency for interest to rise and wages to fall.[9] The marginal laborer has passed over into the extra-marginal "not-laborer," choosing to subsist entirely upon his *rentes.* Consequently an expansion of credit operates, on the one hand, through rising wages to draw into active employment many members of this reserve army, including women and children, and thus to induce a fuller utilization of existing plant capacity; and on the other, through rising prices, to transfer income from the fixed salary and *rentier* group to entrepreneurs. The stream of goods is both broadened and lengthened: more of everything is produced and more capitalistic, more roundabout

[4] *Ibid.*, p. 51.
[5] *Ibid.*, p. 120.   (Italics author's.)
[6] *Ibid.*, p. 121.
[7] *Ibid.*, pp. 131-132.
[8] *Ibid.*, p. 130.
[9] *Ibid.*, p. 139.

methods are employed. Not saving but altered distribution produces these results—distribution changed "interpersonally" by the forced rise of wages and fall of interest, and "intertemporally," by the forced deflection of goods out of present consumption. "Credit produces goods out of nothing, in that, without it, they would not have been produced." [10]

A by-product of this expansion of production may be [11] a rise of prices for consumers' relatively to producers' goods. But the expansion could persist as long as new credit drew additional labor power into production.[12] Experience shows, however, that ordinarily before this point is reached the rising conjuncture is broken off by a universal glut. How can this be accounted for? Simply by the fact that in the period of high earnings the laborer, having a fairly fixed standard of living, saves instead of spending his income; "circulating deposits metamorphose into savings accounts"; and the disappearance of this demand precipitates a fall in prices, production, and employment.[13] But a way lies open to the state to prevent this termination of the boom either by continued interest reductions through the central bank, enabling the producer to hold his finished products, or by removing the interest burden entirely through the purchase and storage of the goods on government account.[14] ". . . theoretically, at any rate, the assumption of the possibility of a 'perpetual boom' does not belong to the realm of Utopia." [15] Whether or not to purchase greater and greater production by expropriating the salaried and *rentier* classes is a question belonging not to economics but to politics.

The course of Hahn's original argument, culminating in a supposed dethronement of frugality and an apotheosis of credit creation, has evoked emphatic denial at every stage. Aside from the identification of capital and money markets and a tendency, decried by Hayek,[16] to recognize no more ultimate determinant of interest

---

[10] *Ibid.*, p. 141.

[11] *Sic, ibid.*, p. 133. Hahn does not seem to appreciate that his previous reasoning calls for "must," and so this sentence is merely a parenthetical observation.

[12] *Ibid.*, p. 145.

[13] *Ibid.*, p. 148.

[14] *Ibid.*, p. 151.

[15] *Ibid.*, p. 159.

[16] *Konjunkturtheorie*, pp. 103-104.

than bank liquidity, Hahn proves to be particularly vulnerable in arguing that capital originates in fundamentally different ways in a cash economy and in a cashless economy. As Neisser, Mannstaedt, and Haberler observe, the difference between the two systems is purely a matter of payment technique: bank deposits function just as money does, and in both cases interest is paid for the surrender of purchasing power, not, as Hahn would have it, for the cession of money in the earlier and for "confidence" in the modern system.[17] To go below the merely superficial phenomena of credit and cash exchange media, we must agree with Lampe that it is quite as possible for coinage in a cash economy to make purchasing power available without saving as for credit creation to accomplish the same end in a bank deposit regime.[18] By consequence, if capital comes into being in another way in the latter than in the former, it will have to be on other grounds than merely the creation of new purchasing power.

That the existing volume of bank deposits originates preponderately from loans is of course a far cry from the proposition that capital formation proceeds from credit creation and not from saving. It is not surprising, therefore, to find that Hahn tries to support the latter notion by some other argument than this flimsy confusion. Demand, he says, precedes production. But the really surprising thing is that this homely truth, equally valid for cash and credit economies, should somehow demonstrate that capital formation does not nowadays proceed from saving. Probably, as Lampe suggests, Hahn has unwittingly fallen victim to an ambiguity in his term "demand." If demand be interpreted as applying to the products of a capital instrument, it is of course apparent that the instrument would not be produced unless such a demand were *expected*. On the other hand, without demand in another sense, that is, *actually available* purchasing power in the form of a bank deposit, the entrepreneur could not undertake production at all. But Hahn,

[17] Neisser, *Tauschwert*, pp. 70-71; Heinrich Mannstaedt, *Ein kritischer Beitrag zur Theorie des Bankkredits*, Jena, 1927, pp. 13-15; Haberler, *Archiv* 56, p. 814.
[18] Adolf Lampe, *Zur Theorie des Sparprozesses und der Kreditschöpfung*, Jena, 1926, pp. 134-135.

who says his proposition pertains to the first sort of demand, actually applies it also to the second, i.e., he assumes that whenever a bank extends credit to a customer, a *sure* market must exist for the capital good and its products. Of course, even if every bank loan did result in economically useful capital-good formation, it would not be true that "no capital good can be produced without credit creation," as Hahn states literally,[19] unless, furthermore, *no* new capital were produced on the basis of bank loans of accumulated savings. It is not necessary to argue against this absurd proposition inasmuch as Hahn himself blows hot and cold within the confines of a single paragraph. Admitting that current production proceeds out of "a certain stock of goods produced in the past capable of covering the need for nourishment, clothing, and shelter," he concludes, "*If this certain stock is present,* then the founding of new enterprises is independent of the supply of capital!" [20] Indeed, far from supporting the earlier dictum that capital formation is *solely* the product of credit creation, Hahn's description of the period of rising conjuncture indicates at the utmost that new credit *increases* the quantity of capital, and even then he concedes that this does *not* invariably transpire. And so the thesis of a totally new origin of capital is abandoned by the author himself.

The theory of business cycles, based upon the more modest claim of a productive effect of expanding bank credit, has been most adversely criticized at three points: the course of wages relative to prices during the upswing, the cause of crises, and the final outcome of the whole evolution. Hahn, it will be remembered, relies upon *mounting* wage rates to activate the industrial reserve army during boom times. To object, as Haberler does, that this contradicts his admission that consumption goods are enhanced in price does not dispose of the matter,[21] because Hahn argues that through the competitive tendency of prices toward cost, consumption costs are indeed raised by the increase of nominal wages, but this is partly

[19] *Volkswirtschaftliche Theorie,* p. 121. "*Ohne Krediteinräumung*" might be ambiguous were it not for the previous statement "*Krediteinräumung ist also Schaffung kaufkräftiger Nachfrage*" (*ibid.,* p. 120. Italics mine).

[20] *Ibid.,* p. 142. (Italics mine.)

[21] *Archiv* 56, p. 817.

offset by the low interest charges which generated the upward movement.[22] On purely *a priori* grounds one might agree with Lampe that forced saving imposed merely upon the small class of non-laboring and non-entrepreneurial *rentiers* would scarcely support an increase of real income for the whole wage-earning population.[23] Or again, simply deductively, one may object that Hahn has given to laborers the conjunctural gains which were supposed to be in the hands of entrepreneurs, supplying the motivating factor in the whole upward movement. But the most effective answer would be Burchardt's appeal to the fact that real wages lag,[24] if economists could be more certain that the statistical evidence is clearly in this direction. If Hahn had not relied upon a strictly rationalistic calculus to account for the existence of the reserve army in the first place—that technical progress so raises interest rates as to induce the *rentier* to prefer idleness—and had instead attributed ordinary unemployment to economic friction and inertia, he might more easily have accounted for increased employment and output attending *falling* real wages in the period of recovery. But unless real wages actually decline, the amount of forced saving would not be such as to lend much color to Hahn's expectation of a substantial increase in capital.

Furthermore, if forced saving supplies the driving power to a period of industrial expansion, why should not the voluntary savings of laborers, which Hahn supposes on the increase in the late stages of boom times, support the expansion indefinitely? It is enigmatic why he should believe that banks allow savings deposits to pile up without investing them, when the universal characteristic of the system according to his account is extending more credit than it receives.[25] This version of the overinvestment theory, it will be observed, rests not upon the fading out of forced saving, but upon the (altogether improbable) growth of hoards.

[22] *Volkswirtschaftliche Theorie*, p. 137.

[23] *Sparprozess*, p. 161.

[24] Fritz Burchardt, "Entwicklungsgeschichte der monetären Konjunkturtheorie," *Welt. Arch.* 28, p. 131.

[25] An objection levied by Burchardt, *loc. cit.*, and by Haberler, *Archiv* 56, p. 818.

No single feature of the entire structure has occasioned a more general outcry than Hahn's suggestion that proper authoritarian measures at the time of impending crisis might support a "perpetual high conjuncture." It scarcely requires an academic economist [26] to point out that either continued injections of credit at progressively lower interest charges or the purchase and storage of unmarketable products by the state would signify a nationalizing of industry, and that even such drastic measures would only intensify the final debacle, the more the longer they persisted.[27] Far from leading to a progressive diversion of resources into capital form, as Lampe suggests,[28] such policies mean outright and violent inflation, and the disappearance of all accumulation.

Finally the question presents itself whether, aside from such attempts to protract the boom indefinitely, artificial credit creation attending the ordinary cycle leaves society at the end better provided with usable capital. The answer naturally varies from the enthusiastic affirmative of Hahn's own followers to the categoric denials of the Vienna school. Midway lie the appraisals of the majority of special Hahn critics whom we have just mentioned. While maintaining that credit extension *per se* means only capital displacement, Diehl concedes that it may lead to an increase of capital formation, depending upon the success of the ventures it fosters.[29] Lampe, as we have seen, proposes the same test. Considerably more skeptical is Haberler,[30] for whom the "spark of truth" in the doctrine of the productive effect of "inflationary" credit is first, that it prevents declining prices in a progressive society, and secondly, that it overcomes the frictional resistance of an indolent entrepreneurial community. But the new undertakings called into being by inflation would not persist longer, with the return of interest to its natural level, than the life of their fixed capital equipment. Mannstaedt concludes that in a free exchange economy where banks

[26] Diehl, *Theoretische Nationalökonomie*, III, 582.

[27] *Cf.* Wilhelm Röpke, "Kredit und Konjunktur," *Jhrb. für N. & S.* 126, p. 263.

[28] *Sparprozess*, pp. 152-158.

[29] *Theoretische Nationalökonomie*, III, 571.

[30] *Archiv* 56, pp. 817-818.

exercise control only through prices, any policy may be thwarted
by a tendency for the public to react upon these prices negatively;
in other words, though banks may give an initial impulse toward
the liberation of productive factors through credit creation, ultimate success depends on the public's voluntary continuance of the
additional saving.[31] This is practically what Lampe and Diehl
have said: the answer depends on whether the ventures based upon
forced saving succeed. It is certainly not a foregone conclusion, as
Hahn assumes, that even while the artificial depression of interest
persists, the new produce will cover interest and depreciation costs,
nor *pro tanto* that this will be the case if the cessation of the forcing
is accompanied by a sag in the magnitude of saved income.

Since the appearance of the first and second editions of the
Volkswirtschaftliche Theorie, Hahn has abated his radicalism at certain points and at others altered the supporting argument. Most
noteworthy is the disappearance of the idea of maintaining a "perpetual boom." Although proposals to overcome glutted markets by
state assumption of interest changes or by inflation were repeated
as late as 1926[32] their omission in Hahn's widely read contribution
to the *Handwörterbuch* on "Kredit"[33] is a matter of general comment. In the third and completely revised edition of his magnum
opus,[34] Hahn retains nearly all of the catchwords around which the
underlying theory was originally developed. But there are some
very significant departures. Although we still read that "every
increase of credit increases goods through a change in their distribution," we discover also that even aside from such debacles as
the German inflation, the stimulating effect of credit sometimes
proves to be quite short-lived.[35] Credit expansion now becomes an
"essential condition" for the development of cycles, not the unique
cause.[36] But most notably, the explanation of crises from laborers'
savings, or rather hoards, disappears completely. There is some

[31] *Kritischer Beitrag,* pp. 30-31.
[32] According to Diehl, in Hahn's article "Krisenbekämpfung durch Diskont-
politik und Kreditkontrolle," *Soziale Praxis* 37, p. 931.
[33] *Hdwb. der Staats.,* 4th ed., Jena, 1923, V, 944-953.
[34] *Volkswirtschaftliche Theorie des Bankkredits,* 3rd ed., Tübingen, 1930.
[35] *Ibid.,* pp. 125, 152.
[36] *Ibid.,* p. 154.

evidence that the reason is an uncertainty on Hahn's part as to whether real wages advance as much above the standard of living as he had imagined in boom times.[37] Be that as it may, crises occur simply because a time must "necessarily" come when the stimulus of conjunctural gains to entrepreneurs has exhausted itself.[38] Although he continually lays great stress upon "intertemporal and interpersonal changes in distribution" wrought by artificially low bank rates, Hahn does not recognize that this distortion of productive factors into the capital category can itself account for a breakdown. In this he resembles Schumpeter, and it may be ventured that the failure to perceive the dangers of overinvestment accounts for the sanguine attitude of both writers toward the outcome of credit inflation.

A section on Hahn should not close without reference, at least, to his study of German bank series over the period 1900-13.[39] Here Hahn writes as a practical banker, and the analysis has been widely recommended. From the angle of the history of German theory, however, the early and more radical writings of Hahn are more significant, presenting a bold thesis [40] which gives rise to an equally bold antithesis on the part of the Vienna group.

[37] *Ibid.*, pp. 119, 123-124. The increase of labor supply is sometimes made to turn merely upon the "illusion of a constant value of money."

[38] *Ibid.*, p. 146.

[39] "Zur Frage des volkswirtschaftlichen Erkenntisinhalts der Bankbilanzziffern," *Geld und Kredit, Neue Folge,* Tübingen, 1929, pp. 149-189.

[40] An illustration of the "idiot fringe" which all theories possess is afforded by Hans Honegger's *Der schöpferische Kredit,* Jena, 1929. Capital is necessary to production only when it has to be pledged as collateral for a loan. So long as confidence persists, there is no limit to the profitable extension of bank credit. The entire pamphlet is a panegyric to "creative credit."

II

Translation of Gottfried Haberler, Albert Hahn's *Volkswirtschaftliche Theorie des Bankkredits* (*Archiv für Sozialwissenschaft und Sozialpolitik,* 1927, vol. 57, pp. 803 ff.) *

Undoubtedly Albert Hahn deserves a prominent place in the history of the most recent German monetary theory. His complaint
that science has not heeded his book (p. ix, preface to the second
edition) would not be valid now. One could practically say that of
late a Hahn literature has developed, inasmuch as scarcely a book
is published today on money and credit that does not discuss
Hahn's teachings at length. His theory is indeed worthy of the
greatest attention. For in the field of credit and banking it revo-
lutionizes the accepted views based upon the classical economists.
Starting from Schumpeter's ideas, but making them more radical
and extreme, Hahn has very skillfully and in an original manner
taken up a case before the forum of science that one had been
accustomed to consider completely settled (although the ideas
still haunted popular economics). With splendid dialectic which
handles in masterly fashion all the weapons in the arsenal of modern theory, Hahn attempts to rehabilitate completely the capital
and credit theory associated with the names of Law and Macleod.
He heads his book with the following quotation from Macleod:
"A bank is not an institution to receive and to lend money, but an
institution to create credit."

The second part of the book, entitled "The World of Credit and
Goods," discusses the productive effects of credit. According to
Hahn, to these teachings, whether or not they emanate from natural
or monetary-economic ideas, and whatever concept of capital they

* All italics are Haberler's. Numbers in parentheses after quotations refer
to pages in Hahn's book.

may have, "the opinion is peculiar that the amount of credit available in the economy and therewith also . . . as a matter of principle the interest rate . . . depend upon the goods existing at any time and created in the preceding production period. . . . It will be the main object of what follows to prove the fallacy of this concept" (109).[1]

Hahn begins his positive statements with this sentence: "Capital formation is not a consequence of saving, but of granting credit. *Granting credit is primary to the production of capital*" (120). This statement seems indeed to contradict every principle of economics. However, we should never let Hahn confuse us with his paradoxical expressions. Essentially at least the second sentence, that granting credit is primary to the production of capital, is nothing but a not very apt expression for a self-evident matter. Let us not forget that we still talk of an economy depleted of cash. Hahn says correctly that the production of capital is merely a part of the production of goods. "Granting credit, however, means granting *purchasing power*" (120). The introduction of a production process is therefore accomplished in an economy depleted of cash in such a way that funds are placed at the disposal of the entrepreneur—regardless of their origin or whether they can be increased at will—thus enabling him "to buy machinery, etc., to pay wages, in other words, to develop demand for the means of production" (120). Before starting a production process, one must have the money necessary to acquire the needed means of production unless one already possesses them, which happens so seldom in a modern economy that one can neglect the possibility. Since in an economy depleted of cash these funds are in the form of bank credit, one may say that *granting credit*—that is, granting a banking account—is primary to the *production of capital*.

Whereas this sentence is obvious and self-evident, Hahn's further statement—that the adoption of more devious ways of production is entirely independent of building up savings—is quite objectionable. We, on the contrary, are of the opinion that it makes

---

[1] The reader must believe us when we say that the passages are quoted word for word, and have not been taken out of their context in order to distort the author's views.

a fundamental difference whether the credit to purchase means of production originates in savings or has to be created *ad hoc* (inflationary credit); in the latter case, reactions ensue that considerably limit the expansion of production. It is embarrassing to be called on to demonstrate constantly such well-known facts. However, we should not shirk the trouble inasmuch as in these quite vulnerable statements of Hahn there is a spark of truth that should be salvaged.

Through pages 122-52 Hahn depicts the course of a credit inflation, i.e., of a credit expansion that goes beyond the savings base. Its survey is difficult because Hahn fails to describe the process step by step chronologically as it happens, but dissects the problem into several not too well-chosen subquestions: 1. Effects of credit on the *composition of goods* (should be "on the *composition of the stock of goods* of a nation"); 2. Effects on the prices of goods; 3. Effects on the quantity of goods; 4. Influence on capital and national wealth.

Reduction of the interest rate leads to credit expansion. Thus unprofitable new enterprises and investments become profitable. Longer production detours are taken and "the composition of the goods of a nation changes . . . so that there are fewer perishable and more durable goods, more capital equipment and semifinished goods" (129). However, credit expansion has yet another effect. "Production detours naturally cause a temporary, but quite noticeable, scarcity of goods for current consumption, for which the future alone compensates" (130). Moreover, granting credit brings a general price increase which is stronger the longer the production detours introduced.

While at the time of the classical economists a *price increase* was the *sole effect* of credit expansion, nowadays it increases production also—for two reasons: 1. "The techniques were so primitive . . . that increased demand for goods could be satisfied only if labor too was proportionately increased" (130), while today's techniques allow a definitely greater production from an insignificant addition of labor. The second reason is to be found in the fact that nowadays there is "*an immense pool of unemployed, part-time employed, and persons who can be induced to work harder*" (136), whereas at the time of the classical economists the entire popula-

tion almost without exception was always at work in production.
Thus Hahn makes the daring statement: *"The establishment of new
producing enterprises does not depend upon a more or a less large
reserve of capital; therefore the adoption of new production detours
can never be hindered by a lack of capital, because the necessary
capital can always be produced by credit.* . . . As long as its other
prerequisites were met by the nature of the country,[2] production
has never been hindered by lack of essential factories or tools. If
there were no factories, they . . . were simply built" (142). Once
again, however, Hahn qualifies his statement. "Of course, no factories could have been built unless means of subsistence for the
workmen during construction as well as the necessary tools had
existed." This, however, would be no impediment. "No doubt,
the present stands on the shoulders of the past in that the people
participating in the production process . . . cannot eat, clothe
themselves, work . . . or have a roof over their heads unless in the
past a certain stock of goods has been created. *However, if this
certain stock of goods . . . exists*[!], the creation of new enterprises
is independent of the capital reserve" (152). After having clearly
demonstrated that a reserve of capital is entirely superfluous for the
establishment of new enterprises, Hahn completes his exposition by
explaining: "For an increase of enterprises does not presume the
existence of a *bigger* stock of capital. The size of capital stocks
does not determine whether more or less labor is employed" (142).

In reply it may be objected that the length of a production de-
tour depends upon the existing stock of the means of subsistence,
nay, is practically proportional to the size of the stock of goods,
because obviously one thousand laborers require more clothes, food,
and living quarters than one hundred men, and because after all
it makes a difference whether they have to live on them a month,
a year, or two years. One cannot brush this consideration aside
with the remark that "if worst comes to worst, the price of current
goods will rise" (142). Nor can the following sentence be deemed
a satisfactory explanation: "The size of the capital stock does not
determine whether the labor force can be employed to a smaller

[2] This condition must be interpreted restrictively according to the sense of
the sentence.

or greater extent. A nation working intensely does not necessarily require more food, clothes, or living quarters than a partly employed nation" (142-43).

However, still other far-reaching considerations are against Hahn's thesis. First, it is very doubtful that a modern economy actually has at its disposal a tremendous labor reserve and that through credit inflation a significant proportion of this reserve can be employed. Hahn is of the opinion that higher wages spur people to work harder. They do not always do so. His statement that *real* wages rise, by the way, strikingly contradicts his former statement about the scarcity of current goods. Does he think that the scarcity affects only capitalists and rentiers? It is also possible that on higher wages one can retire sooner or be satisfied with an *eight*-hour working day while formerly one deemed a *nine*-hour day necessary. It may indeed be correct that rentiers and persons on fixed salaries are prompted to work because their incomes have been reduced by the rise in living costs, but not until prices have risen *considerably*. Then all the disadvantages of inflation emerge— Hahn does not even mention them—disadvantages that might curtail production more than taking new workers into the production process would further it. At present, since the great inflationary period, there is no excuse for neglecting the devastating economic consequences of monetary depreciation (which need not be discussed further). The important difference is simply that a production expansion financed by savings does not lead to price increases and thus no such countereffects are brought about. Hahn barely touches the decisive question how it actually happens that enterprises not profitable before credit inflation become profitable afterward and are able to remain in existence. The truth is that enterprises based upon inflationary credit can survive only as long as credit inflation continues. As soon as credit expansion stops and the rate of interest returns to its natural level they lose the basis of their profitability; they may still go on until their fixed capital is used up, then disappear. However, if credit continues to be created in order to keep these undertakings alive artificially, it would naturally bring about a progressive monetary depreciation which would eventually lead to a complete disorganization of the economy—how, does not have to be explained nowadays.

One can think of only two situations in which through credit inflation a permanent incorporation of new enterprises into the production process of an economy is conceivable: 1. If the sole effect of a credit inflation in an expanding economy (Hahn mentions this situation in passing but fails to recognize its special feature) is to arrest a necessary price decline, no countereffects are created that otherwise would destroy the profitability of the new enterprise. 2. If improvements in production methods that are profitable in themselves cannot be introduced because of "frictions" such as indolence or lack of entrepreneurial spirit, they can be forced by inflationary bank credit. As they are profitable and not introduced merely on account of temporary difficulties, such new undertakings survive even after credit inflation has been discontinued.

This is the spark of truth in the doctrine of the productive effects of inflationary credit. The second instance may be quite important in practice, even though compared with savings activity it hardly matters. When we discuss savings we do not have in mind only the little fellow's bank account; the big bank, too, saves by not distributing part of its profits in the form of dividends, and applying it to productive use.

In Hahn's system savings not only do not stimulate, but, on the contrary, impede production. According to him, there is only one limit to the beneficial effect of credit expansion on production: "When new credit cannot put new labor into the service of production," a further expansion of credit does not effect further production increases (145). If, as experience teaches us, this limit is never reached, but a recession starts before full employment is attained, the cause can be found in the fact that consumption does not follow the increased production. This again is the result of the savings activity. "Checking accounts are transformed into savings accounts, are consolidated (i.e., stay in the account), and no longer create demand in the market for goods. Therefore, as production no longer meets a corresponding consumption, the flow of goods begins to stop" (147-48).

There are two weighty arguments against this theory: 1. Funds one desires to save are not hoarded—even in an economy without cash—but are "invested" (for instance, in stocks), because of the higher rate of interest, so that respending takes place automatically. Consequently, there is no lack, but merely a displacement of demand. 2. Hahn himself keeps emphasizing that banks "regularly grant more credit than flows to them in the form of savings" (e.g., p. 63). Nevertheless, from his viewpoint he is right in wanting to fight economic crises by the vigorous creation of credit, ultimately for the account of the government (155).

However, it is entirely inconceivable how Hahn can maintain that inflationary credit spurs savings activity, that "savings increase not only pro rata with the credit granted but overproportionately" (153). Would a credit expansion which, according to Hahn, first raises prices, and secondly reduces the supply of current goods, induce people to limit consumption voluntarily still more than they are forced to already by higher prices, and to undergo willingly the inflation losses by not spending the depreciating currency?

III

The Gold Exchange Paradox *

The views most commonly held in the present discussion on the problem of stabilization may be summarized as follows: Advocates of stabilization argue that the disturbances and divergences to which the world economy is subject today are attributable primarily to the fact that the exchanges are not stable; those who oppose the idea of stabilization consider the causal sequence to be in the very opposite direction, urging that the first step to take is to bring about a rough equalization of the divergent elements, notably the difference in the purchasing power parity between different countries. They assert that a stabilization, if at all desirable, should be the final phase of a kind of experimental period during which one must needs have restored rational purchasing-power parity conditions, whereas the advocates of stabilization desire forthwith the binding of the exchange ratios as a prerequisite *if the purchasing power parity is to be restored,* which, however, they do not consider to be in itself absolutely essential. "When the Council of the B.I.S. contemplate (as in their last report) a return to a régime of fixed gold parities, they are living in an unreal world, a fool's world!" In this recent utterance of Keynes [1] the views of the opposition reach their highest pitch of intensity.

* Appeared first in *Index,* Review of Swennska Handelsbanken, 1936. It should not be forgotten that the article deals with the situation after the devaluation of the dollar and the pound in the thirties. At that time the problem was whether gold currencies *without* currency restrictions, not whether paper currencies *with* currency restrictions, should be devaluated. However, whether an artificial exchange rate can and should be maintained by *trade* restrictions, and whether internal inflation is compatible with external stabilization, is the problem of some European countries today as it was in 1936. The article was written in German and translated into English by the editors of *Index.*

[1] John Maynard Keynes, in *Lloyds Bank Monthly Review,* No. 68.

Even if, like the author of these lines, one accepts the arguments of the antistabilizationists, one must nevertheless admit that the English economists in particular have on one point thoroughly misjudged the situation. Assuming that what they consider to be common sense will obviously appear to be so too in the eyes of others, they have for some time past been forecasting an early devaluation of the gold currencies. This has not yet taken place, however, and, at any rate as far as Switzerland and Holland are concerned, it is extremely doubtful whether such a step is imminent. Those who entertain a different view on this point underestimate the strength of the antidevaluationist ideas and of tradition in these gold-bloc countries. They forget that in this no less than in other spheres it is not always the logically tenable ideologies that determine the issue.

Whether, however, one believes that the present exchange conditions in the world will be of long or of short duration, these conditions, which have in any case lasted for years, merit theoretical analysis with a view to ascertaining how far those exchanges which are today firmly linked to gold are really to be regarded as gold exchanges in the classical sense of the term.

Among the gold currencies, those which are subject to exchange control and only thereby maintain their old or a more or less reduced parity have no doubt shown the greatest changes. It is a moot question whether these exchanges are still to be regarded, even in the less strict sense of the term, as gold exchanges. On this point the views of the country concerned and those of foreign countries mostly differ. Perhaps these currencies might conveniently be termed *formal gold currencies*, seeing that the exchange rate, which is fixed officially in relation to other exchanges, is essentially of only formal significance. For the foreign exchange cannot freely be obtained at the official rate for the purpose of adjusting items either in the trade balance or in the balance of payments in general. Debt and interest payments as well as capital transfers to abroad are prohibited or regulated in some way or other. Foreign exchange to finance imports is not sold at the official rate on a scale sufficient to meet every demand but is rationed, while for the exports-exchange it is in reality not the official rate but, thanks to subsidies and premiums, a lower rate that applies. Thus, the official rate is not the price at which an adjustment is effected between supply and demand, the "parity" rate becoming in actual fact a purely formal one. It is difficult therefore to understand why any such rate is maintained at all. However, we shall not discuss that aspect of the matter here.

To the monetary theorist the real gold exchanges that still exist are of far greater interest. For, however paradoxical it may sound, it may well be asked, even in regard to them, whether they are still gold exchanges in the traditional sense.

Opinions on the essential nature of the gold exchanges are as widely divergent as most economic doctrines. Few perhaps will contradict the statement that Ricardo's views, as propounded in those passages of his works in which he deals as an exponent of the quantity theory with monetary and banking problems,[2] are to be regarded as the best thought out and still the most widely held in the world today. We shall only mention en passant here the fact that in other passages [3] he bases the value of gold and money on the amount of labor they contain, a theory which is untenable and in conflict with the theory just mentioned.

In the view of Ricardo as an exponent of the quantity theory, the essence and aim of a gold exchange is to maintain the purchasing power of the domestic currency in relation to foreign gold currencies. To him a gold currency is an international currency—and this not so much for the reason that one can buy for it anywhere in the world as because its mechanism guarantees that one can buy as much for it at home as abroad. To him it is the currency that possesses an internationally anchored purchasing power. The mechanism that guarantees its safe anchorage works, as everyone knows, in the following manner: If, in consequence of the increasing abundance of money, or, as it would nowadays be expressed, in

[2] David Ricardo, *The High Price of Bullion*, London, 1810.
[3] David Ricardo, *On the Principles of Political Economy and Taxation*, London, 1817, Pt. 1, sect. 1.

consequence of an expansion of credit, the prices in a country begin to rise, the exports will go down and the imports will increase. In order to cover the deficit in the trade balance, gold will flow out of the country. This will contract the gold-exporting country's quantity of money, or credit, so that prices will fall, while the gold balances abroad will increase, with the effect of raising prices there. The process goes on in this manner until the purchasing power parity—as Ricardo would say were he to use our present-day form of expression—has been restored.

A gold standard in Ricardo's view—and indeed in any common-sense view—is a standard subject to the following rules: both at home and abroad gold can freely be sold and bought at a fixed price. If the domestic price level rises, then gold as the cheapest export commodity is shipped abroad. This process lets loose forces which tend to deflation in the home country and to inflation abroad. This is the sole purpose that gold serves: by being transferred from one country to another it exercises internationally a stabilizing effect on the value of money.

The question whether the present gold-bloc currencies are still gold currencies in the classical sense may thus be reduced to the question whether the "rules of the game" are still being followed.

Hitherto the central banks of the gold-bloc countries have redeemed their notes with gold or gold exchanges on anyone's demand. Consequently the gold-bloc exchanges have so far never fallen to any appreciable extent below the gold export point. Therefore there seems to be little reason to doubt that the rules just quoted are actually being followed. If, however, we look more closely into the circumstances under which the export of gold takes place, we find that, as soon as it assumes substantial proportions, this export principally meets the demand for gold which arises when people begin to lose confidence in their own currency. The function of gold exports has chiefly been to finance the flight of capital to gold or to other exchanges that are to be had for gold. This, however, is a purpose that Ricardo (for instance) never even thought of and which indeed can hardly be regarded as legitimate. On the other hand, as regards the export of gold for the purpose of adjusting differences in purchasing power, it is certainly true that gold is sometimes exported to finance deficits in the trade balance. But these deficits are never anything like proportionate to the difference in purchasing power. By means of a complicated and refined system of tariffs and quotas—compared with which the erstwhile high-tariff countries now seem like a free-trade paradise—such imports are excluded as would otherwise inundate the country owing to the difference in purchasing power, and deficits in the trade balance and in the balance of payment are prevented. The rules of the gold exchanges have not been suspended. But this is true only in a very formal sense; for the chief contestants in the game are never able to insist on the rules' being respected. By taking measures in the sphere of *trade policy*, measures in that of *gold policy* can be avoided.

The domestic price level is maintained by keeping out a one-sided flow of imports—in protection of home enterprise, which would otherwise find it impossible to compete with the cheaper import goods. For if the prices at home were on a level with those abroad there would be no need for import restrictions. At the same time, however, the "gold automatism" that is the true purpose of every gold exchange is put out of function. As nevertheless the gold exchange is maintained, it is possible to observe as in many other spheres of social life the following very interesting phenomenon: What was originally a means becomes an end in itself and the original aim is no longer sought after—indeed in the present connection it is directly counteracted. But this involves the transition of the gold currency from an international exchange to a national one. Without transferring both his capital and himself abroad the citizen cannot use his gold for making purchases on the world market in conformity with its international purchasing power; he is prevented from doing so by import prohibitions and quota systems. He can disburse his gold only by converting it into the local currency—i.e., on the basis of the essentially lower domestic purchasing power. Out of this arises a paradoxical situation: The gold in the countries of the gold bloc possesses its full international purchasing power only in the hands of those who go to countries with a sterling or dollar exchange, not in the hands of those who remain at home. It may be said, therefore, that the gold exchange for the maintenance of which so many sacrifices are made in the countries of the gold bloc is there subject to a system of control which theoretically, in spite of all disparities as regards practical consequences, differs only quantitatively, not qualitatively, from the control exercised in countries with an exchange control system. These gold exchanges, then, may perhaps be termed *denatured gold exchanges.*

If the above reasoning is correct, it means that there are at present in the world two gold-exchange spheres, the French-Netherlands-Swiss and the British-American. (I here leave out of account the fact that the Bank of England, while it buys and sells gold, lets the buying and selling prices fluctuate within certain limits.) Between those spheres with a devalued and those with a nondevalued gold exchange there are differences in purchasing power, but these differences cannot be adjusted owing to difficulties being placed in the way of intercourse. The most striking peculiarity about this state of affairs is a tendency of the two spheres to adopt an increasingly strong autarchic attitude towards each other. For it is possible by means of a quota system to reduce imports but not to increase exports, since you can prevent the citizens of your own country from buying cheaply abroad but you cannot compel the foreigner to buy in a dear market. Likewise, for the same reason any attempt to bring exports up to a level with imports by means of reciprocal trade treaties is bound to fail. A policy aiming at an artificial restriction of a country's imports, or else at making them by means of reciprocal agreements dependent upon the willingness of foreign countries to accept whatever that country wishes to export, may, on the whole (apart from certain exceptional cases), possibly succeed in preventing changes in *the net result of the trade balance* but is bound at the same time to force the trade *turnover* down to an ever lower and lower level. It is, however, of interest to note that the autarchic tendencies cannot go beyond certain limits. As soon as it is realized that the situation means ruin to all those branches of industry which are producing for visible or invisible export, it becomes necessary to subsidize that export. Indeed, in the non-devalued countries the export industries are now largely working with the aid of export premiums, while on behalf of those export industries which are not yet subsidized similar schemes have been drawn up which by force of circumstances will no doubt have to be put into practice. Ultimately, of course, these subsidies have to be paid for by the public in the form of increased taxes or enhanced prices. From the point of view of the consumers, therefore, the system acts as a devaluation, and it does in fact represent an indirect devaluation.

To the important question how long a system of this kind can be kept going it may be replied that theoretically there is no reason, from the purely technical point of view of the exchange problem, why such a system must break down. But from the practical and the political points of view the matter naturally becomes more complicated: The permanent depression which the system must for many reasons necessarily and unavoidably involve gives rise to factors of social tension whose scope is often underestimated. The perhaps not inevitable, but in any case possible, consequences of such tension have lately become apparent in France: Instead of the theoretically correct, but for reasons of practical politics utopian, way out through price and budgetary deflation, which Laval wished to follow, the opposite extreme, price and budgetary inflation for the sake of "creating work," is more and more insisted upon. This leads—the road via devaluation being blocked by obstacles of an internal politicopsychological nature—to what is from the point of view of monetary theory the most paradoxical of all demands, the demand for "an expansion of credit without devaluation." But any such policy is bound to result, vis-à-vis abroad, in differences in purchasing power, the consequences of which cannot any longer be counteracted by the present system of trade restrictions. After some time it is bound, owing to the trade balance becoming more and more adverse, to lead to a heavy drainage of gold, even if, contrary to expectation, the authorities should succeed, by "creating an atmosphere of confidence," in preventing the balance of payments from becoming increasingly unfavorable through the flight of capital. If they continue to pursue this policy, it will inevitably lead to exchange control—or devaluation. It is, however, the same with devaluation as with the Sibylline Books—the longer the delay the higher the price owing to the destruction of existing values. And yet, if devaluation is adopted at all, it will be adopted only at the very last moment. For the creditors make the currency laws, whereas the debtors do not always bring about a revolution, although they sometimes do. This no doubt explains why history can hardly produce a single instance in which the policy of the opposite extreme—the policy of adjustment and deflation, such as Laval tried to pursue—has ever been carried to a successful conclusion.

As regards Switzerland and Holland, there can be no doubt that a change in the policy of those two countries—if at all likely—is possible only under far more severe economic pressure than they are being subjected to at the present time.

The gold exchange which the United States has introduced at least temporarily by fixing the buying and selling price of gold at $35 per ounce is likewise more of a paradox than is generally imagined. If we are really to grasp its implications we must first of all distinguish between its effect in relation to the countries of the gold bloc on the one hand and countries possessing a paper currency on the other.

1. As regards the former, it may be said that the fact of the United States' having reverted to the system of fixed buying and selling prices for gold is of no real practical significance. For the importance of the gold automatism described above can only be a subordinate one. As a matter of fact, an *efflux* from the United States of such gold as is obtainable at a fixed price with the object of preventing a decline in the purchasing power of the dollar is quite out of the question, because at the new parity the dollar has a far higher purchasing power than the gold-bloc currencies have, and, unless a violent inflation in the United States is conceivable, this higher purchasing power will undoubtedly last for years. On the other hand gold automatism does not work in the contrary direction either. In the gold-bloc countries there can be no drainage of gold to the United States, with a resultant lowering of prices in those countries, because such a movement of gold is rendered impossible by their tariff and quota systems. Consequently, the true aim of the gold exchange—the adjustment of the international purchasing power differences—will not be achieved in the intercourse

between the United States and the countries of the gold bloc. The fixed price of gold in the United States is of practical importance only in that a Frenchman, for instance, who desires to transfer his capital to the United States procures the dollar, via gold, at a price that is far too low in proportion to its purchasing power. He pays only 16 francs for the dollar instead of 26 francs as he did before the devaluation in the United States. This, however, is a factor that, from the American point of view, can hardly be of any decisive importance. The gold-bloc country may of course find these gold movements, caused by transfer of capital to that country in which the purchasing power is greatest, a problem, for such movements cannot be stopped by quotas and tariff regulations—as is the case with transfers of capital effected in the ordinary course of trade— but only by exchange control.

2. Seeing that the countries of the gold bloc are nowadays merely small islands in a sea of devaluation, it is in practice, of course, a far more important question how the new American gold currency functions vis-à-vis the paper currencies. If we regard without prejudice the function of the new dollar exchange, especially vis-à-vis the pound sterling, we shall find to our surprise that it depends primarily on the Bank of England whether the gold automatism is to come into play, whereas the American exchange authorities have no influence whatsoever in the matter. We might perhaps, there- fore, call it a *casual gold exchange,* seeing that from the American point of view it is actually a matter of chance whether it functions as a gold exchange or not. It will be so only on condition that the Bank of England, or the British Exchange Equalization Fund, does not allow its own gold price to fluctuate parallel to the dollar's movements in relation to the pound. In other words, if in conse- quence of a tendency to a rise in prices in the United States sterling rises in terms of the dollar, this will lead to an efflux of gold from the United States only when, in order to prevent this tendency from spreading to England, the Bank of England maintains its buying price for gold unchanged or at any rate refrains from lowering it by as much as the dollar falls in terms of the pound. In the event of the opposite tendency in the United States, the contrary will be the case. Only if the price of gold remains absolutely or relatively

unchanged does gold fetch the highest price as an article imported into England and cost the lowest price as an article exported from England. Otherwise the pound rises and falls in relation to the dollar without giving rise to such a drainage of gold as would serve to adjust the purchasing power. The British tactics at the moment seem to be to keep the price of gold stabilized within certain limits. Whether there will be any change in this policy in future, when any tendencies to inflation in the United States appear to make it desirable that the sterling-dollar rate should go up, it is impossible to know, any more than we can know whether the contingency we have thus assumed will ever become a reality. In any case it should be clear how comparatively unimportant and incidental is the part played by the American gold as affecting the adjustment of the purchasing-power parity vis-à-vis the countries of the sterling bloc.

It might perhaps be said, then, that the huge stocks of gold in the United States are only of decorative importance. However, one of the primary functions of gold is also, of course, to represent the permanence of value in time and space. On this ancient and apparently eternal question we may venture to make a few brief remarks—merely with reference to the immediate future. The theoretical knowledge that the value of gold depends on the value of money in a far greater degree than vice versa is without doubt fairly common nowadays. For, after all, gold is worth only exactly as much as the price bid in the open market by the highest bidder among the note-issuing banks. Nonetheless, if we dispassionately examine all the relative facts we need not consider the value of gold to be threatened. So long as the overwhelming majority of the governors of the note-issuing banks believe that they are bound to link their currencies to the gold value which they themselves have previously fixed—so that the currencies may, so to speak, drag themselves by their hair out of the quicksand of worthlessness—for just so long will the "gold prejudice" be valid. It need not even be anticipated that the value of gold will go down to any appreciable extent in the near future. In the United States it will only be under very exceptional circumstances that any lowering of the value of gold will be undertaken. Nor is it likely in England that any appreciable reduction in the price of gold will be permitted, seeing that such a step would entail a rise in the sterling rate in terms of the dollar. On the other hand, neither in the United States nor in England is any new increase in the price of gold to be expected. For people have apparently come to realize the following facts, which are really self-evident: A one-sided increase in the value of gold can, as far as the world economy is concerned, lead only to increased tension in the matter of international purchasing-power differences—that is to say, to enhanced difficulties in the way of world trade. And, for the internal economy, an increase along such lines is neither necessary nor sufficient when one wishes to bring about a rise of the domestic price level.

IV

Table of Contents of *Geld und Kredit*

Tübingen, 1924

V

Table of Contents of *Geld und Kredit, Neue Folge*

Tübingen, 1929

VI

List of Articles and Pamphlets Published Since the Appearance of *Geld und Kredit, Neue Folge*, 1929, But Not Included in This Volume

(Articles in dailies are not included)

1. Ist Arbeitslosigkeit unvermeidlich?, Berlin, 1930.
2. Kredit und Krise, Tübingen, 1931.
3. Die "verfügbaren Mittel" der Börse, Zeitschrift für National-ökonomie, 1935. Bd. 6, H. 5.
4. Geldzins und Effekten-preise, Schweizerische Zeitschrift für Volkswirtschaft und Statistik, 1936. Bd. 72, H. 1.
5. German Experience with Stocks and Inflation (in collaboration with Joseph Soudek), The Bankers Magazine, July, 1942.
6. Idle Money in Stock Markets, Trusts and Estates, May, 1943.
7. Deficit Spending and Private Enterprise, Chamber of Commerce of the United States, 1944, Bulletin 8.